Let there be Lite!

Let there be Lite!

An Illuminating Guide to Delicious Low-Fat Cooking

Jay Disney

THE OVERLOOK PRESS

WOODSTOCK • NEW YORK

First published in 1995 by
The Overlook Press
Lewis Hollow Road
Woodstock, New York 12498

Library of Congress Cataloging-in-Publication Data

Disney, Jay
Let there be lite! : an illuminating guide to delicious low-fat
cooking / Jay Disney.
    p. cm.
Includes index.
1. Cookery, International. 2. Low-fat diet—Recipes.
I. Title.
TX725.A1D49   1995
641.5'638—dc20
94-37368
CIP

ISBN: 0-87951-576-7
Manufactured in the United States of America
Book design by Bernard Schleifer
Typeset by AeroType, Inc.
First Edition

Contents

6. VEGETARIAN

7. FISH AND SEAFOOD

8. CHICKEN AND TURKEY

9. MEAT

10. VEGETABLES, SALADS AND SIDE DISHES

II. DESSERTS AND MISCELLANEOUS

12. INFORMATION AND SAMPLE MENUS

13. THE DOG CHAPTER
OR, *The Lowest Point in my Culinary History*

To **Lou,**
my personal *sous-chef.*

ACKNOWLEDGMENTS

Bonnie Leslie, whose weekly pep sessions helped me finish this book.

And **Camille D'Ambrose Bates** for lending me her critical eye, keen discerning mind, and ever-sharp blue pencil.

And **Jeff McMillen.**

And the quartet without whom this would not be possible, **Michael Hornburg, Hermann Lademann, Gene Taft,** and a very special thanks to **Tracy Carns,** the editorial director of **The Overlook Press.**

Introduction

WOULDN'T IT BE wonderful if a low-fat "diet" was an elected choice rather than an edict passed down by a physician?

One of my goals in writing this book was to shy away from the word and the American conception of "diet"; this term has been much overused and misapplied in the past fifty years, with our current definition probably coming into vogue in the 1920s when flappers needed to be extraordinarily thin to wear the drop-waisted dresses to emulate the hyperstylized Art Deco graphics of the era. A typical tenet of the Art Moderne movement was to stress a new "streamlining" look over the newly passé Edwardian curves. Artists such as Erté designed dresses that were geometrically lush when viewed from a two-dimensional medium (paper), but when translating those ideas to three-dimensional women a problem happened; namely, women had curves—and very few women had legs four feet long and necks that sat a graceful eleven inches from their shoulders! But that didn't stop young women everywhere from trying to cultivate that two-dimensional look by starving themselves so that they would be razor-thin and come as near as possible to the unreal Art Deco ideal. Nowadays "diet" still implies deprivation of favorite foods, starving oneself by only being allowed carrot and celery sticks, bland, boring menus, and expensive, frozen prepackaged meals. We should change this conception immediately! The word diet means "what we eat." But a more modern definition is that diet is not only a way of eating, but is also a way of thinking. It is a way of living. To change a diet not only alters what foods we ingest, but should realign our thinking so that we reassess what we put into our bodies and— more importantly—why. What we eat affects what we feel, how we feel, and how we operate as a living organism; to blindly ignore the real, specific cause-and-effect results of how food influences the body and mind is madness. To alter a lifelong program of established eating habits is not easy, but it is helpful if there is agreement and solace in the mind as to *why* one is changing one's eating habits. Many people are forced because of health reasons to make radical alterations in diet, but they still crave the junk and heavy fat-laden foods of their past, either because of habit or because they've not been introduced to *good* low-fat cooking.

Is This a Diet Book?

No. And yes. This book's mission is to make low-fat cooking recognizable and fun, showing how you can easily and painlessly have a low-fat diet, and most importantly, not feel as if you're missing anything. None of the recipes are labor intensive or difficult and none require any special chef training or techniques. The purpose is to provide for cooks at any level the necessary tools to prepare delicious and healthy meals. It is my belief that the everyday cook is a person who advances in culinary skills by degrees and is egged along in their culinary development with each successful venture into the realm of "exploring something new for dinner." It is imperative that the recipes breed success, and the first step toward a healthier diet is to expose the cook to the basics of low-fat cooking. *Let There Be Lite!* guides both the beginning and the novice cook to everyday, satisfying meals to enjoy with family and lovingly share with friends.

JAY DISNEY
Dallas 1995

1

A Short History of Traveling Lite, or Life's Funny That Way . . .

I NEVER INTENDED TO be the president of a corporation, but there you are. Even in my wildest dreams I never thought I'd be living in Texas either, but Life has a funny way of putting you somewhere and in some position you never dreamt possible.

"Would you be interested in cooking for one of my clients?" Larry asked me years ago.

"Whaddya mean?" I responded in an unnaturally articulate grunt.

Larry Lane, a friend and fitness instructor, added, "Well, this client of mine is overweight, and she's exercising and doing everything she can do by herself, but she can't cook. I don't mean she doesn't *like* to cook, she really *can't* cook. She said to me today, 'If I could just get someone to fix low-fat meals for me I'd eat them.' She's really frustrated, because the minute she gets home it's her downfall—since she can't cook she relies on all of the old reliables, you know, fast-food stuff. She can't lose weight because she eats all the wrong things."

"So what exactly is it you want me to do?" I asked.

"Cook for her. Make some low-fat meals so that she can lose weight."

"Cook for her . . . you mean like every night?"

"Yeah."

There was a nanosecond of pause in contemplation of the proposal, then I blurted, "There's not enough money in the entire world to make me cook for someone every night." All I could envision was myself chained to someone else's stove the rest of my life.

Larry regrouped. "Well, maybe . . . well, how about going in once a week and cooking for her just the entrées?"

Now we were talking turkey. "Once a week—? Go in and fix *just* the entrées?"

"Yeah—well, *anything* is better than what she's doing now. You could go in the morning and get everything prepared for the evening."

It seemed innocent enough, so I said, "Okay."

And that was the beginning of my Unexpected Journey into the World of Business.

Larry's old client and my new client, Betty S——, was thrilled not only with my cooking, but with how much easier her life had become. Betty told everyone she knew about this "wonderful new service," and within two weeks I was booked solid cooking low-fat entrées for wealthy Dallasites. Within two months Larry and I formed an official partnership to offer this service and got set to begin hiring employees, but first we needed a name.

"What about LITE SERVICE ?" Larry asked.

"LITE SERVICE ? What on earth is that supposed to mean? We replace lightbulbs?"

"No—like ROOM SERVICE, except it's light food."

A silence. "Next . . . " I droned.

"Well, how about something like . . . SPA COOKING?" Larry asked.

"Why not call it A SHARP STICK IN YOUR EYE—just as appetizing."

"It's not at all the same! It's a food service like you'd get at a spa—it makes perfect sense."

"Except that we're not a spa. And we're not a food service. We're a *chef* service specializing in low-fat food."

"All the more reason to focus on the healthy aspect of the business." A brief pause. Larry continued, "HEALTHY TIMES?"

"Isn't there a dog biscuit named that? Or something to relieve constipation?"

"What's wrong with HEALTHY TIMES?"

"Nothing except it sounds so . . . *healthy*. Wheat bran and all that. Health might be healthy, but it isn't appetizing."

Larry pondered aloud, "HEALTHY TIMES, HEALTH ON WHEELS, chef . . . health . . . gourmet . . . spa . . . travel . . . lite . . . "

A divine inspiration hit me. "What about LITE MOTIF?" I asked.

"What?"

"LITE MOTIF—except this is spelled L-I-T-E motif, not L-E-I-T motif."

"I don't get it."

"You don't get it? What don't you get?"

"Any of it."

"Any of it? It's a play on words. A leitmotif, l-e-i-t-m-o-t-i-f, from the German," I explained, spelling as I went, "is a recurring literary or musical theme; in this case, we do a 'lite' play on standard foods, hence, a LITE

MOTIF. L-I-T-E motif. So our business leitmotif would be lite cooking—get it?"

Larry looked at me blankly.

"Well, there's got to be someone else around here who knows what a leitmotif is." Another blank stare. "Well, if we were in India we could call ourselves CURRY IN A HURRY. . . ."

Larry mused on silently.

"How about COOKING GO LIGHTLY?" I said.

"Nah. Too cute."

"How about . . . CHEFS WITH ATTITUDE? No? At least with that name we couldn't be accused of not having Truth in Advertising. Hmmm."

Finally it was decided that we would become TRAVELING LITE. The chef would go into a client's home, that is, *travel*, and then cook "lite" food. *Not* a travel company specializing in lightweight luggage.

Within six months we formed a corporation and added that magical "Inc." to our name, TRAVELING LITE, INC. Life's funny. What started out being a stopgap measure for me wound up becoming a full-time job. Who would have guessed that having a once-a-week chef would have been so popular?

I look back to that moment when Larry asked me to cook for Betty with amazement at how one seemingly innocent action turned into a business opportunity that I couldn't have thought up by myself to save my soul.

Now, years later, I still think LITE MOTIF is a great name. But so is TRAVELING LITE.

2

How to Cook for the Week in Three Hours

"I dare say you never even spoke to Time!"

"Perhaps not," Alice cautiously replied: "but I know I
have to beat time when I learn music."

"Ah! that accounts for it," said the Hatter. "He won't
stand beating. Now, if you only kept on good terms with
him, he'd do almost anything you liked with the clock."

Lewis Carroll, *Alice's Adventures in Wonderland*

WHAT IS THE age-old question that haunts almost every household and is a major source of anxiety at the end of a long day's work?

"What's for dinner?" Or, in the case with Alice who beat Time, *"What's for tea?"*

With the increase of dual-income households, the issue of dinner becomes quite a sticky point since both partners are equally busy, equally tired, and have an equally limited amount of spare time. Many people opt for the frozen-food alternative, others for ordering food in; still others spend an enormous amount of money and time going nightly to restaurants. One simple solution to this problem of dinner is to spend a small amount of time in preparation for the week ahead; by utilizing a few hours on the weekend you can have a leisurely week of meals without stress or hassle, and rest assured that you're eating the healthiest food around. Not only is this the healthiest route, but it is by far the least expensive.

One of the best methods of saving time, energy, and frustration during the week is to prepare four to five different entrées at one time; you then have homemade meals ready for the week ahead. For example, let's say that you prepare five entrées on Sunday afternoon and put them in the refrigerator—when you get home on Monday you've got your main course ready, and with the simple addition of a salad or steamed vegetable you've made a complete dinner within 30 minutes. Many of the recipes in this book freeze beautifully, and many will keep for two to three days without any problem since they are in a "preserving" marinade. By "preserving marinade" I mean a marinade which contains any of the following: lemon juice, lime juice, salt, tamari, vinegar, or prepared mustard. Each of these ingredients hinders or eliminates the growth of many harmful bacteria, as well as begins the breaking-down process of proteins, causing tenderer meats. A longer marinating peroid also means that more of the flavor of the marinade will enter the meat.

"How do I go about this?" you ask. There are two methods listed below, the first for a solo cook and the second for multiple cooks. In either case the methodology is the same and is as easy as 1-2-3.

First, organize your week's menus. Let's say you've picked:

Monday:	**Shrimp Kabobs with Bay**
Tuesday:	**Parmesan Chicken Breasts**
Wednesday:	**Spinach Lasagna**
Thursday:	**Hearty Navy Bean Soup**
Friday:	**Black Bean Enchiladas**

Second, you need to purchase the necessary groceries.

Third, select a period of undisturbed time when you can cook. Gather the ingredients you need and prepare to cook. The process of preparing several entrées at once is not difficult if you organize properly. For example, if you have three recipes that call for chopped onions, use your food processor and chop all of the onions at once. Peel and set aside all of the garlic at one time. In other words, use your time *efficiently*. Look at what you've selected and start with the most labor intensive, or one that takes the longest time to cook. Move on next to another item while the first is cooking. The simplest item should be left for last since it will take the least amount of time. There is nothing difficult about this process—you will merely be juggling several items according to the difficulty of preparation and the length of time it takes to prepare.

To Illustrate

Judging from the selected menus above, you will need to prepare the filling for the enchiladas first since it will take at least 45 minutes to cook and time to cool. The tomato sauce and the filling for the lasagna should be prepared while the black beans are cooking, then it's time to assemble and make the soup. While all of these are cooking merrily on the stove, you can trim the chicken breasts and process the breadcrumbs (still keeping an eye on the stove, taking items off of the heat when necessary). Finish breading the chicken breasts and place the uncooked, covered breasts in the refrigerator. Next, assemble the fillings for the enchiladas and fill them; garnish and cover the enchiladas and refrigerate. Taste the soup to see if it is done; if so, turn off the heat and allow it to cool. Next, assemble the lasagna, cover, and refrigerate. Then prepare and skewer the shrimp; cover and refrigerate. And last, refrigerate the cooled soup.

Now, you will notice that the shrimp and chicken are not cooked; this is fine. The object is to have the freshest food possible, so you will want to cook the shrimp on Monday night. "Why not cook the shrimp Sunday and reheat it on Monday?" you ask. Reheated food simply isn't as tasty as food cooked for the first time. Reheated shrimp and chicken dry out easily and become tough. As long as you schedule the uncooked foods at the beginning of the week you should have no problem with spoilage. Any fish or seafood should be eaten within 24 hours; raw chicken and meats should be eaten within one to three days. Once again, any chance of unhealthy bacterial growth will not only be inhibited by the marinade, but will be eliminated by the cooking process—heat kills bacteria. If something unexpected happens and you cannot cook the meal(s) you have prepared, freeze them. In this case, the chicken, soup, enchiladas, and lasagna all freeze perfectly. So if a hot date comes up on Friday night, no need to worry about the enchiladas—freeze them! Or better yet, ask your date over for homemade enchiladas—talk about making a good impression!

If preparing five entrées seems daunting at first, start out making three; adjust the number of entrées to your schedule. Some people religiously go out to dinner on Friday night, so for those people preparing only four entrées is sufficient. Having a couple of items in your freezer is also extremely helpful when life becomes too hectic—once again, a modicum of preparation will make your life so much easier!

And remember, the more you practice the better you'll get. When you get addicted to the simplicity of returning home and having a meal waiting, the little amount of time spent on the weekend preparing it will seem trivial to the rewards.

The second way to go about cooking for the week when you have a partner or family is to get everyone involved; set aside several hours on a weekend and invite everyone to help. The idea of how you organize your time and how you prepare the entrées is the same for one cook as it is for four, only there are more people involved. By spending quality time working together toward a common goal in the kitchen, new bonds are formed not only between family members but educationally it shows how to cook, how to cooperate, how to prepare low-fat food, how to chop vegetables, and what effort goes into preparing a meal. By knowing the steps involved in cooking, children will become more appreciative of what is served them, particularly when they helped make it. Many vegetables and unusual dishes that children otherwise wouldn't touch suddenly become palatable when they've seen how it was made, and when they've helped as a member of the family to make dinner. Sometimes the pickiest child can turn over a new leaf and eat everything in sight once they've become a participant in the kitchen!

About the Nutritional Analysis

The nutritional analysis software for *Let There Be Lite!* was Recipe Master 1.1, by Richard D. Lasky, Ph.D., Big Byte Software for Hypercard. It was a program that was particularly easy to custom-fit to my needs, enabling me to enter new nutritional information where the database proved insufficient. Unfortunately, there was at the time of this writing *no nutritional information available* (at least none that *I* could find) for certain items used in the recipes, such as ancho chilies, or chili paste with garlic. In these and other cases, I substituted items which I felt were close to the original ingredient; as an example, for chili paste with garlic I would substitute small amounts of garlic, toasted sesame oil, vinegar, and chili peppers. As a result, I can only say that *all nutritional counts are approximate*. I have endeavored to give the best nutritional analyses available to me, but someone else running the same recipe through a different nutritional analysis program may come out with slightly different results, particularly when the type of meat or fish is up to the reader's discretion and depends on availability. The nutritional count for Seafood Gumbo, for example, will differ widely depending on how oily or lean a fish is selected, just as a beef dish will vary depending on which cut is chosen.

Besides which, *relax*!!! It's not that important!

3

A Discourse on Low-Fat "Techniques" and Living

OR,

JAY GETS ON HIS SOAPBOX

FIRST AND FOREMOST: **FAT IS NOT YOUR ENEMY.**

Why do I make that statement?

Many times I've been asked, "Are these recipes *nonfat*?" and I must explain that practically everything we eat has some fat in it—even cucumbers contain a miniscule amount of fat. In my opinion we have a fatal flaw in our society, namely that the minute it is reported that a "high-fat diet is bad for you" we immediately jump to the reverse conclusion, filling in the syllogism with the seemingly logical but erroneous notion, "If a high-fat diet is bad for you, then a nonfat diet must be healthiest of all."

Wrong.

The human organism must have fat. It must have fat to maintain healthy daily functions. The misguided goal of a nonfat diet is not only impossible but dangerous for your health. Everyone has read the reports about the diseases caused by and the dangers of having a high-fat diet, but too infrequently is it written that there is *nothing inherently wrong with fat*. Fat is a part of our diet, it is a part of our life—without fat we couldn't exist. Health problems such as heart disease are not the result of fat itself, but a chronic high-fat diet; health problems are not caused by one high-fat meal per month, or five high-fat meals per year, but a habitual, chronic high-fat diet. The current goal is to reduce the daily intake of fat to an easy, manageable level, somewhere between the 15 to 30% range (that is, 15 to 30% of the daily calories come from fat).

Remember this statement: **FAT IS NOT THE ENEMY**. Too *much* fat is the enemy. So let's begin with a healthy attitude toward fat. To recap: There is nothing wrong with fat. There is everything wrong with *too much* fat.

'Nuf said about that.

I'm often also asked during cooking classes about *low-fat cooking techniques*, a question that rather baffles me. I can't think of any techniques per se—just one maxim for low-fat cooking:

> **The only maxim for low-fat cooking I can think of:** Don't try to make a super high-fat recipe into a low-fat recipe. It won't work. Save the high-fat recipe for special occasions and enjoy every bite. (More on **The Maxim** later.)

There are many authors who will espouse mere *substitutions* in recipes as *techniques*, that is, substituting chicken or vegetable stock for cream or butter. My fear with literally suggesting "substitute item A for item B" is that the reader will become dependent upon such a chart. Cooking is a creative and free-form undertaking—or, rather, it *should* be a creative undertaking. I would rather suggest where to look for low-fat substitutions, enabling the cook to see what they have on hand and invent for themselves their own chart of "substitute item A for item B." This is the only way to really learn the nuts and bolts of where to cut fat, as well as empower the cook to take responsibility for his or her own diet. The idea of experimentation in the kitchen is paramount; what's the worst that can happen? You prepare a highly indigestible meal and you order Chinese takeout. Big deal.

Low-fat cooking, by my personal definition of the term, includes nothing more or nothing less than regular, run-of-the-mill cooking. Low-fat cooking merely adjusts one's way of *thinking* about the cooking process. A stir-fry is a stir-fry is a stir-fry; the vegetables remain the same, the cooking process remains the same, the only thing that changes is either the quantity of added oil or the amount of fat-laden items, such as meats.

What does this mean in practical terms? It means to *think*. Think through where the obvious fat is in a recipe and try to cut down the amount. It is amazing how great a difference there is between one tablespoon of oil and one teaspoon; one tablespoon of oil has 120 calories and 13.6 grams of fat, whereas one teaspoon of oil has 40 calories and 4.53 grams of fat. To make a simple reduction of added oil in a recipe causes a startling change in the overall fat content. For example, if you're making a vegetable stir-fry that calls for 2 tablespoons of oil, your overall calorie/fat content might be, say, 540 calories and 16 grams of fat (27% calories from fat); if you reduce the oil to *one teaspoon*, the figures drop to 340 calories and 6.93 grams of fat (18% calories from fat).

First and foremost, look at the obvious. When you see a recipe that calls for a quarter cup of oil for sautéing a cup of onions, ask yourself, *Why? Why* is it necessary to have that much oil? Could I get by with just 1 tablespoon? Could I get by with just Pam®? Could I get by with a bit of both, like, a teaspoon of oil and a spritz of Pam®? In this case, the cooking process remains identical; the only thing that has changed is the amount of oil.

How does this affect your average recipe? First reduce or eliminate the apparent fat, wherever possible. Be sure to trim all meats thoroughly. Second, reduce high-fat items, such as meats, nuts, creams, cheeses, milk, and so on, from the written amount to a smaller portion. Substitute additional vegetables or grains for the high-fat reduction if desired.

But what about merely replacing a new nonfat product for a high-fat item? This is unquestionably an alternative, but an alternative that is akin to walking through nettles. You may emerge unscathed, but then again you may be stung!

Let's face it. Many new nonfat items on the market (nonfat cheeses, sour cream, cream cheeses, etc.) simply don't taste as good as the higher fat products. The public has become so frustrated with promising nonfat alternatives whose claims exceed their performance (namely taste) that they frequently throw their hands up in despair.

Before tearing out your hair and reaching for a quart of Häagen Dazs® chocolate chocolate-chip, let's assess low-fat and nonfat products. Unfortunately many nonfat items don't behave the same as their high-fat counterparts. Take for example the infamous nonfat cheeses that don't melt, or the nonfat sour creams that taste like gelatinous curdled yogurt, or the nonfat cream cheeses that can't be heated above room temperature. Ultimately, if the reduced-fat product doesn't taste good, you won't be satisfied and won't eat it.

I advocate a compromise.

To wit, I personally find that using Pam® alone doesn't give the same taste as sautéing in oil. Pam® is a great product, but there is unquestionably a taste and physical reaction that occurs when using oil that Pam® can't replicate. Does that mean I don't use Pam®? Not at all. I couple Pam® with a small bit of oil. That action alone reduces the amount of fat from, say, two tablespoons to *one teaspoon* and still gives the taste of sautéing in oil yet giving the benefits of using Pam®! This isn't a technique of cooking, it is merely a way of readjusting the way one thinks of sautéing.

By the same token, when making a recipe that calls for a half cup of sour cream, try using one-quarter cup "light" sour cream and one quarter cup nonfat sour cream. Concurrently, when you need a cup of cheese, try using one-third cup regular cheese and two-thirds cup reduced or nonfat cheese. A culinary compromise embraces one undeniable fact: you'll never be able to replicate the taste of the high-fat item, so why fight it? Why not accept the fact that low-fat items not only don't have the same *taste* as high-fat items, they don't have the same *quality* either, so why not deal with it accordingly? If you want to have the taste of real cheese, use real cheese for part of the amount and substitute a low-fat version for the remaining part. You'll be surprised at how well this simple idea works! (Once again, this isn't a *technique*—it's just a different way of approaching the way one thinks of cutting fat.)

Returning to **The Maxim** (*see* page 12) . . . My own experience tells me that trying to drastically cut back the fat in a recipe usually alters the recipe, and not necessarily with the best of results—particularly if the recipe is unnaturally high in fat to begin with. Sometimes using a low-fat or nonfat item (such as reduced-fat sour cream or cheese) causes a plastic taste which many people not surprisingly find offensive.

For example, it is my opinion that it is impossible to prepare a low-fat Alfredo sauce; by definition an Alfredo sauce has butter, heavy cream, and lots of Parmesan cheese. How on earth could you attempt to make this sauce reducing the fat? It's nothing *but* fat! I would say, "If you want an Alfredo sauce, have Alfredo sauce and know what you're eating." By having conscious knowledge that you're ingesting a very high-fat dish you may: a) eat less than you ordinarily would, or b) eat it happily with full approval of what you're eating and not feel guilty about it.

I can hear someone screaming, "Eat a high-fat item *happily?* I thought this was a low-fat cookbook!"

And indeed it is. But we must consider the philosophy of eating. Why do we eat? Beyond the obvious necessity of maintaining the organism we reside in, what experiential and spiritual levels do we nurture by eating? We commune with family, friends, and loved ones while eating; this is a spiritual connection which supercedes the basic act of eating; we form a bond between the physical motion of eating and the act of sharing. The stages and preparation of a meal connotes an act of caring; the act of sharing one's meal with others is an act of love; the appreciation of that meal is one of thanks and blessing. The ritual of eating can be a very special time to relax, enjoy, and reassess one's life on a daily level.

But in today's society we're not only inundated with advertisments screaming that "Product A will make you thinner quicker," "Product B will make you sexier," "Product C will make people love you," but we are constantly in search of the *faster* way to eat, the *faster* way to exercise, the *faster* way to live. Such insanity! We've become a country where we connote eating with "torture" and consider taking the time to eat a meal "a waste." We have been brainwashed into associating the very basic act of sharing and loving with deprivation of food, of forcing unpalatable items down one's throat so we can be "sexier . . . thinner . . . more attractive." We are not only a nation of fast-food junkies, but one wherein we eat fast-food *on the run!* We don't even allow ourselves the time to sit down and eat fast food! The notion of slowing down and savoring a meal—a communion with loved ones—has become the oddity instead of the norm.

What does this have to do with low-fat eating? Low-fat cuisine unquestionably plays a role in keeping a fit, healthy body; but what of the mind? What about the psychological role of a low-fat diet? What about the analysis of one's eating routine in regard to having a happy, healthy life?

We are dangerously close to becoming a society in which we don't want to take responsibility for our lives. We want someone else to make the decisions for us. We want Mr. X to give us a diet that will be delicious, filling, indulgent, inexpensive, meet all of our wildest fat fantasies, be absolutely and completely nutritious, yet still have only three calories! Very few people want to hear the statement, "You are responsible for what you put in your mouth."

I believe in moderation. I believe in following a low-fat diet *whenever possible*. For example, if you're invited over to dine with some special friends and they prepare a high-fat dinner, what should you do? Do you cause a big stink and insult your host and hostess by asking if they have anything *else* to eat? Do you sit mutely looking at your plate, moving around the food but eating nothing? What are you to do? Answer: Enjoy yourself. Enjoy the company, the talk, the *meal*. Life is too short to be obsessed with constantly counting grams of fat and calories. Live in the moment—enjoy and savor the experience of a communion with friends. Tomorrow you'll be back at home and can cook a low-fat meal. No harm done. You will have: a) indulged yourself in having a lovely dinner prepared by caring people, b) had a wonderful time with friends, and c) allowed yourself the time to enjoy life. Let's say you've begun a low-fat regimen and have been faithfully following it for six months; eating one high-fat meal will not "undo" all the good you've done. Your system will be in a much better condition to process the high-fat meal than it was before. Don't kick yourself in the head for going "off the wagon"—there *is* no wagon! Diet is a cumulative, ever-changing, ever-evolving part of our lives. Almost everyone will at one time or another make the statement, "Yeah . . . I used to be able to eat that, but now it disagrees with me." We as organisms change as we age, yet we somehow simplistically expect our diet to always remain the same!

Becoming neurotically obsessed with the total grams of fat you are "allotted" per day is not the answer for a healthy life; becoming unnaturally aware of grams of fat can lead to stress, anxiety, and anger. A healthy attitude toward exercise, diet, and life is of utmost importance. Fat in and of itself is not your enemy, nor is it evil. Allow yourself the occasional indulgence without guilt. Follow your own path of diet whenever possible. And enjoy yourself!

4
Questions and Answers

*T*HROUGH MY BUSINESS and cooking classes I've often been quizzed about nutrition, fat, and cooking; here are some of the most common questions.

I don't understand the difference between all the fats and cholesterol. Please explain.

To begin with, cholesterol refers to "animal fat." Any fat that doesn't come from an animal by definition has no cholesterol. Olive oil, canola oil, and sunflower oil have no cholesterol since they are pure *vegetable* fats. A bottle of vegetable oil with a label that states "No Cholesterol" is inane; vegetable oil and cholesterol have mutually exclusive definitions.

In the world of fats, there are three categories: saturated, mono-unsaturated, and polyunsaturated. The reason they are called this is because of their molecular makeup, so put on your Chemistry Thinking Caps. If you have a mental image of all fats as starting out being saturated, then the molecular chain is full and can hold no more; it is sated, or saturated. A monounsaturated fat, then, is one in which each molecular chain is one atom short of being saturated, hence its name: **mono** (one) **un** (not) **saturated** (full), or one atom short of saturation. (Or, each molecular chain forms **one** [mono] double bond.) Polyunsaturated, then, follows the same rule: **poly** (two or more) **un** (not) **saturated** (full), or a fat molecule which is two or more atoms short of being saturated. (Or, each molecular chain forms **two or more** [poly] double bonds.)

Now that you're thoroughly confused, let me bring out the visual aids.

The following illustrates the kinds of fats, their molecular chains, where they can be found, and how they affect your cholesterol level.

SATURATED:

carbon and hydrogen atoms in a complete chain. Saturated fats are usually hard at room temperature.

Commonly found in: *animal fats, some vegetable fats, solid fat at room temperature. Butter, cheese, shortening, meats, lard, margarine (see hydrogenated fats below).*

```
    H   H   H   H   H H   H   H   H
    |   |   |   |   |  |   |   |   |
H - C - C - C - C - C - C - C - C - C
    |   |   |   |   |  |   |   |   |
    H   H H   H   H H   H   H   H
```

Saturated fats raise cholesterol levels.

MONOUNSATURATED:

molecular fat chain with two hydrogen atoms short of saturation, forming one double bond. Monounsaturated fats are usually liquid at room temperature.

Commonly found in: *vegetables oils, liquid at room temperature. Most notably olive oil, canola oil, high-oleic safflower and high-oleic sunflower oils.*

```
    H   H   H   H   H   H   H   H H
    |   |   |   |   |   |   |   | |
H - C - C - C - C - C = C - C - C - C
    |   |   |   |   |   |   |   | |
    H   H   H   H               H   H   H
```

Monounsaturated fats lower LDL cholesterol without changing HDL cholesterol levels. (The difference between LDL and HDL cholesterol is explained below.)

POLYUNSATURATED:

molecular fat chain with four or more hydrogen atoms short of saturation, forming two or more double bonds. Polyunsaturated fats are liquid at room temperature.

Commonly found in: *vegetable oils, liquid at room temperature. Corn oil, soy oil, sunflower oil, safflower oil.*

```
    H   H   H   H   H   H   H H   H
    |   |   |   |   |   |   | |   |
H - C - C - C = C - C - C = C - C - C
    |   |   |   |   |   |   | |   |
    H   H       H               H   H
```

Polyunsaturated fats lower *both* LDL and HDL cholesterol levels.

Hydrogenation and partially hydrogenated fats: a process in which poly-unsaturated fats are subjected to high temperatures and bombarded with trace elements (such as nickel or copper) to squeeze hydrogen atoms into the open spaces, thereby making a normally unsaturated fat behave and look like a saturated fat at room temperature. Unfortunately, during this pro-cess the fatty acid molecules get twisted into strange shapes; these are then called *trans-fatty acids.* Since they are technically unsaturated, they enter the same biochemical pathways as other polyunsaturates, but they behave differently: the body is fooled into thinking that these trans-fats will do es-sentially what fatty acids do. Trans-fats tend to accumulate in heart tissue. Trans-fats are almost *never* present in nature.

HDL and LDL cholesterol:
HDL (high-density lipoproteins) cholesterol is commonly called "good cholesterol."
LDL (low-density lipoproteins) cholesterol is common called "bad cholesterol."

Here is a mnemonic device for remembering the difference between HDL and LDL cholesterol: imagine bad cholesterol (low-density) as being globby, soft lumps of fat that will stick to the sides of your veins and arteries since it is soft, *i.e.,* low-density. On the other hand, imagine good choles-terol (high-density) as being hard pieces surging through your veins, scrap-ing away bits of globby fat as it goes along its way through the circulatory system. The hard, high-density fat cleans away soft, low-density fat.

The most recent studies suggest that even HDL cholesterol ("good cholesterol") in large quantities is not beneficial; once again, the adage "Everything in moderation" rings true.

Why all the fuss about fat?

Unlike many other aspects of our diet, fat is the single most important *correctable* source for improving one's health. In studies around the world, excess dietary fat has been directly linked to breast cancer, colon cancer, arteriosclerosis, blood clotting, and heart disease, to name but a few. Monitoring one's fat intake is most important because it is one of the few ways in which we can live a longer, healthier life merely through diet.

What about saturated fats?

Some studies suggest that saturated fats, whether from vegetable or animal sources, compound the problem of fighting cholesterol—even to the point where a noncholesterol saturated fat (such as vegetable shorten-ing) can *increase* your serum cholesterol level. (The most common satu-

19

rated fats are butter, lard, shortening, coconut oil, and hydrogenated fats.) The fewer saturated fats you eat, the better. Even an all-vegetable shortening that claims "no cholesterol" is still a saturated fat and should be avoided if you can substitute a better fat, such as olive oil, canola oil, high-oleic safflower or high-oleic sunflower oil.

If a product says "no cholesterol," it means the same thing as "no fat," right?

Wrong. "No cholesterol" means exactly that—no cholesterol. Although cholesterol is indeed fat, it is *animal fat*—only products that are made of (or come from) animals can contain cholesterol. Meats, poultry, fish, seafood, eggs, lard, and milk products (including cheeses)—only these can contain cholesterol since they are either animals or animal products.

But plant products also contain fat. Nuts, for example, are quite high in fat but contain no cholesterol (obviously, since they are *plant* products and not *animal* products). A bottle of olive oil may say "No Cholesterol" but in fact contains 100% fat! Don't be misled by advertising! A container of vegetable shortening may say "No Cholesterol," yet it is really nothing but hydrogenated vegetable fat, one of the worst kinds of fat to be eating. Don't use cholesterol as a guideline for reducing fats. If you reduce your overall fat intake then you will be automatically reducing your cholesterol intake—but that equation doesn't work in the reverse! Just because you reduce your cholesterol (animal fat) intake does *not* mean you're reducing your fat (plant fat) intake.

To recap: Cholesterol is fat, but not all fats contain cholesterol. By reducing your *overall* fat intake you are automatically lowering your cholesterol intake.

How do I use the nutritional information provided at the bottom of the recipes?

The primary reason the nutritional information is provided is to allow you to figure your total intake of fat per day (or per meal). The most current analyses pertaining to fat report that we should keep our daily caloric intake from fat at or under 30%. This is a confusing way to say that no more than 30% of our daily calories should come from fat. How does it all work?

To figure the percentage of calories from fat:

1) Take the total grams of fat and multiply it by nine (since there are nine calories in a gram of fat):

$$\text{Fat grams} \times 9 = N$$

2) Next take the number ("N") and divide it by the total calories per serving:

N ÷ calories = % of calories from fat

EXAMPLE: For Mexican Quiche:

6.9 (grams of fat per serving) × 9 (calories per gram) = 62.1

62.1 ÷ 252 (calories per serving) = .25, or 25% of the calories per serving
come from fat

The above procedure is a guideline only; depending on the dish, the percentages can be confusing and misleading. To illustrate, let's look at Baba Ganoush using the formula above. Its percentages per ounce would read:

2.1 g × 9 = 18.9

18.9 ÷ 30.3 = .62, or 62% calories from fat

The first reaction would be, "Gosh! Sixty-two percent of the calories come from fat—that must be loaded with fat—I can't eat that!" But herein lies the problem with statistics. What's more important than the percentage is the actual *total grams* of fat, which in this case is only 2.1 grams (less than a teaspoon of oil) of fat, extremely low by anyone's standards. So although the percentage of fat-to-calories is rather high, even if you were to eat three servings you would have consumed less than 7 grams of fat total, a total less than if you'd eaten potato chips. So a modicum of common sense should always be invoked, thinking not only about the percentage of calories to fat, but about the total amount of fat consumed.

So how many grams of fat should I be getting per day?

Yikes! What a loaded question!

There's no one answer. Every person's recommended caloric needs are based upon their sex, age, height, weight, general health, and level of activity, among other things. To say that everyone should be getting X grams of fat is impossible. If you're serious about monitoring your daily grams of fat, I would strongly urge you to: a) visit your doctor before you consider any kind of alteration to your diet, and b) purchase a book with the latest health guidelines available, complete with charts to assess your personal needs and requirements based upon age, sex, weight, height, etc.

The chart below is just an average idea of what is recommended— the fat-gram column is the maximum you should be ingesting on a daily basis, if you want to stay at that magic "30% of calories from fat" guideline. It certainly wouldn't hurt to try to stay well below it.

	Calories per day	*Should not exceed this number of grams of fat per day*
Women age 22–50:	1800–2000	60 g–65 g
Women age 51 + :	1600–1800	53 g–60 g

(This is based on a woman standing about 5'4" tall and weighing 130 pounds.)

	Calories per day	*Should not exceed this number of grams of fat per day*
Men age 22–50:	2500–2700	82 g–90 g
Men age 51 + :	2200–2400	73 g–80 g

(This is based on a man standing about 5'9" tall and weighing 155 pounds.)

What about the fat content of the entire meal?

Two other things need to be mentioned: 1) serving size, and 2) side dishes and snacks. The serving size is important because even low-fat entrées cease to be low-fat if you're eating three portions. Serving size is imperative to monitoring fat, especially since an entrée does not constitute the entire meal. For instance, a piece of chicken (4 ounces white meat roasted, 196 calories, 5.1 g fat, with 23% calories from fat) is well under the 30% guideline until you accompany it with a baked potato heavily laced with butter and cheese and hot eggy corn bread slathered in butter! As a general rule of thumb, side dishes should also conform to the same guidelines as the entrée.

What is "light" olive oil?

Don't be misled by the label. "Light" olive oil is exactly the same as any other olive oil except that the taste is lighter. The only possible reason I can think of for purchasing light olive oil is that you don't like the taste of regular extra virgin olive oil.

I noticed that in some of your recipes you say to add both Pam® and oil? Why?

This is simply for taste. Pam® is a wonderful product, but it doesn't fully replicate the taste or quality of sautéing. I find by using a small amount of oil with Pam® you can get more of a real sautéed taste—and taste is the bottom line, *n'est-ce pas?*

If I cut out starchy foods like potatoes, pasta, and breads, will I lose weight and reduce my overall fat level?

Huh?!?! We're talking apples and oranges here. Starchy foods, like the ones you mentioned, are usually very low in fat and are an excellent source of complex carbohydrates (that is, energy). Fat, on the other hand, is fat. They're completely different things. There's nothing wrong with including pasta or potatoes on a weight-reducing diet since they are low in fat, as long as you're not slathering the potatoes with butter and the pasta with cream sauces. In fact, the carbohydrates may even raise your energy level and help you get through your exercise routine with greater ease, allowing you to lose weight faster.

Are grocery store diet foods better for a low-fat diet?

Not as far as I'm concerned. Most commercial "diet" products are loaded with chemicals and additives, things which are there to try to fool you into thinking you're getting something you're not. Just because a product has fewer calories doesn't make it *healthier*; in my opinion, it is far "healthier" to use less of a real food product than to use more of a hyperprocessed item saturated with chemicals.

I notice your recipes are "lite" with meat—why?

Americans on the whole think we need more meat protein than we actually do. We were raised eating meat morning, noon, and night and were led to expect an entire T-bone steak or a quarter of a chicken as a single portion; this is an extremely high quantity of meat. The average person only needs about 12 grams of complete protein per day. Four ounces (a quantity most people would find skimpy) of chicken breast contains 35.1 grams of protein—four ounces of red snapper contains 23.2 grams of protein! Luckily the Food and Drug Administration (FDA) now endorses a grain and vegetable based diet supplemented with meat (if desired), and not vice versa.

What about sugar and salt?

Unless you have a specific physical problem, such as hypertension or diabetes, both are fine as long as you use them in moderation, coupled with a well-rounded, healthy diet and exercise regime.

Is a vegetarian diet lower in fat than a meat-based diet?

Not necessarily, particularly if you substitute eggs, cheese, and nuts for the meat. A surprising part of our fat intake comes from vegetable sources anyway—salad oils, shortenings, nut butters, etc. As with any "diet," it is as healthy as you want to make it.

23

Do vegetarians eat eggs?

There are three major "sects" of vegetarians: 1) ovo-lacto vegetarians: those who eat eggs and dairy products as well as vegetables; 2) lacto-vegetarians: those who eat dairy products and vegetables but no eggs; and 3) vegans: those who eat only vegetable products. Of course, probably the easiest way for most people is to set a general guideline for yourself (such as "I'm going to eat dairy products but not eggs") and then use that as a rule of thumb. The best answer I've ever heard when someone was asked, "Are you a vegetarian?" was "Yes, whenever possible." Sometimes meals are out of your control, especially if you're a guest somewhere, or traveling in a foreign country. If a friend invites you over for afternoon tea and serves you a cookie with egg in it, don't have an apoplectic fit, just enjoy the cookie and be done with it—otherwise you'll let your self-imposed diet dictate your life and make you paranoid about everything you put in your mouth, instead of enjoying life and being thankful that you've got a friend who thinks enough of you to invite you over for afternoon tea.

I notice some of your recipes have odd amounts of beans—like 1½ cups. How am I supposed to make just 1½ cups of cooked beans?

One and one-half cups of beans is roughly one 15-ounce can's worth. I've specified the measure amount in the recipe, but if you want you can just think of 1½ cups as "one can."

If I eat a low-fat diet, will I be healthy?

A low-fat diet should be accompanied by an exercise program and, if possible, a holistic approach to life. Diet and exercise are only two facets of a healthy lifestyle. Other things to consider: stress, interpersonal relationships, environment (both at work and at home), psychological baggage which can be exorcised—a healthy person has a healthy outlook on life, not just a healthy diet.

Isn't Pam® an artificial product?

It depends on what you term "artificial." Nonaerosol Pam® contains oil, lecithin, and alcohol. Oil is natural (whether it be corn, canola, or olive), lecithin is natural (a derivative of the soy bean), and so is alcohol (derived from corn for clarity and acting as a preservative). Besides being the active agent in Pam® that prevents sticking, lecithin, when taken in supplement form, has been linked in some studies with the lowering of cholesterol levels. Regular aerosol Pam® also contains a propellant, a mixture of isobutane, n-butane, and propane, all gases which exist in the atmosphere—which tells me nothing since I'm not an atmospheric scientist. Even though the Pam® people assured me that the propellant didn't harm the atmosphere and contained no CFC's, still . . . how much of these gases do we need to be spritzing around the house? So for my own purposes, I usually stick to the nonaerosol variety and rest assured that I'm ingesting a natural product and being eco-friendly.

What shouldn't I eat?

Eat anything you like in moderation. Eggs, butter, cheese, bacon—you name it, there is nothing inherently wrong or bad in any food as long as it is eaten in moderation. Julia Child was asked, "What foods shouldn't we eat?" and she replied, "Eat anything you like in moderation, moderation, moderation!" How very true!

I'm so frustrated with nutrition! One minute I read that olive oil is good for you, the next that it's not so good as they thought; ten years ago they said that salt and sugar were the enemy, then they reneged on that later. Why should I believe anyone? If I believe all the reports, everything gives you cancer!

I understand your frustration and sympathize. Unfortunately for all concerned, nutrition is a very young science and scientists are still figuring out how it works. And herein lies one of the problems with dissecting one part of the package known as "health"—individual parts of it demonstrate various results depending on the study and the context. What is most important, in my humble opinion, is not to focus obsessively on the individual components of health but the totality. A classic example of this is how several years ago studies reported that HDL cholesterol (good) was exactly that, good; now, studies suggest that too much HDL cholesterol may not be as good as earlier reported. People feel betrayed by this information; but what can you do? If you follow the advice of the "experts" and maintain a balanced diet, then very little can go wrong. If you follow the advice of the "experts" and go off the deep end radically altering your lifestyle and diet, you could end up in the hospital. (Remember the high-protein liquid diet of years past?) The only advice I can give is to do your best at maintaining a healthy diet, take all new nutritional information you read with a grain of moderation (notice I didn't say "a grain of salt"), and keep your sense of humor.

Soups

- *How to Make Defatted Chicken Stock*

  Beef and Barley Stew
  Black Bean Soup
  Broccoli Soup
  Chervil-laced Carrot Soup
  Creamy Corn Chowder
  Gazpacho
  Seafood Gumbo
  Lebanese Lentil Soup
  Hearty Navy Bean Soup
  Summer Split-Pea Soup
  Pleasant Peasant Stew
  Red Pepper Soup
  Chilled Sorrel Soup
  Sparkling Spinach Soup
  Vietnamese Chicken Soup
  Tomato-Ginger Soup
  Wild Rice Soup

I CAN'T THINK OF a more satisfying or soul-healing food than soup. It evokes humankind's earliest beginnings, heating whatever was available in a primitive pot—meat, bones, leaves, and newly discovered vegetables. I can envision families from the past three thousand years gathered 'round a steaming bowlful with a big chunk of freshly baked bread, dipping the bread in the bowl periodically, finishing off by sopping up any broth with the last bit of bread; families in what would become Asia, Europe, and the Americas, communing at what would evolve into the "dinner table." The universality of soup is truly an amazing anthropological event; it crosses all cultures, all social boundaries, all barriers; the humble yet nourishing soup!

Even today when autumn is approaching and the days are beginning to show signs of decline with the cooler-than-expected nip in the air, or when the gray gloom of a wet and rainy day has set into a damp evening, nothing but *nothing* revives the spirit like stoking a roaring fire in the hearth and partaking of one of the simplest yet best meals, soup and bread. Soup not only is a first-class way to heat your bones from the inside out; it comforts when mild cases of depression set in. Somehow soup is reminiscent of having the warm and caring arms of Mother wrapped around you, whispering, "Everything's all right! Momma's here to take care of you now!"

Perhaps I seem oversentimental about soup, but so many times I've heard people state: "I like soup for lunch, but not for dinner. I don't consider soup a *meal*."

Oh my.

I just hope they never come to my house for dinner some cold evening! I couldn't imagine anything better!

How to Make Defatted Chicken Stock

Question: Why should anyone make chicken stock when you can buy it?

First off, when you buy stock you're buying whatever else is in the can—salt, MSG, maltodextrose, artificial color, BHT, hydrolyzed protein, the infamous "flavor enhancer," and the list goes on and on. Fat is the least of the worries one encounters with canned stock.

Chicken stock is simplicity itself to make and is quite economical. By saving chicken bones in the freezer you can accumulate enough to make a big pot of delicious stock (another reason to buy chicken breasts *with* bones and do the boning yourself!). There's nothing complicated about this process and no real measurements are needed. The best stock comes from the highest proportion of bones and meat to water; that is, the more bones you have in a pot the more taste there will be. If you're in the mood to make stock and are lacking bones, you may wish to ask your butcher if he or she has any leftover chicken bones which they usually give away at minimal or no cost. If not, simply purchase a couple of packages of chicken wings or chicken "drummettes," the part of the chicken wing that resembles a miniature chicken leg. These are loaded with flavor and are quite inexpensive. Some ancient Chinese recipes call for using an entire chicken just for making stock, which is fine—but a bit expensive I think, since the chicken meat is then thrown away because it has lost its flavor.

This "recipe" is amazingly delicious by itself without the addition of onions, carrots, or herbs; and since there are no seasonings except salt, there is nothing to mask the taste. After you have made the stock, you may wish to add other flavorings, such as a bouquet garni or vegetables, but for your basic chicken stock, this can't be beat.

You will need:

> **chicken bones and/or chicken "drummettes" or wings**
> **water**
> **a big pot**
> **salt**
> **a large sieve or colander that fits into a large bowl, or a slotted spoon**

Place as many chicken bones and/or chicken drummettes or wings as you can in a large pot (or small pot, if you're making a small amount of stock). Fill the pot with just enough water to come an inch over the bones. Put the pot over moderate heat and bring it to a boil; as soon as the boiling point has been reached, reduce the heat to low and simmer for 60 minutes. (If you're making a very large amount of stock, you may wish to increase the cooking time to 2 hours.) Skim off and discard any scum that may arise during the first 10 to 15 minutes of cooking. During the cooking process you should always have enough water just to cover the bones; if too much liquid evaporates, fill the pot with additional water just so the bones are covered. Occasionally you may wish to mash down and break up the bones so that you won't have to keep adding liquid.

After the 60 minutes is up, turn off the heat. There will be fat on the surface of the broth as well as a potful of cooked bones. Let the broth cool for 20 minutes before you proceed.

Now you have a couple of options:

One) You can fit a large sieve in an appropriately large bowl and carefully pour the broth into the sieve; then you merely lift the sieve up and you'll have a bowlful of broth and fat, and a colander full of bones.

Two) You can scoop out the bones with a slotted spoon and set them aside.

Either way, the object of the exercise is to remove the bones. After the bones have been removed, skim off any fat from the surface of the broth with a spoon—you won't be able to get all of the fat, but don't worry about that now. When you've removed as much fat as you can, add salt gradually to taste. If you have a quart of stock, try 1 teaspoon of salt to begin with, then taste. You may wish to add more salt, but remember Kitchen Maxim #552: *You can always add salt—you can never take it away.* It's always better to be a bit miserly with the salt at this stage. When you're satisfied with the taste, refrigerate the stock. When it is quite cold, the fat will have coagulated on the surface and will be hard; now is the time to easily remove the remaining fat. When you've removed all of the fat on the surface, you've removed all of the fat there is! You now have defatted chicken stock! Homemade chicken stock is gelatinous when it is cold; this is natural. Cooking the chicken bones for an extended period is the reason it turns jellylike, and when the stock is brought to room temperature (or barely heated), it will return to a liquid state.

But what are you to do with the bones? If you wish, and this is by no means mandatory, you may remove any leftover pieces of meat from the breast bones and from the wings. These pieces don't have much taste by themselves but can be used as a filler for soups, chicken pot pies, or as a treat for your pet. Otherwise throw the bones away.

As you can see, making chicken stock is by no means difficult. You fill the pot, bring it to a simmer, cook, strain, and refrigerate. None of these steps are in themselves time-consuming, and making stock is even easier when you're already in the kitchen working on something else. Stock preparation is always a secondary task in the kitchen, though a vital one. If you're used to canned stock, you'll be shocked at the utter difference between mass-produced stock and your delicious, homemade stock. Homemade stock also gives you the peace of mind knowing that you're using pure ingredients without artificial additives and chemicals.

31

Beef and Barley Stew

SERVES 4 TO 6

This soulful soup is uplifting and comforting on a cool day, besides being nutritious, hearty, and completely satisfying. Nothing more is needed but a loaf of warm homemade bread.

1	**teaspoon olive oil and Pam®**
½	**pound lean beef tips or stewing beef**
½	**cup pearled barley**
1	**cup chopped onion**
1	**clove garlic, minced (optional)**
1	**cup chopped carrots**
1	**cup chopped celery**
1	**bay leaf**
1	**teaspoon marjoram (optional)**
½	**teaspoon thyme**
3 to 4	**cups defatted, full-flavored beef stock**
1	**cup red wine, or ⅔ cup red wine and ⅓ cup fine port**
1½	**cups cooked navy beans (if canned, drained and rinsed)**
	chopped parsley for garnish

Note: It's probably best to purchase a better quality of beef than usual for soup, because traditional stewing beef takes quite a long time to become tender. If you use a cheaper cut you will have mushy vegetables by the time the meat becomes edible.

Heat the oil and Pam® over a moderate flame in a large saucepan or Dutch oven; add the beef. Brown the beef on all sides as much as you can; don't worry if it sticks to the pan. Add the barley, onions, and garlic, stirring and cooking until the onion is soft, approximately 5 to 7 minutes. Next add the carrots, celery, herbs, stock, wine(s), and navy beans. Bring the soup to a simmer and cook gently for 30 minutes. After 30 minutes, taste the soup to see if the barley has cooked through; if the mixture becomes too thick, add water or wine to thin it out; it should have the consistency of a stew. When the beef has cooked sufficiently to cut easily and is tender, remove the soup from heat.

Serve with hot bread, garnishing with parsley.

Per 12-ounce serving:

Calories: 324
Carbohydrates: 29.3 g
Protein: 20.9 g
Fat Total: 4.9 g
Fat Saturated: 1.4 g

Variations

- Add 1 can of chopped tomatoes.
- Add 2 cups large diced potatoes along with the carrots.
- Add 2 cups sliced mushrooms along with the onions.
- For a vegetarian version, eliminate the beef and beef stock; add instead vegetable stock or a mixture of vegetable stock and tomato juice.

Black Bean Soup

SERVES 4 TO 6

Bracing and delicious. Be sure to try the Variation at the bottom of the recipe — it completely changes the taste of the soup!

	Pam®
1	**small onion**
1 to 2	**cloves garlic, minced**
1	**teaspoon olive oil**
1	**18-ounce can of Italian plum tomatoes, chopped, seeded, and drained**
⅓	**cup each green and red pepper**
1	**bay leaf**
3 to 4	**cups defatted, flavorful chicken stock**
½	**teaspoon thyme**
1	**teaspoon basil**
1	**cup white wine or vermouth or red wine**
	juice of half a lemon
	up to 4 cups (roughly 3 15-ounce cans) cooked black beans (see note below)
	tamari or soy sauce to taste (approximately 1 tablespoon maximum)
2	**tablespoons fresh chopped parsley**
1	**chicken breast, diced (optional)**

Note: This recipe can be vastly different depending on what quality of soup you are aiming for; thick or thin, summer or winter, etc. If you want a thinner soup with recognizable pieces, use a total of 1½ cups (1 can) of drained, cooked black beans. If you wish to have a heartier, thicker soup, use the entire amount of cooked black beans, pureeing 3 cups (2 cans) and leaving the remainder (or the other can) whole.

Place a large, heavy pot over moderate heat; when the pot is hot, spray it with Pam®. Immediately add the oil, onions, and garlic. Sauté the onions and garlic for several minutes until the onion is soft and translucent. Add the plum tomatoes, peppers, bay, chicken stock, thyme, basil, wine, and lemon. Bring the soup to the simmering point and let simmer for 10 to 15 minutes. Add the beans (see note above) and cook another 10 to 15 minutes. Taste for seasoning; add tamari if it needs a bit of extra flavoring, parsley, and the optional chicken. Let the pot remain cooking until the chicken bits are just done. Remove from heat.

Serve with hot, crusty bread and a salad. If desired, garnish hot soup with grated low-fat cheddar or jack cheese.

This soup keeps perfectly in the refrigerator for several days; to serve, simply reheat gently.

Variations

- Instead of using bay, basil, and thyme, use ½ teaspoon curry powder, 1 teaspoon ground cumin, 1 teaspoon chili powder, and ⅛ teaspoon cayenne.

Serving four:

Calories: 384
Carbohydrates: 47.8 g
Protein: 31.3 g
Total Fat: 4.0 g
Saturated Fat: .83 g

Serving six:

Calories: 256
Carbohydrates: 31.9 g
Protein: 20.8 g
Fat Total: 2.7 g
Fat Saturated: .55 g

Broccoli Soup

SERVES 4

Broccoli soup is another much-neglected item which is nutritious, unusual, and simple. It has a smooth, creamy consistency with little chunks of broccoli and mushrooms floating about, and is lovely to have after or during a minor illness; the bright-green color is appealing, and the warm, comforting taste is healing.

1	**teaspoon olive oil or butter and Pam®**
1	**cup onion, finely minced**
1	**clove garlic, minced (optional)**
1½	**cups mushrooms, finely diced**
1	**cup celery, diced**
3	**tablespoons flour**
½	**cup white wine or vermouth**
½	**cup milk, skim or low-fat**
3 to 4	**cups flavorful, defatted chicken stock**
3	**tablespoons chopped fresh basil**
½	**teaspoon marjoram**
¼	**teaspoon ground nutmeg**
2 to 3	**cups broccoli, broken into small florets**
	salt and pepper

In a large pot heat the oil or butter over a medium flame; when hot, spray some Pam® in with the oil and add the onions and optional garlic, cooking for 5 minutes or so, until the onion is soft and translucent. Add the mushrooms and celery and continue cooking for another 2 to 3 minutes, then add the flour. Stir and cook the flour with the vegetables for 1 minute. Add the wine, milk, and chicken stock, stirring well to separate the flour granules, bringing the soup to the simmering point. Add the basil, marjoram, and nutmeg and continue simmering for 15 to 20 minutes. Add the broccoli and return to the simmering point. Place 1 to 1½ cups of the soup in a food processor or blender and puree until it is nearly smooth; return the puree to the pot. (If desired, you can completely puree all of soup for a smooth, pale-green creamy soup.) Taste for seasoning.

Serve hot with a baguette or warm French bread and a salad, garnishing with a dollop of sour cream and a sprig of fresh basil or parsley, or with a splash of fresh lemon and/or a sprinkling of Parmesan cheese.

Per serving:

Calories: 205
Carbohydrates: 29.9 g
Protein: 14.8 g
Fat Total: 1.8 g
Fat Saturated: .28 g

Chervil-Laced Carrot Soup

SERVES 4

Bright yellow speckled with green and fragrant with chervil, this light and attractive soup is an uncommon treat. Chervil is a very delicately leaved herb and subtle in taste, almost like a very pale anise or tarragon. Chervil traditionally used to be eaten (and may still be eaten for all I know) after Lent on Holy Thursday as a restorative. Perhaps this soup will become a new Easter tradition . . . ?

1	**teaspoon butter with Pam®**
3 to 4	**cups carrots, julienned**
¼	**cup flour**
3 to 4	**cups strong defatted chicken stock**
½	**cup vermouth**
½	**cup chopped fresh chervil**
	salt and pepper to taste
	nonfat yogurt or nonfat sour cream
	sprigs of fresh chervil or fresh parsley

Heat the butter and Pam® in a saucepan over a moderate flame; when hot, reduce the flame to medium-low and add the carrots, sautéing for 8 minutes until tender. Add the flour, stirring well to make sure there are no lumps, then add the stock and wine. Bring the soup to the simmering point and cook gently for 20 minutes.

Place the soup in a food processor and puree until smooth; return the soup to the pan and add the chopped chervil. Bring just to the simmer again, add salt and pepper, and taste for seasoning. Serve hot (or cold) with a dollop of yogurt or sour cream and a sprig of fresh chervil.

Variations

- Add 1 teaspoon curry powder.
- Use fresh dill instead of chervil, but only add ⅓ cup instead of the ½ cup fresh herb.

Per serving:

Calories: 148
Carbohydrates: 20.9 g
Protein: 6.6 g
Fat Total: 0.8 g
Fat Saturated: 0.1 g

Creamy Corn Chowder

SERVES 4

Quite rich and creamy, this chowder is a lovely first course. Bright yellow with a few dots of red and green, it is eye-catching and attractive.

Pam®
½   **cup minced onion**
2   **tablespoons flour**
½   **teaspoon ground cumin**
     the corn from 4 to 6 fresh ears of corn, either yellow or white (if using white corn, you may wish to add ½ teaspoon turmeric to give it more of a yellow color)
3   **cups flavorful defatted chicken stock**
1   **cup skim milk**
⅛ to ¼   **teaspoon cayenne**
6 to 8   **ounces nonfat sour cream (see note below)**
½   **cup red bell pepper, diced into ¼-inch cubes**
     salt to taste

     parsley or cilantro as garnish, if desired

*Note: You can either mix all of the sour cream in the soup at one time, or use part of it in the soup and serve 2-tablespoon dollops in each bowl as it is served as garnish.

In a large pan, sauté the onion with Pam® over medium-low heat, covered, until the onion is soft and translucent. Add the flour and cumin, stirring and allowing the flour to cook for a minute or so. Add the corn and chicken stock, bringing the soup to a simmer and allowing it to cook for 10 minutes, scraping the flour from the bottom and incorporating it into the soup. Remove the pan from the heat. Using a slotted spoon, remove and puree one-half to two-thirds of the soup in a food processor or blender until the desired consistency is reached; it should still retain pieces of corn and not be a totally smooth puree. Return the partially pureed mixture to the pot and to the medium flame. Add the milk, cayenne, and sour cream (*see* note above). Bring the soup to the simmering point; as soon as the soup is hot, add the diced red bell pepper. Remove from heat and let the soup stand, covered, for 2 to 3 minutes. Taste for seasoning, adding salt if necessary. Serve with additional dollops of sour cream, and garnish with cilantro or parsley leaves.

Per serving:

Calories: 219
Carbohydrates: 41.4 g
Protein: 11.9 g
Fat Total: 1.9 g
Fat Saturated: 0.3 g

Gazpacho

SERVES 4

España! I was lucky enough to spend a month in Spain and tour the country from Madrid to Toledo to Granada to Seville to Ronda to Barcelona to Santiago de Compostela! (And then, back to Madrid!) A typical cross-country trip, seeing and tasting the local cuisines firsthand. Spanish cooking, like the countryside itself, is rough-hewn and peasanty; this is not an insult, for the freshest food prepared in the simplest manner is beyond reproach. I suppose I ate more of the National Soup of Spain at the beginning of my trip than I should have, for by the time I reached Andalusia (where eating gazpacho is de rigeur), I felt full to my eyeballs with it and couldn't swallow another spoonful!

This is not the famous Andalusian version which is a pale orange soup base into which chopped cucumber, peppers, tomatoes, and hard-cooked egg are added at the dinner table. This is a basic yet lovely gazpacho, easily and quickly prepared—nutritious and refreshing.

Per serving:

Calories: 81.7
Carbohydrates: 19 g
Protein: 2.9 g
Fat Total: .7 g
Fat Saturated: .094 g

2	**cups tomatoes, peeled, seeded, and chopped**
1	**small cucumber, peeled and seeded**
1	**small green or red pepper**
2	**green onions**
1 to 2	**cloves garlic, minced or put through a garlic press**
2	**tablespoons fresh chopped basil**
1	**teaspoon ground cumin**
3 or 4	**tablespoons chopped parsley**
2	**tablespoons chopped cilantro**
3	**cups tomato juice**
2	**tablespoons lemon juice**
2	**tablespoons balsamic vinegar**
2	**tablespoons Worcestershire sauce**
½	**teaspoon freshly ground black pepper**
	salt to taste
	cayenne or Tabasco® to taste

Combine the tomatoes, cucumber, pepper, green onion, and garlic in a food processor and blend until the pieces are small but still recognizable (that is, the size of a grain of rice or an oat groat). Place the chopped mixture into a large bowl and add the remaining ingredients. Taste for seasoning, then chill the soup for several hours before serving. Garnish with chopped cilantro or chopped fresh basil and croutons.

Variations

- For a lighter soup, add 1 cup ice water.
- For a heartier soup, garnish with chopped hard-cooked egg. This adds fat and cholesterol but tastes good.
- For a creamier soup, add a dollop of nonfat sour cream or yogurt as a garnish.

Seafood Gumbo

SERVES 4

Gumbo is one of those wonderful, hearty, rich stews which screams COMFORT FOOD! I'm sure many gumbo recipes use 8 ounces of butter to brown the flour, but so much added fat really isn't necessary. This can be made ahead of time and refrigerated or even frozen.

Per serving:

Calories: 353
Carbohydrates: 38.7 g
Protein: 28.2 g
Fat Total: 6.2 g
Fat Saturated: 1.9 g

1	**tablespoon butter**
1	**teaspoon olive oil**
2	**tablespoons flour**
1	**cup onion, finely chopped**
2	**cloves garlic, minced**
1	**cup celery, chopped**
1	**cup okra, cut into ¼-inch rounds**
1½	**cups tomatoes, peeled, seeded, and chopped or 1 18-ounce can tomatoes, drained and chopped**
1	**cup corn, fresh or frozen**
1½	**cups green and red peppers, diced**
¼ to ½	**teaspoon cayenne (depending on how much heat you want)**
1	**teaspoon each basil, oregano, and thyme**
1	**bay leaf**
3	**tablespoons parsley**
1	**8- to 12-ounce jar clam juice**
3	**cups defatted chicken stock**
1	**cup vermouth**
2	**tablespoons lemon juice**
	assorted fish and seafood: ¼ pound shrimp (peeled and deveined), ¼ pound scallops, ¼ pound lean white fish cut into bite-sized pieces, ¼ pound crab meat (optional)
1	**tablespoon gumbo filé**

Place a large pot over medium heat and melt the butter with the olive oil. Sprinkle in the flour and continue to cook until the roux has turned a light nut brown, approximately 3 to 5 minutes. Add the onion and garlic to the roux and continue cooking and stirring until the onion has softened. Add the celery and okra, stirring often. (The okra will make this look truly disgusting, but it's supposed to look like that. Trust me!) Add the tomatoes, corn, green and red bell peppers, herbs, and seasonings; stir and cook another minute or so. Add the clam juice, chicken stock, vermouth, and lemon. Bring to a simmer and let cook for 20 minutes.

Taste for seasoning. The gumbo should be rich and flavorful and the vegetables should be quite done. Add the cut-up fish and seafood pieces, leaving at the simmering point just long enough to cook the seafood through, around 3 to 5 minutes. Remove the gumbo from the heat. Sprinkle the filé powder on top and stir well.

Serve immediately, or allow to cool. Simply reheat gently and serve with a salad.

Lebanese Lentil Soup

SERVES 4

Simple yet bracing—an ideal cold-weather lunch accompanied with pita bread sandwiches. As you can see, the amount of lentils is a matter of choice: the lesser amount results in a thinner soup; the greater in a more stewlike product.

1 to 2	**cups red lentils, soaked in warm water for 1 to 2 hours**
1	**teaspoon olive oil and Pam®**
1 to 1½	**cups onions, finely minced**
1	**clove garlic, minced**
2	**cups tomato juice**
1 to 1½	**cups strong defatted stock, chicken or vegetable**
1	**tablespoon ground coriander**
1	**teaspoon ground cumin**
	salt and pepper
2 to 3	**tablespoons chopped cilantro or mint for garnish**

Soak the lentils in warm water for 1 to 2 hours. Drain the soaked beans, rinsing well, then set aside.

Heat the oil and Pam® in a large saucepan over a medium flame; when hot, add the onion. Sauté the onion for about 5 minutes until tender, stirring occasionally. Add the garlic and the drained lentils, stirring and sautéing for another few minutes. Add the tomato juice, stock, ground coriander, and cumin; bring the soup to the simmering point. Cover and cook for 30 to 40 minutes, or until the lentils are done and soft. Taste for seasoning.

Serve hot with a garnish of cilantro and/or fresh mint.

Variation

- Use curry powder instead of cumin and add 1 teaspoon finely minced gingerroot.

Per serving:

Calories: 242
Carbohydrates: 41.8 g
Protein: 16.2 g
Fat Total: 2.5 g
Fat Saturated: 0.3 g

Hearty Navy Bean Soup

SERVES 4

Savory and satisfying, this chicken-bean soup would be a lovely first course for an informal dinner, or another autumn treat.

2	**teaspoons olive oil**
1	**small onion, finely chopped**
2	**stalks celery, diced (less if stalks are very large)**
2	**carrots, ¼-inch diced**
1	**clove garlic, minced**
3½	**cups chicken stock, defatted**
½ to ⅔	**cup white wine or dry vermouth**
1	**bay leaf**
1	**teaspoon thyme**
¼	**teaspoon tarragon**
¼	**teaspoon basil**
2	**tablespoons chopped parsley**
3	**cups navy beans (if canned, drained and rinsed)**
1	**chicken breast, diced**
⅓	**cup fresh chopped tomato**

In a large soup pot, sauté onion in olive oil over medium flame until it is translucent and soft. Add the celery, carrots, and garlic, continuing to cook for another minute or so. Add the chicken stock, wine, bay, thyme, tarragon, basil, and parsley; bring the soup to the simmering point. Add 1½ cups of the navy beans to the soup pot. Place the remaining navy beans in a food processor and puree until smooth. Add the pureed beans to the soup, stirring well. Let the soup simmer for 20 minutes or so; taste for seasoning. Add the diced chicken breast and tomato and cook until chicken is just done, around 3 minutes.

Serve immediately with a garnish of fresh parsley and with large salad and/or garlic toast.

Per 12-ounce serving:

Calories: 347
Carbohydrates: 49.8 g
Protein: 24.8 g
Fat Total: 3.5 g
Fat Saturated: .64 g

Summer Split-Pea Soup

SERVES 4

What would the world do without soups? Perfect for lunch and dinner; in Japan, soups are served at breakfast! That mysterious feeling we associate with "comfort food" is certainly entwined with homemade soup!

Please note that the split peas need to be presoaked.

1	**teaspoon olive oil and Pam®**
1	**medium onion, finely chopped**
1	**clove garlic, minced**
1	**cup split peas, soaked overnight, then rinsed well**
1	**tablespoon tomato paste**
3 to 4	**cups defatted chicken, beef, or vegetable stock**
½	**cup tomato, peeled, seeded, and chopped**
2	**new red potatoes, diced into ¼-inch pieces**
½	**cup diced zucchini or yellow crookneck squash**
¼	**cup chopped fresh basil**
	salt and pepper to taste
	nonfat yogurt
	basil leaves

Per serving:

Calories: 233
Carbohydrates: 41.3 g
Protein: 14 g
Fat Total: 1.9 g
Fat Saturated: .27 g

Heat the oil in a large saucepan over a medium flame. When hot, spray with Pam® and add the onions and garlic, sautéing and stirring until the onion has softened, around 2 minutes. Add the drained split peas, tomato paste, and stock. Bring to a simmer and cook for 30 minutes or so, until the peas are almost cooked. Remove the soup from the heat and allow to cool for 5 to 10 minutes. Place the split pea mixture into a food processor or blender and puree until completely smooth. Return pea puree to the soup pot and add the tomato and potatoes, simmering until the potatoes have softened and the split peas are completely done, another 15 minutes or so.

Add the zucchini and basil, cooking for no more than 2 additional minutes. Taste for seasoning, adding salt and pepper if desired.

Serve warm with a dollop of nonfat yogurt and a fresh basil leaf as garnish; serve with fresh bread or a bright green salad.

Variations

- Add 2 tablespoons finely chopped Canadian bacon along with the onion and garlic.
- For vegetarians, add 1 tablespoon smoked yeast to the pureed peas and use vegetable stock.

Pleasant Peasant Stew

SERVES 4 TO 6

Serving four:

Calories: 321
Carbohydrates: 54.6 g
Protein: 17.6 g
Fat Total: 3.8 g
Fat Saturated: .44 g

Serving six:

Calories: 214
Carbohydrates: 36.4 g
Protein: 11.7 g
Fat Total: 2.6 g
Fat Saturated: .29 g

The name of this stew reminds me of one of my favorite "I Love Lucy" episodes, wherein Lucy writes an operetta for the Wednesday Afternoon Women's Club (that meets on Tuesday). The operetta was called "The Pleasant Peasant." In it, Lucy played the snaggletoothed Queen of the Gypsies, Ethel was the ingenue Lily of the Valley, Ricky was "typecast" as the Good Prince Lancelot, and Fred got to be the gouty Innkeeper of the Inn on the River Out.

They just don't write 'em like that anymore!

2	**teaspoons olive oil**
2	**cups chopped onions**
2 to 3	**tablespoons curry powder (depending on how much you like curry powder)**
1	**cup chopped celery**
2	**cloves garlic, minced or put through a garlic press**
1	**18-ounce can tomatoes, chopped (including juice from can)**
1	**cup brown or green lentils**
1	**bay leaf**
1	**teaspoon each thyme and marjoram**
4	**cups defatted stock or water, or a mixture of both**
2 to 3	**tablespoons tamari or soy sauce**
3	**tablespoons sherry or white wine**
½	**cup uncooked rice (brown or white) or barley**

nonfat yogurt or nonfat sour cream

Heat the oil in a large, heavy Dutch oven over a moderate flame; when hot, add the onions and cook until they are soft and translucent, about 3 minutes. Add the curry powder, celery, garlic, tomatoes, lentils, bay leaf, thyme, marjoram, stock, tamari, and sherry. Bring to the simmering point and cover, cooking for 30 minutes over low heat.

Add the rice; continue to simmer until rice and lentils are done, approximately 20 minutes more.

Serve hot in bowls and top with a dollop of nonfat yogurt or nonfat sour cream.

Red Pepper Soup

SERVES 4

Cold soups are outstanding in hot weather, and this refreshing alternative to the omnipresent gazpacho is quite pretty in appearance—deep scarlet, a dollop of white, and a graceful basil leaf for dynamics!

2	**teaspoons olive oil**
1	**clove garlic, minced**
½	**cup onion, finely minced**
5	**red bell peppers, roasted, peeled, and chopped** (see note below)
½	**cup tomato, peeled, seeded, and chopped**
3	**tablespoons fresh basil**
	a pinch of herbes de Provence
3	**cups (approximately) defatted chicken stock or vegetable stock**
½	**cup vermouth or white wine**
1	**tablespoon balsamic vinegar**
	salt to taste
	nonfat sour cream
	fresh parsley or basil sprigs

Note: To roast, hold each pepper over an open flame (or under a broiler) using tongs, until the pepper is completely charred and black on the outside, turning as necessary. When the pepper is black, wrap it in a paper towel and place the wrapped pepper in a large cloth towel. Let the peppers sit for 20 minutes or so, then remove them from their wrappings and wash the charred skin away under cool, running water. Seed and chop the roasted pepper.

Place a large pan over a medium flame and heat olive oil briefly. Add the onion and garlic, cooking until the onion is soft, around 3 to 5 minutes. Remove the pan from heat.

Place the onion-garlic mixture, roasted and seeded peppers, tomato, and basil in a food processor and blend until you have almost a complete puree; it is fine if some of the pieces remain the size of a split pea. Return this mixture to the soup pot and add the herbes de Provence, stock, wine, and vinegar. Bring to a simmer, allowing the soup to remain at the simmer for 8 to 10 minutes. Take the soup off the heat, cover, and let cool. When the soup is room temperature, salt it to taste. Chill the soup.

Serve the soup cold or cool with a dollop of nonfat yogurt or sour cream, and garnish with additional fresh basil sprigs.

Variations

- Serve hot by reheating gently before serving.
- Use fresh thyme instead of basil.

Per serving:

Calories: 112
Carbohydrates: 13.7 g
Protein: 4.7 g
Fat Total: 2.6 g
Fat Saturated: .36 g

43

Chilled Sorrel Soup

SERVES 4

Sorrel is a lovely, leafy green belonging to the buckwheat family, resembling pale spring-green spinach in appearance and with a distinct lemony tang originating from the oxalate in its veins. The taste is almost identical to the common wood sorrel, Oxalis acetosella.

This soup would be a fitting beginning for a St. Patrick's Day dinner or for a Midsummer's Feast, glorifying the availability and freshness of seasonal produce. A must for summer brunches.

1 cucumber, peeled, seeded, and grated
1 clove garlic
3 cups strong defatted chicken stock
2 cups sorrel leaves, trimmed and washed
⅔ cup nonfat yogurt or nonfat sour cream
salt and pepper to taste

parsley, chervil, or (if available) wood sorrel for garnish

Bring the cucumber, garlic, and stock to a simmer in a soup pot over medium flame; cook until the cucumber is tender, around 5 to 10 minutes. Remove the soup from the heat and allow to sit for 5 minutes. Place the fresh sorrel leaves into a food processor; add the warm soup base and blend until smooth. Empty the soup into a large bowl.

Add the yogurt or sour cream, salt, and pepper; mix well, using a whisk if necessary. Taste for seasoning, keeping in mind that a cold soup needs more salt than a heated soup. Chill when you are satisfied with the seasoning.

Serve cold with a garnish of parsley, chervil, or the lovely trifoliate wood sorrel.

Per serving:

Calories: 74.9
Carbohydrates: 6.4 g
Protein: 6.5 g
Fat Total: .5 g
Fat Saturated: .075 g

Sparkling Spinach Soup

SERVES 4

Yet another lovely green soup, this potage is delicious, unusual, and simple to prepare.

1	**pound spinach, trimmed and washed**
2	**teaspoons butter or olive oil**
4	**green onions, finely minced**
1	**small clove garlic, minced**
2	**tablespoons flour**
2	**cups defatted, full-flavored chicken stock**
½	**cup vermouth**
1	**cup skim milk**
½	**cup nonfat sour cream**
¼	**cup fresh basil, chopped**
½	**teaspoon thyme**
	salt and pepper to taste
	fresh lemon juice
	chopped fresh parsley

Place a kettle of water (2 quarts or so) on the stove and bring to a boil.

Place the stemmed and washed spinach in a large colander or sieve. When the kettle of water is boiling, pour the hot water over the fresh spinach slowly, turning the spinach as necessary. The spinach will turn from medium green to a deep, vivid green and will wilt. Immediately rinse the blanched spinach in cold water. When the spinach is cool, squeeze out any excess liquid. Chop roughly and set aside.

In a large pan, heat the butter over a medium flame; add the onions and garlic. Stir and cook the onions and garlic briefly, then add the flour and cook for 1 minute, scraping the bottom of the pan as you go. Add the remaining ingredients, including the blanched spinach. Bring the soup just to a simmer, then remove from the heat.

Using a slotted spoon, place three-quarters of the spinach and onions in a food processor with some (½ to 1 cup or so) of the liquid. Process until the mixture is a smooth puree. Return the smooth spinach puree to the soup pan and stir. Taste for seasoning, adding salt and pepper as necessary. Serve the soup hot or warm with a sprinkling of freshly chopped parsley and a small squirt of fresh lemon juice.

Vietnamese Chicken Soup

SERVES 4

This will wake you up and get you moving on a cold evening! It's also great instead of the traditional chicken soup for illnesses, but only if you're suffering from a head cold or respiratory problem, as the hot pepper is not recommended for an upset stomach. Garlic is wonderful for sicknesses, being an inhibitor of viruses and bacteria, ginger aids the circulatory system and warms you from the inside out, and the hot pepper clears the sinuses and gets the blood flowing. But don't wait until you're sick to try this—it's delicious!

1	**teaspoon flavorless oil (such as canola)**
2 to 3	**garlic cloves, minced or put through a garlic press**
2 to 3	**green onions, diced**
1	**teaspoon finely minced gingerroot**
1 to 2	**small hot peppers (finely minced) or**
	¼ teaspoon cayenne or ½ teaspoon crushed red pepper flakes
1	**cup sliced mushrooms**
3	**cups defatted chicken stock**
½ to 1	**cup white wine**
3	**tablespoons lemon juice**
2 to 3	**tablespoons red wine vinegar**
1 to 3	**teaspoons sugar or honey (optional)**
⅓	**cup diced, peeled, and seeded tomato**
½	**teaspoon toasted sesame oil**
	one-half chicken breast, thinly sliced
⅔	**cup small broccoli florets**
½	**cup sliced snow peas**
¼	**cup chopped cilantro (loose, not packed)**

In a large saucepan, heat 1 teaspoon oil over moderate heat and then add the garlic, green onions, gingerroot, and hot peppers. Sauté for a bit (around 1 minute) until the garlic has become more opaque and lost its raw look. (If desired, you may even toast the garlic a bit until it is lightly nut brown.) Add the mushrooms and sauté for an additional 30 seconds, then add the chicken stock, wine, lemon juice, vinegar, and sugar. Stir and bring to the simmering point. Add the tomato, sesame oil, and sliced

Per serving:

Calories: 124
Carbohydrates: 12.2 g
Protein: 10.4 g
Fat Total: 2.2 g
Fat Saturated: .26 g

chicken breast. Stir again, and allow to cook until chicken has cooked through, around 3 minutes. Add the broccoli and snow peas and immediately remove from the heat. Cover the soup and let it cool a bit (3 minutes), then add the cilantro. Taste for seasoning—it should be hot, garlicky, and tangy!

Serve immediately or cover and refrigerate. Garnish with freshly chopped cilantro.

Variations

- Add ¼ cup bean sprouts to soup.
- Add ½ cup diced shrimp to soup along with or instead of chicken breast.

Tomato-Ginger Soup

SERVES 4

Tired of bland tomato soups? Try this one—it is flavorful and bracing.

Per serving:

Calories: 98.4
Carbohydrates: 16.8 g
Protein: 5.3 g
Fat Total: 1.8 g
Fat Saturated: .22 g

1	**teaspoon oil and Pam®**
1	**small onion, minced**
2	**cloves garlic, minced or put through a garlic press**
2	**stalks celery, finely diced**
1	**tablespoon finely shredded and minced gingerroot**
1	**very large (28-ounce) can tomatoes (chopped), or 3 to 4 cups peeled, seeded, and chopped fresh ripe tomatoes**
2	**cups flavorful defatted stock (chicken, beef, or vegetable)**
½	**teaspoon basil**
1 to 2	**tablespoons tamari**
	nonfat sour cream

Place a large saucepan over medium heat; when the pan is hot, add the oil and spray with Pam®. Immediately add the onion and garlic. Cook and stir until the onion is soft and tender, around 3 to 5 minutes, then add the celery, gingerroot, tomatoes, stock, and basil. Bring the soup to a simmer. Remove the soup from heat and allow to stand and cool for 5 minutes. Place the soup in a food processor or blender and puree briefly until the soup is not quite so chunky, but not a complete puree either. It should be the consistency of gazpacho. Taste for seasoning; adding tamari as needed.

Serve hot with a dollop of nonfat sour cream. Garnish with fresh parsley, basil, or cilantro.

Variation

- Add 1 teaspoon garam masala or fragrant curry powder just before pureeing.

Wild Rice Soup

SERVES 4

This soup is a fall or winter treat, a very nutritious bowlful speckled with rice and vegetables. If you use vegetable stock and eliminate the optional chicken breast, you've got a wonderful vegetarian version with complete protein.

½	**cup wild rice**
	water and 1 teaspoon salt
1	**cup strong defatted chicken, beef, or vegetable stock**
1	**small onion, finely chopped**
1	**tablespoon olive oil**
2	**stalks celery, diced (less if stalks are very large)**
2	**carrots, diced**
1	**clove garlic, minced**
3 to 4	**cups full-flavored defatted chicken, beef, or vegetable stock**
½ to ⅔	**cup white wine or dry vermouth**
1	**bay leaf**
1	**teaspoon thyme**
¼	**teaspoon tarragon**
¼	**teaspoon basil**
2	**tablespoons chopped parsley**
1½	**cups cooked navy beans (if canned, drained and rinsed)**
1	**boneless, skinless chicken breast, diced (optional)**

Fill a heavy sauce pan with 1 to 2 quarts of water and add 1 teaspoon salt; bring the water to a boil. Add the wild rice and boil for 8 minutes, then drain the rice in a colander or sieve. Next place the semicooked wild rice in a small saucepan with a tight-fitting lid and add 1 cup of flavorful stock; bring to the simmering point and cover. Cook over a low flame until the liquid has been absorbed, around 20 to 30 minutes, checking as necessary. Remove from heat when the rice is done (or the liquid is all gone), but keep the pan tightly covered.

In a large soup pot, sauté the onion in olive oil over a medium flame until the onion is translucent and soft, around 3 to 5 minutes. Add the celery, carrots, and garlic; continue cooking and stirring for another minute or so. Add the stock, wine, bay leaf, thyme, tarragon, basil, and parsley, bringing the soup to the simmering point. Meanwhile, puree the navy beans in a food processor until completely smooth, then add the puree to the soup. Next add the cooked wild rice and let the soup simmer for 20 minutes or so, then taste for seasoning. Add the optional diced chicken breast and cook until chicken is just done, around 3 minutes.

Serve immediately, or cool and refrigerate; reheat gently before eating. Serve with large green salad and garlic toast.

Per serving:

Calories: 380
Carbohydrates: 47.8 g
Protein: 28.4 g
Fat Total: 5 g
Fat Saturated: .8 g

Vegetarian

- *Having Vegetarians for Dinner . . . ?*

  Mexican Quiche
  Quiche Athenée
  Spinach-Stuffed Pasta Shells
  Spinach Lasagna
  Savory Stuffed Potatoes
  Lentil Veggies Au Gratin
  Black Bean Enchiladas
  Imperial Navies
  Indian Chickpeas in a Savory Sauce
  Eggplant Parmesan
  Chinese "Hot" Noodles
  "Fried" Rice
  Kingston Town Beans 'n' Rice
  Lentil Lasagna
  Stuffed Peppers
  Fresh Pasta Sauce with Zucchini
  Vegetarian Chili
  Vegetarian "Hamburgers"

Having Vegetarians for Dinner . . . ?

VEGETARIANS, when cooked properly, give you a full day's supply of complete protein.

OH! Having vegetarians *over* for dinner!! Now that's something completely different.

For a great many people, the notion of subsisting on a vegetable-based diet seems unthinkable. "It can't possibly be healthy—humans *need* meat" is frequently heard, or "Where do you get your protein?" "I can always spot vegetarians—they're the pale, sickly looking ones . . ." Vegetarian diets have been a part of humankind for millenia; cultures have not only survived but flourished on a meatless diet. And for those of you who scoff at vegetarians, you may as well gird your loins and get used to the idea because vegetarianism is unquestionably on the rise and has become a large part of mainstream American society, increasing year by year. (I feel myself getting up on my soapbox . . .)

The catalysts for electing a vegetarian diet are varied and deeply personal; be they religious, medical, ethical, or merely idiosyncratic, the reasons should nonetheless be respected. It is unconscionably rude, inconsiderate, and downright wrong to serve meat if you know that you're entertaining vegetarians, and allow them no meatless alternative. I'm reminded of a dinner I attended wherein each dish from appetizer to salad to main course to side dishes contained some kind of meat—and the poor vegetarian guests had no alternative but to choose between breaking their regimen or go hungry and insult the host, as there was no way to "eat around the meat." "But," you ask, "hadn't the host deliberately and with malice aforethought insulted his guests?" Alas, that's another issue entirely. To be fair, perhaps the host didn't know that some of the guests were vegetarians. When in doubt, as a good host, ask your vegetarian guest(s) what they would like to have ahead of time—vegetarians are more than sympathetic with the position they've put their host into, and require very little in way of preparation for the evening's repast. And a gathering of friends sharing a common meal should be a moment of pleasure, not a moment of deep-seated political statements on either the host's part or the guest's part.

There are few rules about vegetarianism, but the most important are *protein* and *vitamin B-12*. A great many plant products are high in protein, but they're incomplete proteins. There's no great mystery about how to combine a complete vegetable protein; just eat a grain and a legume at the same time. Bingo, complete protein. If you're having vegetarians over for dinner, just be sure to serve something that includes a legume product and a grain product. This is extremely easy to do; for example, if you serve hummus with pita bread triangles as an appetizer, you've served a complete vegetarian protein. The hummus is made of chickpeas and the pita comes from wheat flour. Or you could serve a split-pea soup with hot, homemade biscuits—once again, a bean (split pea, a legume) and a grain. Many cuisines (Indian, Chinese, Japanese) use novel ingredients such as bean flours (like *besan*, a chickpea flour from India) that allow you even greater flexibility with vegetarian combinations. You could make some hot dinner rolls combining wheat flour and chickpea flour, or you could make a light minestrone soup with pasta noodles—both complete proteins. In India you could have *besan* dumplings served with a yogurt sauce accompanied by a rice pilaf: beans (chickpea flour), rice (grain), and yogurt (vitamin B-12)! I could go on making lists for days—it is really quite simple and easy!

It is not necessary to serve *whole* beans or grains, just something made *from* beans or grains. Bread, be it corn bread, wheat bread, rolls, or oatcakes, all count as a grain. Tofu, tempeh, and miso all count as a bean since they're derived from soybeans.

It would also be nice to serve something with B-12, such as a dairy product, cheese, or egg; not only do these products contain B-12, they are complete proteins in themselves. Yet some vegetarians won't eat any animal products at all, so be warned. If you happen to ask a vegan over to dinner, trust him or her to supply the B-12 themselves by taking a vitamin pill. There's only so much you're expected to do, after all! However, if you're a very kind host, nutritional yeast and yeast products (Marmite, Vegemite, smoked torula yeast) are good vegetarian sources of vitamin B-12, as well as the soy-based tempeh.

Just to make your life easier, here's a quick list of legumes and grains. The bean part is easy—anything that says "bean" after it is a bean!

LEGUMES

beans (azuki, Anasazi, black, navy, red, kidney, pinto, soy, lima, great northern, cannelli)
garbanzo (chickpea)
split peas (any variety)
lentils (any variety)
tofu, tempeh, miso
dried bean curd sheets
flours made from the above

GRAINS

wheat (includes pasta)
rice (all varieties)
corn
barley
buckwheat
oats
amaranth
quinoa
teff
rye
millet
sorghum
flour made from the above items
seitan (wheat meat or wheat gluten)

And remember, a vegetarian complete protein can also be found in all dairy products, eggs, and cheeses.

Mexican Quiche

SERVES 6

Yummy. I particularly like it when the tortilla "crust" gets crunchy along the edges! If you're not a fan of crispy tortillas, try a polenta crust instead.

1	**cup chopped onion**
2	**cloves garlic, minced or put through a garlic press**
1	**teaspoon oil and Pam®**
1	**ancho chili, rehydrated and chopped (optional)**
½	**green or red bell pepper**
3	**tablespoons tomato paste**
1	**teaspoon honey or sugar**
1	**teaspoon chili powder**
1	**teaspoon cumin**
⅛ to ¼	**teaspoon cayenne (optional)**
½	**teaspoon salt**
1½	**cups pinto, kidney, or black beans**
½	**cup egg whites and ¼ cup low-fat buttermilk or ⅔ cup egg substitute**
½	**cup nonfat cottage cheese**
½	**cup reduced-fat cheddar cheese**
6 to 8	**corn tortillas**
	one 9-inch pie dish, sprayed with Pam®

Sauté the onion and garlic in oil and Pam® over medium flame until onion is soft and translucent; add the chili, bell pepper, tomato paste, honey, chili powder, cumin, optional cayenne, salt, and stir. Continue sautéing, and after a minute or so, add the beans and bring the mixture to a boil. Turn off the heat and allow it to cool.

Preheat the oven to 375°.

Spray the baking dish with Pam®. Place one tortilla directly in the bottom of the pan. Next, place a tortilla so that its tip lays on the center of the baking dish (that is, you've got one tortilla in the middle, then you start to put in more tortillas to cover the sides of the dish). Layer the tortillas one next to the other around the sides, to create a "crust" totally covering the bottom and sides of the dish. The tortilla crust should look something like the petals of a flower, each overlapping onto the other.

Mix the eggs and cheeses with the cooled bean mixture. Pour the mixture over the tortillas and bake for 40 to 50 minutes, until top has risen, browned and the mixture has set. Garnish with chopped cilantro or parsley.

Serve with a generous dollop of salsa rojo (*see* page 216) on top and/or a dollop of nonfat sour cream.

Per serving:

Calories: 252
Carbohydrates: 32.7 g
Protein: 17.2 g
Fat Total: 6.9 g
Fat Saturated: .46 g

Quiche Athenée

SERVES 6

I never had anything like this when I was in Greece. Too bad, too—it's great! The crust is reminiscent of the hippie-style health food of the '60s and '70s, full of sweet earthy flavor and whole grains.

Per serving:

Calories: 213
Carbohydrates: 25.9 g
Protein: 14.6 g
Fat Total: 6.5 g
Fat Saturated: 2.6 g

FOR THE CRUST:

1½   **cups rolled oats (quick or long cooking)**
½   **cup wheat germ**
    up to ¾ cup buttermilk
1   **teaspoon salt**
1   **teaspoon thyme or oregano (optional)**
1   **clove garlic, very finely minced (optional)**

FOR THE FILLING:

1   **10- to 16-ounce package chopped frozen spinach, thawed and squeezed to remove excess liquid**
3   **green onions, finely chopped**
1   **whole egg and 3 egg whites plus more buttermilk to total 1 cup of liquid**
½   **cup nonfat yogurt**
¼   **cup crumbled feta cheese**
2   **cloves garlic, minced**
1   **teaspoon oregano**
½   **teaspoon thyme**
¼   **teaspoon ground allspice**
½   **teaspoon salt (optional)**

  Pam®
1   **8-inch pie dish**

Preheat the oven to 375°.

Mix the crust ingredients in a bowl; the mixture should be crumbly but moist (looking rather like clumps of granola), so add the buttermilk gradually, mixing as you go. If the mixture doesn't stick together at all, add a bit more buttermilk until it does. Place the crust mixture into an 8-inch pie dish that has been sprayed heavily with Pam®, and press the oatmeal into a "crust" along the bottom and sides, first using a fork to equally distribute the crumbly crust mixture and then using your dampened fingers.

Mix the remaining filling ingredients in a large bowl and place (gently) into the crust. Bake the quiche uncovered for 35 to 40 minutes, until it is just set. The center should rise and it may even brown slightly on top. Remove from the oven and allow to cool.

Either eat at room temperature or while still warm. To reheat, bake uncovered at 325° for 20 minutes until just warm.

Spinach-Stuffed Pasta Shells

SERVES 4 TO 6

This is more "fun" for children than lasagna, even though the ingredients are al-most identical. Stuffed shells seem much more elegant, too—and they freeze excellently.

1	**16-ounce box of large pasta shells**
	Basic Tomato Sauce (see page 219)
1	**teaspoon olive oil**
½	**teaspoon fennel seed, optional**
4 to 6	**green onions**
2	**cloves garlic, minced or put through a garlic press**
¼	**cup white, dry vermouth or white wine**
1	**16-ounce package frozen spinach, either chopped or whole leaf, thawed and drained**
⅛	**teaspoon ground nutmeg**
1½	**teaspoons dried basil, or 3 tablespoons chopped fresh basil**
½	**teaspoon dried oregano, or 2 teaspoons chopped fresh oregano**
	juice of ½ lemon
⅔ to ¾	**cup nonfat cottage cheese or nonfat ricotta cheese**
⅓ to ½	**cup nonfat sour cream (optional)**
¼	**cup freshly grated Parmesan cheese**
2 to 4	**ounces low-fat mozzarella cheese, grated**
	salt and freshly ground black pepper

one square or oblong baking dish (approximately 8 × 8 inches or 9 × 12 inches) sprayed with Pam®

Per serving:

Calories: 411
Carbohydrates: 55.1 g
Protein: 22 g
Fat Total: 9.7 g
Fat Saturated: 4.4 g

Fill a large stockpot (1 to 2 gallons) with water, salting the water if desired. Bring the water to the boil, then add the pasta shells. Boil the pasta shells for about 5 to 8 minutes until they are just pliable but are *not* done; they should be malleable enough to enable you to open and stuff them. When the shells are barely soft, remove them from the heat, drain in a colander, and rinse in cold water. Let the shells sit in a colander until ready for use.

Prepare the Basic Tomato Sauce.

In a sauté pan, heat 1 teaspoon olive oil and the optional fennel seed over a moderate flame; when hot, add the minced garlic and green onions. Sauté the onions and garlic a bit until the onion is tender, then add the vermouth. Next add the spinach, nutmeg, basil, oregano, and lemon juice. Cook briefly (2 to 4 minutes or so) until spinach is warmed through and some of the liquid has reduced. Taste for seasoning; it may need some salt and pepper, but don't oversalt at this point because you'll be adding Parmesan cheese later. Set the spinach aside to cool slightly.

Spray a square or oblong baking dish with Pam®.

Next, in a large bowl mix the cheeses together, then add the cooled spinach mixture. Blend the spinach and cheese together and taste for seasoning, adding salt or herbs as necessary.

Assemble all of your ingredients in front of you: the Basic Tomato Sauce, the pasta shells, the spinach-cheese mixture, and the prepared baking dish.

Fill the pasta shells with approximately 2 tablespoons of spinach-cheese mixture and place in the baking dish, continuing until the spinach-cheese mixture is used up. Spoon the Basic Tomato Sauce over the filled shells, then garnish with an added sprinkling of Parmesan cheese and/or more mozzarella cheese. Sprinkle with some dried basil or oregano—½ teaspoon or so. Cover the dish with foil. (The stuffed pasta shells could now be refrigerated for a couple of days or so until needed.)

Bake covered in a preheated 350° oven for 30 minutes, then uncovered for an additional 15 to 20 minutes until the top has browned lightly and the shells are hot. Remove from the oven and allow the shells to stand for 10 minutes before serving. Serve with a salad and hot garlic toast.

Spinach Lasagna

SERVES 4 TO 6

Great Myth Of Italian Cooking #1: that it is necessary to cook lasagna noodles before using them. The moisture in the casserole is sufficient to soften and cook the noodles as they bake; the result is you have noodles which are al dente and not mushy. I can hear some traditional Italian cooks scoffing at this notion, but all I have to say is, "Try it!!"

Basic Tomato Sauce (see page 219)

1	**teaspoon olive oil and Pam®**
⅔	**cup onion, finely chopped**
2	**cloves garlic, minced**
2	**10-ounce packages frozen spinach, thawed and drained**

1   tablespoon lemon juice

1   teaspoon salt

2   teaspoons basil, plus an additional ½ teaspoon at the end

½   teaspoon oregano

4   tablespoons parsley (optional)
    few grindings of fresh black pepper
    uncooked lasagna noodles

6   ounces low-fat mozzarella, grated

⅓   cup finest quality Parmesan cheese

1   cup nonfat ricotta or nonfat cottage cheese (see Variation)

½   cup nonfat sour cream (optional)

2   tablespoons or so dry vermouth

    one square (8- × 8-inch) baking dish sprayed with Pam®

Per serving of 6:

Calories: 388
Carbohydrates: 42.9 g
Protein: 26.5 g
Fat Total: 11.3 g
Fat Saturated: 5.8 g

Prepare the Basic Tomato Sauce, then allow it to cool.

Place a sauté pan over moderate heat and add the olive oil, Pam®, onion, and garlic. Cook, stirring occasionally, until the onion has softened and become somewhat translucent, around 3 to 5 minutes. Add the spinach, salt, and lemon juice. Continue cooking until the spinach is warmed through; add the basil, oregano, optional parsley, and pepper. Set aside to cool.

Spray a square baking dish with Pam®; assemble the rest of the ingredients in front of you.

Spoon a tiny bit of Tomato Sauce (2 tablespoons or so) into bottom of prepared baking dish and spread it around (it does not have to cover the bottom entirely). Place a layer of uncooked lasagna noodles in next, breaking them to fit into the pan, then one-third of the spinach mixture, spreading as evenly as possible. Next sprinkle a bit of Parmesan cheese on top, then one-third of the mozzarella cheese, and one-third of the ricotta (or cottage cheese). Next, spoon ⅓ cup or so of Basic Tomato Sauce into pan, and repeat the procedure until everything is used up, trying to end up with cheese and tomato sauce on top. Sprinkle any leftover liquid from the spinach and the vermouth on top of the lasagna, the additional ½ teaspoon of basil, and then cover with foil. (You can refrigerate the lasagna now and eat it at a later time—it'll keep for several days without any harm.)

Bake the lasagna covered in a preheated oven at 350° for 40 minutes; then remove the foil and bake an additional 10 to 15 minutes until top cheese has browned and the lasagna is bubbly. Remove the hot lasagna from the oven and allow to cool for 10 to 15 minutes. Cut it into equal squares and serve with salad.

Variation

- Place the ricotta cheese and sour cream with 1 to 2 cups of fresh basil into a food processor and make a smooth puree; add ½ teaspoon nutmeg and a bit of salt. Use this mixture instead of the plain ricotta.

Savory Stuffed Potatoes

SERVES 4

For many people, the idea of having a dinner without meat is incomprehensible. These potatoes are filling, tasty, and are a perfect introduction to the idea of vegetarian living. They are also great as a winter lunch with a cup of hot soup. Besides all of this, they freeze perfectly!

Per serving:

Calories: 471
Carbohydrates: 62.5 g
Protein: 26.9 g
Fat Total: 12.1 g
Fat Saturated: 4.1 g

4	**russet potatoes**
	Pam®
1	**cup onion, finely diced**
1	**clove garlic, minced**
1½	**cups broccoli florets, cut into ¼-inch pieces**
1	**cup carrots, diced into ⅛-inch pieces or shredded**
1	**teaspoon each thyme, oregano, and basil**
½	**teaspoon pepper**
½	**cup nonfat cottage cheese**
⅓	**cup Parmesan cheese**
½	**cup reduced-fat cheddar cheese**
4	**tablespoons parsley, finely chopped**
1 to 3	**teaspoons salt, or to taste**
	nonfat sour cream, if desired

Scrub the potatoes under running cool water until they're clean. Bake the scrubbed potatoes at 400° until done, approximately 50 to 60 minutes depending on the size of the potato, then remove the hot potatoes from the oven and allow them to cool.

Over a medium flame, sauté the onion and garlic in a heavy skillet sprayed with Pam® until the onion is soft, around 3 to 5 minutes. Add the carrots and broccoli, cooking for another minute or two. It may be necessary to add a tablespoon or two of water if the vegetables begin to stick to the pan. When the carrots and broccoli have softened slightly, add the herbs and pepper. Remove the pan from the heat.

Slice the cooked, cooled potatoes down the middle and scoop the insides into a large bowl, reserving the potato shells. Discard one cup of baked insides, reserving it for soup, vegetable stock, or whatever. (You will be stuffing the potatoes again, and since you will be adding other vegetables, you will need to eliminate some of the potato in order to make room for the other items.) Add the onion-broccoli mixture to the bowl and stir briefly with the potatoes; let the mixture cool, then add the cheeses and parsley. Fold everything together carefully, then taste for seasoning; you will need to add salt. When the seasoning is right, place the cheese-potato-broccoli mixture into reserved skins, filling well, and place the stuffed potato in a ceramic dish and cover. (You can refrigerate the stuffed potatoes now and eat them at a later time—they'll keep for a couple of days perfectly.)

Bake covered at 350° for 25 minutes; then remove the cover and bake an additional 15 to 20 minutes. Garnish with additional fresh parsley, a sprinkling of Parmesan cheese, or a dollop of nonfat sour cream. Serve with salad.

Lentil Veggies Au Gratin

SERVES 4

I love peasanty foods that create a homey, comforting feeling. I'm amazed at how having "comfort food" can erase a mild case of the blues or a bad day at work! Beans, onions, vegetables, and herbs combine here to make a gentle, soothing, satisfying meal. Perfect with a loaf of hot, fresh sourdough bread.

You can chop the vegetables however you wish; personally, I prefer big chunks that you can sink your teeth into.

1½	**cups lentils, rinsed and picked over**
2½	**cups defatted stock (chicken, beef, or vegetable) or water**
1	**bay leaf**
½	**teaspoon each thyme, marjoram, and basil (or sage)**
1	**teaspoon olive oil and Pam®**
2	**cups onions, finely minced**
2	**cloves garlic, minced or put through a garlic press**
1	**18-ounce can Italian plum tomatoes, chopped, including juice**
2	**carrots, chopped**
2	**stalks celery, chopped**
1	**green pepper, chopped**
4	**ounces (approximately ½ to ¾ cup) low-fat cheddar cheese, shredded**
	1 square baking dish (8 × 8 inches)

Place the lentils, stock, bay leaf, and herbs into a heavy saucepan. Bring the lentils to a simmer and cook covered for 30 minutes, until just done. It is fine if there is some leftover liquid remaining in the saucepan.

Meanwhile, in a heavy sauté pan, heat the olive oil and Pam® over a medium-low flame; add the onions and cook until they have browned lightly, around 20 minutes. Next add the garlic, tomatoes, carrots, celery, and green pepper, cooking for one minute. Remove the onions and veggies from the heat.

Coat a baking dish with Pam®. Mix the cooked lentils and vegetables together and spread the mixture evenly in the baking dish. Sprinkle the cheese over the lentils and veggies, then cover the dish. (You can refrigerate the casserole now and eat it at a later time—the casserole will keep for a couple of days without any harm.)

Bake the casserole covered at 375° for 30 to 45 minutes until everything is hot and the vegetables have cooked through. If desired, remove the foil and broil for 5 minutes until cheese has browned lightly.

Serve immediately.

Per serving:

Calories: 357
Carbohydrates: 47.7 g
Protein: 25.6 g
Fat Total: 7.5 g
Fat Saturated: .33 g

Black Bean Enchiladas

SERVES 4

Often when I've ordered enchiladas in restaurants I've left the table feeling as if I'd just eaten lead bullets. These are light and healthy, filling but not leaden. (But perhaps the leaden feeling is the result of my ingesting massive amounts of chips and salsa before the entrée arrives.) These are easy to make ahead of time and freeze perfectly. Try them with your meat-eating friends—they won't even miss the meat!

FOR THE BEAN FILLING:

1	ancho chili, roasted, chopped, and rehydrated
1	teaspoon oil and Pam®
½	medium onion, finely chopped
2	cloves garlic, minced or put through a garlic press
½ to 1	tomato, peeled, seeded, and chopped
1	tablespoon soy sauce or tamari
1	tablespoon lemon juice (optional)
1	tablespoon Worcestershire sauce (optional)
3	cups cooked black beans, half pureed and half whole (or 2 16-ounce cans of black beans, one drained and rinsed, the other pureed in a blender or food processor)
1	tablespoon ground coriander
1	tablespoon ground cumin
1	teaspoon chili powder
¼	teaspoon curry powder
¼	teaspoon cayenne pepper

FOR THE CHEESE FILLING:

½	cup nonfat sour cream
1	cup nonfat cottage cheese or ricotta cheese
1	cup cilantro leaves, washed thoroughly
1	teaspoon salt
1	teaspoon ground cumin
3	medium tomatillos, husked and washed (optional)
12	corn tortillas, warmed
	picante sauce (salsa rojo; see page 216)
1	oblong baking dish (approximately 9 × 12 inches)

Per serving (two enchiladas):

Calories: 206
Carbohydrates: 36.1 g
Protein: 12.7 g
Fat Total: 2.1 g
Fat Saturated: .18 g

Using metal tongs, hold the ancho chili by the stem and roast over an open flame (or, if using an electric range, hold over a burner after it has been preheated on high) until it is "roasted"—it will blacken and smoke and might expand; it should not, however, be burned. This process may take as little time as 30 seconds or as long as 1 to 2 minutes. After roasting, quickly remove stem and seeds inside (careful—it will be hot!). Fold the chili tightly as possible and slice it into thin strips, then chop the strips into small bits. Place the chopped chili into a small bowl and pour ⅓ cup of hot water over it. Let it stand until needed.

In a large sauté pan (preferably a nonstick pan) heat 1 teaspoon oil over a medium flame; when the pan is hot, spray the pan with Pam®; add the chopped onion and cook until it is translucent and soft, around 3 to 5 minutes. Add the garlic and cook another 30 seconds or so; then add the ancho chili (with soaking liquid) and tomato. Stir and cook for a minute until the tomato begins to soften. Add the soy sauce and optional lemon juice and Worcestershire sauce. Next add the black beans (both the pureed and the whole beans), coriander, cumin, chili powder, curry powder, and cayenne pepper. Bring the bean mixture to a simmer. Reduce heat to low and cook for 30 to 50 minutes or so, stirring occasionally, keeping the beans from sticking to the bottom. At this point you are just getting rid of excess liquid; eventually the beans will begin to get thick and will stick to the bottom of the pan. Continue cooking and scraping the bottom, until the bean mixture starts to become quite thick and heavy. Remove the beans from the heat, keeping in mind that as the beans cool they will thicken a bit more. When cooled, you should end up with a brownish, thick paste. Taste the beans for seasoning, adding soy sauce or more cayenne pepper for spiciness. While the beans are cooking, prepare the cheese filling.

For the cheese filling, place the cottage cheese, sour cream, cilantro, salt, cumin, and optional tomatillos in a food processor and blend until you have a smooth paste. Set aside.

Spray the final baking dish (an oblong pan or ceramic dish) with Pam®.

When the bean mixture has cooled, assemble the cheese mixture, the bean mixture, the salsa, and the baking dish, and proceed with the tortillas.

Heat the tortillas by either: 1) microwaving briefly, 2) wrapping in foil and baking at 300° for 20 minutes, or 3) placing the tortillas in a steamer for 30 seconds. This is an important step; cold tortillas will crack and fall apart if you try to roll them up without warming them first.

When the tortillas are heated and pliable, take a warm tortilla in your hand, spoon 2 to 3 tablespoons or so of the bean mixture into it, spreading the beans around the upper third of the tortilla, then add 1 to 2 tablespoons of the cheese filling. Starting from the end of the tortilla with the filling, roll the tortilla toward the plain side (creating a cylinder with the filling in the center) and place the filled enchilada into the prepared baking dish. Continue until the beans and tortillas are used up. Garnish the top with any leftover cheese filling. Spoon a bit of tomato salsa over the tops of the enchiladas. Cover the baking dish with foil. (You can refrigerate the enchiladas now and eat them at a later time—they'll keep for a couple of days without any harm.)

Bake covered at 350° for 30 to 40 minutes until hot and steamy. Serve immediately with extra salsa and a large salad.

Variations

- Add 1 small can of diced green chilies to bean mixture.
- Add ½ cup diced mushrooms while cooking onions.
- Pour a can of store-bought enchilada sauce over the top before baking.
- Use reduced-fat cheddar cheese instead of the cheese filling.

Imperial Navies

SERVES 4

Many years ago, I had invited some friends over to dinner who had emigrated to America from the (then) Soviet Union. The husband told me about his search for a certain and special "Georgian herb," a fragrant, fresh, leafy green plant that was near and dear to him and reminded him of his native land. Upon his arrival in the U.S., he was heartbroken to think that never again would he find this "wonderful herb." But Lo and Behold! One day when he was wandering through the farmer's market he espied this vestige from Russia tossed between the bitter gourds, Japanese eggplants, and long beans; there it was, his long-lost cilantro! I was surprised (and confused) that cilantro was used in Slavic cookery, but here was living proof that this pungent herb is used worldwide.

This dish uses ingredients easily found around the area of what used to be the Soviet Union, now the republics of Azerbaijan, Russia, Kazakhstan, and Turkmenistan. This hearty recipe is simple, nutritious, and quite satisfying. The amounts aren't terribly important. It highlights cilantro, but you could use parsley instead with great results.

½	**cup uncooked pearled barley or bulgur wheat**
1	**cup shredded green cabbage, julienned turnips, or kohlrabi, or 3 cups chopped kale**
1 to 2	**cups sliced or chopped carrots**
2	**cups chopped tomatoes, peeled and seeded**
3	**cups cooked navy beans**
3	**cups defatted stock (chicken, vegetable, or beef)**
2	**cloves garlic, minced or put through a garlic press**
	salt to taste
½	**cup fresh chopped cilantro or parsley**

Place the barley in the bottom of a heavy Dutch oven. Add the cabbage, carrots, tomatoes, and beans. Stir the garlic into the stock and pour the stock over the vegetables. Bring the mixture barely to a simmer on top of the stove, then bake covered at 350° for 45 minutes to 1 hour, until the mixture is quite hot and the barley has cooked.

Just before serving, stir in the cilantro or parsley and serve in bowls with fresh corn bread.

Per serving:

Calories: 332
Carbohydrates: 63.1 g
Protein: 19.6 g
Fat Total: 1.4 g
Fat Saturated: .28 g

Variations

- Garnish with a large dollop of nonfat yogurt or nonfat sour cream.
- Use a combination of cilantro and parsley and add 1 teaspoon cumin to the beans.

Indian Chickpeas
In a Savory Sauce

SERVES 4

This dish is better after it has sat in the refrigerator for two days or so, allowing the chickpeas to acquire the taste of the sauce.

3	**cloves garlic**
1	**small onion**
1	**1-inch piece of gingerroot**
¼	**cup water**
2	**teaspoons oil**
1 to 2	**teaspoons ground cumin seeds**
1 to 2	**teaspoons ground coriander seeds**
1	**teaspoon fennel seeds**
1	**teaspoon brown or yellow mustard seeds**
¼	**teaspoon cayenne pepper (optional)**
1½	**cups of chickpeas (garbanzos), drained**
3	**large tomatoes, peeled, seeded, and chopped (or 1 18-ounce can of tomatoes, chopped and drained)**
2	**tablespoons lemon juice**
½	**cup plain nonfat yogurt or nonfat sour cream**

chopped cilantro for garnish
salt and pepper to taste

Place the garlic, onion, gingerroot, and water in a blender or food processor and blend until you have a completely smooth paste. Measure out the cumin, coriander, fennel, and mustard seeds, along with the optional cayenne pepper, placing the spices in a small bowl.

In a large sauté pan, heat 2 teaspoons oil over a medium-high flame until quite hot, then add the spices from bowl; *immediately* take the pan off the heat and add mixture from the blender, averting your face. The onion-garlic mixture will splatter and sputter, so be careful! Return the pan to a medium flame, stirring and sautéing for 10 minutes or so, until the onion mixture has cooked and the water has evaporated. Continue to

Per serving:

Calories: 206
Carbohydrates: 35.6 g
Protein: 8.9 g
Fat Total: 4.4 g
Fat Saturated: .52 g

65

cook for an additional 10 minutes to allow the onion to cook thoroughly. Add the drained chickpeas, tomatoes, and lemon juice. Cook covered over low heat for another 15 minutes, adding a few tablespoons of water if necessary.

(If you are going to let the chickpea mixture sit for a couple of days in the refrigerator, stop the recipe here and remove the pan from the heat and allow it to cool. When you're ready to eat the chickpeas, continue from this point, bringing the chickpea mixture back to the simmering point.)

When ready to serve, take off the heat and allow the chickpeas to cool for 1 minute. Add the yogurt 1 tablespoon at a time, stirring well. Serve immediately with basmati rice (*see* page 212). Garnish with chopped cilantro.

Eggplant Parmesan

SERVES 4 TO 6

Although this recipe is higher in fat than others in this book, it is delicious and (believe it or not) is lower in fat than your regular run-of-the-mill Eggplant Parmesan. Because of the fat, I would be sure to serve it as a side dish rather than as a main course, balancing and supplementing the meal with some sautéed summer squash and an Italian-style rice pilaf.

Per serving of 6:

Calories: 217
Carbohydrates: 17 g
Protein: 14.9 g
Fat Total: 10 g
Fat Saturated: 2.1 g

1	**teaspoon olive oil**
½	**teaspoon fennel seeds**
2 to 3	**large cloves garlic, minced or put through a garlic press**
3	**cups (roughly one 28-ounce can) Italian tomatoes, peeled, seeded, drained, and chopped (either fresh, canned, or a mixture of both)**
¼	**cup dry vermouth or white wine**
2 to 3	**medium eggplants (do not use large, woody eggplants) olive oil and pastry brush or olive oil Pam®**
¼	**cup highest quality Parmesan and/or Romano cheese**
½	**cup breadcrumbs**
3 to 4	**tablespoons chopped parsley**
1½	**teaspoons dried basil or 2 tablespoons fresh chopped basil**
½	**teaspoon dried oregano, or 1 tablespoon fresh chopped oregano**
3 to 6	**ounces grated reduced-fat mozzarella cheese salt and pepper to taste**
	1 square (8- × 8-inch) baking dish, sprayed with Pam®

In a saucepan, heat 1 teaspoon of olive oil over a moderate flame; when the oil is hot, put in the fennel seeds. Cook for 15 seconds or so, allowing them to sizzle but not turn brown, then add the minced garlic, stirring and cooking for about 20 seconds. Add the tomatoes and vermouth and cook for 15 minutes. (If you are using exclusively fresh tomatoes, the cooking time will be approximately 30 minutes.) The sauce should not be too watery, but by the same token it should not be too dry; so continue to cook until some of the liquid has cooked away. Taste for seasoning (that is, salt and pepper); do not oversalt since the Parmesan cheese will add salt. Set aside to cool. The sauce will appear thicker after it has cooled. If you are using exclusively fresh tomatoes, you may wish to add ½ to 1 teaspoon of sugar to the sauce.

Preheat the broiler to high.

Peel the eggplants if the skin seems tough and thick, otherwise just wash and slice the eggplants into ⅜-inch rounds. Place the eggplant slices on a baking sheet and brush with small amount of olive oil on each side or spray with olive oil Pam®. Place the oiled eggplant slices under the broiler and broil until the eggplant turns reddish brown on top; turn each slice over and cook the other side the same way. Remove the slices when they have cooked and set them aside to cool.

Combine the Parmesan cheese and breadcrumbs on a plate. Dip cooked eggplant slices (which will have exuded some juices and will have become slightly wet when cooled) in the cheese and breadcrumb mixture, coating them lightly.

In a baking dish (either nonstick or sprayed with Pam®) arrange a single layer of the eggplant slices; top with ¼ to ⅓ cup of the tomato sauce. Sprinkle on some parsley, basil, and oregano; then place a layer of mozzarella cheese on top. Continue layering until everything is used up, ending with mozzarella cheese. (**Note:** At this point the dish can be covered and refrigerated until ready.) Bake uncovered in the top third of a preheated 400° oven for 35 to 45 minutes, or until the casserole is piping hot and bubbling and the cheese has browned. Remove from the oven and let stand for 8 to 10 minutes before serving. Garnish as desired with additional fresh herbs, fresh pepper, or with a squirt of lemon.

Chinese "Hot" Noodles

SERVES 4

These noodles are served cold, so the "hot" in the title comes from the chili paste! This is outstanding for a hot afternoon's picnic or perfect as a take-along meal for a potluck dinner!

8	**ounces lo mein or other noodle (spaghettini, linguini, or fettucine)**
1	**teaspoon toasted sesame oil**
2	**teaspoons chili paste with garlic (see note below; also see *Ingredients* page 224) or 2 cloves garlic pureed with 1 teaspoon red pepper flakes, ½ teaspoon sesame oil, and ½ teaspoon vinegar**
⅓	**cup red wine vinegar**
⅓	**cup tamari or soy sauce**
1 to 2	**tablespoons sugar or honey**
1	**teaspoon finely grated gingerroot**
½	**red bell pepper, sliced thinly**
½	**green bell pepper, sliced thinly**
1 to 2	**cups broccoli florets**
1 to 2	**cups snow peas**
½ to 1	**cup sliced, seeded cucumber**
3 to 4	**tablespoons chopped cilantro**
1	**teaspoon sesame seeds, raw or toasted**

Note: Chili paste can be found in larger supermarkets in the Asian Foods section, or can be bought in any Chinese, Vietnamese, or Thai market. It is sometimes called Chili Sauce with Garlic.

Boil the noodles in a very large pot of water until nearly done; it is important not to completely cook them so that you can keep them al dente. Drain the noodles into a sieve or colander and rinse in cold water. Toss the drained noodles with the toasted sesame oil. Set them aside until they are needed.

Combine the chili paste, vinegar, soy sauce, sugar, and gingerroot in a bowl, mixing well. (If you're not eating the noodles soon, cover the bowl and place the dressing in the refrigerator. Be sure to have the dressing at room temperature before serving, however.)

Slice the bell peppers into thin pieces, break the broccoli into florets, and clean the snow peas. Next blanch the red and green bell peppers, broccoli, and snow peas in boiling water for 20 to 30 seconds; drain into a colander and rinse under cold water. Drain the vegetables on paper towels. Next peel, seed, and slice the cucumber into thin half-moons.

Place the cooled noodles in a serving dish; arrange vegetables attractively on top. Refrigerate the noodles and vegetables until ready to serve. (Covered, the vegetables and noodles will keep perfectly in the refrigerator for 24 hours.)

Just before serving, spoon the seasoning mixture over the vegetables and noodles, garnishing with cilantro and sesame seeds.

"Fried" Rice

SERVES 4

Recipes for things such as fried rice and vegetable soup seem to me to be pointless, since the point of vegetable soup and fried rice is to use whatever you have on hand in the refrigerator. Even so, here's a recipe to use as a springboard for your own inventions, substituting anywhere you wish with anything you wish. Amounts aren't terribly important.

4   **cups cooked rice, white or brown (preferably day-old rice)**
1   **teaspoon vegetable oil**
½   **teaspoon toasted sesame oil**
2   **cloves garlic, minced**
1   **teaspoon gingerroot, minced or finely shredded**
4   **green onions, chopped**
1   **green or red bell pepper, chopped**
1   **cup broccoli florets**
1   **cup zucchini, cut into thin half-moon shapes**
      tamari to taste
      sherry

Place a wok or large heavy skillet over a medium-high flame; when the pan is hot, add the oil and sesame oil. Immediately add the garlic, gingerroot, and green onions; sauté for 30 seconds. Add the remaining vegetables and stir-fry for an additional 2 minutes or so, adding some tamari (1 tablespoon) or sherry as you go. Add the rice and heat through, then cover. Reduce the heat to low, then sprinkle some tamari (another tablespoon or so) and a tablespoon or two of water over the rice. Continue cooking on low until everything is hot and steamed. Serve immediately when rice is hot and vegetables are just cooked.

Per serving:

Calories: 207
Carbohydrates: 40.6 g
Protein: 4.8 g
Fat Total: 1.9 g
Fat Saturated: .16 g

Variations
- Add 1 cup of cooked, diced shrimp or cooked, shredded chicken breast.
- Add 1 cup bean sprouts and/or water chestnuts.
- Add ½ cup peas or a handful of snow peas.
- Add 2 tablespoons imitation bacon bits just before serving.
- Add cilantro to taste.
- Scramble a couple of eggs; dice into bite-sized pieces, then add at the end.

Kingston Town
Beans 'n' Rice

SERVES 4

This recipe from down Jamaica way definitely shows an Anglo influence; the extreme spiciness found in some Carribean dishes is reduced—but you can always heat things up with more cayenne! And be sure to have lots of daiquiris ready. . . . At least when I come to visit!

Per serving:

Calories: 354
Carbohydrates: 51.2 g
Protein: 18.9 g
Fat Total: 7.7 g
Fat Saturated: .26 g

1	**cup white or brown rice**
1½ to 2	**cups defatted stock (the lesser amount for white rice, the larger for brown)**
1	**teaspoon oregano**
1	**teaspoon olive oil and Pam®**
1½	**cups finely diced onions**
1	**each red and green bell pepper, diced**
1	**chili pepper (fresh), finely diced, or 1 teaspoon dried red pepper flakes**
½ to 1	**teaspoon cayenne (optional)**
2	**cloves garlic, minced or put through a garlic press**
1	**bay leaf**
1½	**cups defatted stock**
1½	**cups cooked red beans**
	salt or tamari to taste
⅓ to ½	**cup crushed tomatoes or tomato puree**
½	**teaspoon ground ginger powder**
½	**teaspoon chili powder**
½	**teaspoon curry powder**
¼	**cup chopped cilantro**
4	**ounces grated low-fat mozzarella cheese or low-fat cheddar cheese**
1	**shallow baking dish, either round, square, or oblong; big enough to hold 2 quarts**

Place the rice, stock, and oregano in a heavy saucepan and bring to a boil; cover and reduce the heat to low. Cook until liquid is absorbed (about 15 to 20 minutes for white rice, around 30 to 40 minutes for brown rice). When the rice is done, take it off the heat and allow it to stand undisturbed for at least 15 minutes.

Heat a heavy sauté pan over a medium flame; when the pan is hot, add the olive oil and spray it with Pam®. Immediately add the onions, bell peppers, chili pepper, optional cayenne, garlic, and bay leaf. Cover and cook until the onions have softened, around 5 minutes, stirring occasionally. Add the red beans and stock, simmering uncovered until the vegetables are barely done. Taste for seasoning and add salt or tamari as needed.

Coat a shallow casserole dish with Pam®. Spread the cooked rice evenly on the bottom. Mix the tomato puree, ground ginger, chili powder, and curry powder together, then pour the tomato mixture over the rice. Add the bean and vegetable mixture, spreading it evenly on top of the rice. Top the beans with the cilantro, then the cheese.

(You can stop at this point, cover, and refrigerate. To reheat after chilling, bake covered at 350° for 45 minutes instead of 30 minutes, then continue as usual.)

Bake the casserole covered at 350° for 30 minutes; then remove the cover and continue to cook for another 10 to 15 minutes. If necessary, broil for 5 to 7 minutes until mixture is hot and bubbly, and the cheese has browned.

Lentil Lasagna

SERVES 4 TO 6

Lentils make a wonderful substitution for the ubiquitous ground beef in lasagna. They are moist and meld excellently with the other ingredients to form a "mock beef." I keep repeating, "Why would anyone want meat?" every time I have a truly delicious vegetarian dish! All lasagnas are free-form casseroles which can be designed to your own tastes. Substitutions are encouraged. One suggestion that immediately comes to mind is to add some smoked Gruyère along with the mozzarella.

Per serving (for 6):

Calories: 418
Carbohydrates: 55.9 g
Protein: 32.6 g
Fat Total: 7.8 g
Fat Saturated: 2 g

1	**cup brown lentils**
1	**2-inch piece of gingerroot**
1	**clove garlic, minced**
⅓	**cup tamari or soy sauce**
3	**cups water**
	Basic Tomato Sauce (see page 219)
½	**teaspoon oregano**
½	**teaspoon thyme**
2 to 3	**cups mushrooms, sliced**
6	**green onions, chopped**
1	**clove garlic, minced or put through a garlic press**
1	**teaspoon oregano**
1	**teaspoon basil**
1½	**cups nonfat ricotta or cottage cheese**
	nonfat sour cream (optional)
¼	**cup Parmesan cheese**
6	**ounces reduced-fat mozzarella cheese**
	regular lasagna noodles
1	**square baking dish (8- × 8-inch)**
	Pam®

71

Pick over the lentils, looking for rocks or pieces of dirt. Place the cleaned lentils in a heavy saucepan and rinse with water, gently swooshing them around and then draining to remove any floating debris or dirt. Chop the gingerroot into two or three large chunks; add the garlic, tamari, gingerroot and water to the lentils. Bring the lentils to the boil over moderately high heat; as soon as it has reached the boiling point, take the pan off of the heat and cover. Allow the lentils to soak in the hot liquid for 30 to 60 minutes.

Prepare the Basic Tomato Sauce. Add the oregano and thyme after it has cooked, then set it aside.

Chop and slice the mushrooms and green onions. Heat a large sauté pan over a medium flame; spray the hot pan with Pam® and add the garlic; when the garlic has cooked for 30 seconds, add the mushrooms and green onions. Cook until the mushrooms have softened, around 2 to 3 minutes. Set aside the mushrooms and onions to cool.

After the lentils have soaked at least 30 minutes, return them to a medium-low flame and bring them to a simmer. As soon as the simmering point has been reached, turn the heat to low and cover, cooking slowly, until the lentils have softened and are done, around 15 to 30 minutes. (**Note:** Due to the variables of cooking dry beans, the cooking time may be longer one time than the next depending on how fresh or old the lentils are. The best method is to simply check the lentils after 20 minutes or so, stirring and testing one or two for doneness. Sometimes it may be necessary to add some more liquid; other times the lentils may be cooked and standing in liquid. None of this really matters; you just need to end up with cooked lentils! How you arrive at a cooking time isn't terribly important. Add liquid as necessary and cook until just done, avoiding mushy, falling-apart lentils.)

Once the lentils are cooked, use a slotted spoon and place them in the sauté pan with the mushroom-onion mixture. Add the oregano and basil and stir, then taste for seasoning; it may be necessary to add salt or tamari. This mixture shouldn't be too dry; some moistness is necessary so the lasagna noodles can absorb the liquid during baking.

In a bowl combine the Parmesan cheese and the 1½ cups of ricotta cheese. (If desired, add up to 1 cup of nonfat sour cream.)

Spray the square pan with Pam®. Assemble the tomato sauce, the lentils, the lasagna noodles, cheese mixture, mozzarella cheese, and the pan.

Place one or two spoonfuls of the lentil mixture in the bottom of the prepared baking dish; next place a layer of uncooked lasagna noodles on top, breaking them to fit the bottom of the pan when necessary. Spread ½ cup of the cheese mixture on top of the noodles. Next spoon on a thin layer of lentils, followed by ½ cup of the tomato sauce, then a sprinkling of mozzarella cheese, then another layer of noodles. Follow in the same manner until you have three layers (for example: lentils on bottom / noodles, cheese, lentils, tomato, mozzarella / noodles, cheese, lentils, tomato, mozzarella / noodles, cheese, lentils, tomato, mozzarella). When you are finished, let the lasagna stand for 15 minutes to check and see how much liquid is remaining in the bottom of the pan: if it is almost or completely dry, add ⅓ cup of dry white wine; if it seems to be moist (that is, if there is ¼ inch of liquid in the bottom), simply cover the lasagna with foil.

(You can stop at this point and refrigerate the lasagna. To reheat after chilling, bake covered at 350° for 60 minutes instead of 45 minutes, then continue as usual.)

Bake covered at 350° for 45 minutes; then remove the foil and bake for an additional 10 to 15 minutes, until the top has browned nicely and the lasagna is hot and bubbly. Remove it from the oven and allow the cooked lasagna to sit and cool for 10 minutes before cutting and serving.

Variations

- Use low-fat provolone cheese instead of mozzarella.
- Add 1 pound of blanched chard or spinach to the lentil mixture, adjusting the seasonings as necessary.
- Add a sprinkling of smoked cheese in each layer, such as smoked Gruyère, Gouda, Bruderbasil, or Tillamook.
- Add a chopped green or red bell pepper along with the mushrooms.

Stuffed Peppers

SERVES 4

Stuffed peppers are great for those times when you're in-between visits to the grocery store and all you've got in the refrigerator is some leftover rice, assorted pieces of half-used vegetables, and no energy to make a rushed trip to the super-market. It's amazing how creative you can be when you're tired! "Aw, what's this . . . ? Half a zucchini? Oh, throw it in the stuffing. . . . When did I buy this? Stick that in too."

Speaking of sticking, someone I barely knew once called me up in a frenzy because they couldn't figure out if their casserole was done—I suppose they called me because they knew I could cook. Wanting to be the Good Samaritan to this poor person who hadn't a clue what to do in the kitchen, I said, "How long has it been in the oven?" "Oh, I'm not sure," he responded, "maybe forty minutes." "It's probably hot by now," I said, "but if you're uncertain, leave it in for another ten minutes. It won't do any harm." "How can I be sure when it's done?" he asked, panic-stricken. "Well," I said, "the best method I've ever found to see whether a casserole is done or not is to stick my finger in it." "Stick your finger in it?!?!?" he screamed into the telephone. "It's not very scientific, I admit," I re-sponded, "but if it's hot, you'll know it."

Strangely, he never called back for more of my cooking tips.

73

2 **large green, red, or yellow bell peppers**
½ **cup mushrooms, sliced and chopped**
¼ **cup green onion, finely minced**
1 **clove garlic, minced**
1 **teaspoon olive oil and Pam®**
2 **tablespoons vermouth**
¼ **cup zucchini, finely diced**
¼ **teaspoon thyme**
1½ **cups cooked rice (white, brown, wild, or any mixture) cooked in defatted stock, preferably day-old**
3 **tablespoons fresh basil, sliced**
¼ **cup Parmesan cheese**
¼ **teaspoon black pepper**
¼ **cup tomato, peeled, seeded, and diced**
¼ **cup vermouth or white wine**
1 **oblong or square baking dish (8 × 8 inches or 9 × 12 inches)**

Wash and slice peppers in half lengthwise, seeding and coring them. Set them aside.

Heat a sauté pan over a medium flame; when the pan is hot add the oil and lightly spray it with Pam®, then add the mushrooms, onion, and garlic. Stir and cook until onion is soft, around 3 to 5 minutes. Add 2 tablespoons vermouth, the zucchini, and thyme. Continue sautéing until the zucchini is barely cooked, around 1 minute, then remove pan from the flame.

In a large bowl place the cooked rice, onion-zucchini mixture, and basil, stirring well. Add the Parmesan cheese, pepper, and tomato; stir again and taste for seasoning. Place ½ cup of the mixture into each pepper half, then place the stuffed peppers into a ceramic dish. Sprinkle some vermouth over the stuffed peppers and cover them with foil.

Bake covered at 350° for 35 to 45 minutes until the peppers are soft and the rice stuffing is hot. (When in doubt, stick your finger in it.)

Variations

- Use feta cheese instead of Parmesan cheese and substitute 1 teaspoon oregano for basil.
- Add ⅓ cup diced, cooked chicken breast to stuffing.
- Add ⅓ cup cooked, seasoned beans or tofu to stuffing.
- Use reduced-fat cheddar cheese for Parmesan cheese.
- Use 2 teaspoons fragrant curry powder instead of fresh basil and substitute ⅓ cup nonfat cottage cheese for Parmesan cheese.

Per serving:

Calories: 189
Carbohydrates: 24.1 g
Protein: 8.9 g
Fat Total: 5.8 g
Fat Saturated: 2.8 g

Fresh Pasta Sauce
with Zucchini

SERVES 4

This easy sauce is perfect for a quick meal when you've got little in the house except some summer squash, pasta, and canned tomatoes.

1	**teaspoon olive oil**
½	**teaspoon fennel seeds**
1 to 2	**cloves garlic, minced or put through a garlic press**
1½	**cups sliced mushrooms**
3 to 4	**cups tomatoes (fresh, canned, or a combination of both), peeled, seeded, and chopped**
⅓	**cup dry white vermouth or white wine**
1	**tablespoon lemon juice (optional)**
1	**cup zucchini, sliced into thin half-moons**
3 to 4	**tablespoons freshly chopped basil**
½	**teaspoon oregano**
3	**tablespoons parsley**
	salt to taste
1	**teaspoon sugar (optional)**
2	**tablespoons chopped Kalamata olives (optional)**
¼	**cup freshest Parmesan cheese**
	fresh black pepper
12	**ounces dried or fresh pasta**

Per serving:

Calories: 430
Carbohydrates: 79.4 g
Protein: 16.2 g
Fat Total: 4.3 g
Fat Saturated: 1.2 g

Heat the olive oil in a saucepan over a medium flame and add the fennel seeds; after they have cooked for 20 seconds add the minced garlic and sliced mushrooms. Stir and cook until the mushrooms have rendered some of their juice, around 3 to 5 minutes. Next add the tomatoes, vermouth, and lemon juice; cook until the tomatoes have softened and the sauce has become thicker. (The cooking time will differ depending on the water content of the tomatoes; fresh tomatoes take longer than canned.) When the sauce has become thicker and the tomatoes are done, add the zucchini, basil, oregano, and parsley. Remove from the heat and taste for seasoning.

Serve the warm sauce over hot, cooked pasta; garnish with Parmesan cheese, Kalamata olives, and freshly ground black pepper.

Variations

- Add ¾ cup red bell pepper along with tomatoes.
- Use yellow crookneck squash instead of zucchini.
- Add one 6-ounce can of drained tuna to sauce just before serving, so that the tuna is warm but hasn't "cooked."

Vegetarian Chili

SERVES 4

The bulgur wheat in this healthy chili resembles ground beef in look and texture; serve it to your carnivore friends and see if they notice the difference! Even if they do notice the difference, they'll still find this a great chili recipe!

Per serving:

Calories: 278
Carbohydrates: 48.8 g
Protein: 12.5 g
Fat Total: 3.3 g
Fat Saturated: .34 g

1	**ancho chili, roasted and chopped**
2	**cups vegetable stock or water**
1	**teaspoon olive oil and Pam®**
1	**small onion, diced**
2	**cloves garlic, minced or put through a garlic press**
1	**cup diced mushrooms**
½ to ¾	**cup each green and red pepper, chopped**
1½	**cups (roughly 1 15-ounce can) beans (black, pinto, or kidney)**
1	**small tin green chilies, drained and chopped**
1	**18-ounce can chopped tomatoes, including the juice**
½	**cup red or white wine**
½	**cup bulgur wheat**
2	**teaspoons cumin**
¼ to 1	**teaspoon cayenne**
1	**tablespoon coriander**
2	**teaspoons chili powder**
½	**teaspoon oregano**
¼	**teaspoon curry powder**
1	**teaspoon Marmite (optional)**
1 to 2	**tablespoons sugar (optional)**
	salt or tamari
	cilantro
	nonfat sour cream

Roast the ancho chili over an open flame until it is hot and slightly charred. Remove the stem, then throw away the seeds inside and chop the roasted chili into small pieces. Place the chopped chili in a small bowl and add ⅓ cup of the vegetable stock. Let it stand for 15 minutes.

In a large pot, heat the olive oil and Pam® over a medium flame. Add the onion and garlic, cooking for 5 minutes or so, until the onion is soft. Add the mushrooms and peppers, cooking and stirring for 3 minutes. Next add the ancho chili with stock and the remaining ingredients; bring the chili to the simmering point. Reduce the flame to very low and let it simmer for 30 to 40 minutes, then taste for seasoning, adding salt or tamari as needed and more chili powder if desired. (You can stop at this point, cover and refrigerate or even freeze the chili.)

Serve hot with fresh chopped cilantro and a dollop of nonfat sour cream. If desired, sprinkle some low-fat cheddar cheese on top as well.

Vegetarian "Hamburgers"

SERVES 4

More and more children are expressing an interest in vegetarianism, and what better way to give them a well-rounded and familiar meal than a veggie burger?

1	**clove garlic, finely minced or put through a garlic press**
⅓	**cup onion, finely chopped**
1	**teaspoon olive oil or toasted sesame oil**
⅓	**cup oatmeal, instant or regular**
1	**cup pureed (mashed) cooked beans, such as lentils, black, or kidney beans**
½	**cup breadcrumbs or a mixture of breadcrumbs and wheat germ (see note below)**
¼	**cup Chilean mushroom powder (optional)**
1	**teaspoon basil**
1	**teaspoon oregano**
1	**teaspoon thyme**
1	**teaspoon fragrant paprika**
½	**teaspoon cumin**
2	**tablespoons tamari**
¼	**teaspoon black pepper**

Note: Depending on how much water the beans contain, it may be necessary to increase or reduce this quantity.

Place a skillet over a medium flame; when hot, spray the pan with Pam®. Add the onion and garlic, cooking and stirring until the onion is soft, around 5 minutes. When the onion is done, remove the skillet from the heat and allow it to cool.

In a large bowl combine all the ingredients; the mixture should be thick and retain its shape. It should not have a batterlike consistency; it should be stiff yet not crumbly. If the mixture is crumbly, knead for one minute. If it is *still* crumbly, add just enough liquid to allow it to stick together. Divide mixture into four equal portions.

Keeping your hands wet, form the mixture into four patties approximately ¼-inch thick. (A thicker patty is infinitely more difficult to cook and turn over.) Place a skillet over a moderately low flame and sauté the patties in a small bit of oil or Pam® until the patties have browned on the bottom. Turn each patty over and brown the other side.

Serve each veggie burger on a toasted English muffin or on a hamburger bun with mustard, ketchup, and whatever else you like. These are quite tasty with a slice of smoked cheese on top, such as smoked Gouda or provolone.

Optional Additions to the Burger Mixture

- 1 teaspoon curry powder or garam masala
- 1 tablespoon chopped parsley
- 1 tablespoon smoked torula yeast
- 1 tablespoon nutritional yeast
- 1 egg

Per serving:

Calories: 215
Carbohydrates: 35.4 g
Protein: 9.2 g
Fat Total: 4.4 g
Fat Saturated: .35 g

Fish and Seafood

- *Fish Cookery: The Basics*

Delicately Braised Fish
Sword-Fish Swordfish
Sole Florentine
Tuna Casserole with Fusilli
Fish Fingers
Indian Fish with Yogurt Sauce
*Orange Roughy with Orange-Ginger
   Flavor*
"Oven-Fried" Catfish
Sautéed Fish with Peppers
Siamese Salmon
Seafood Stir-fry
Shrimp Kabobs with Bay
Szechuan Shrimp
Paella Valenciana
Salmon with Herb Dressing
Ridiculously Simple Japanese Tuna
Indian Spiced Fish
Shrimp Stir-fry
Indian Shrimp with Tomato Sauce
Cantonese Five-Spice Fish
La Ramplas Pescado
Quick Pasta with Red Clam Sauce

Fish Cookery: The Basics

MANY PEOPLE SAY, "I just can't seem to cook fish. It's always an overcooked mess." My response is, "Practice makes perfect."

But what is equally important is to recognize the type of fish you're cooking and use the most appropriate method of cooking. The following are different methods used for cooking fish:

Most added fat:
    Frying
Less added fat:
    Oven roasting
    Sautéing

Least or no added fat:
    Broiling
    Baking
    Poaching
    Grilling
    Boiling

Frying. Cooking in generous amounts of oil or fat until done. Frying is typically thought of as "greasy." Frying usually negates any subtlety of taste (one of the most interesting facets of fish) and is not the best method for cooking most fish types.

Oven roasting. Baking a whole fish at a relatively high temperature until done; depending on the fish, some basting may be necessary. Any type of whole fish may be roasted.

Sautéing. Essentially frying with less oil or fat. A nonstick skillet is best for this, since very delicate or thin fillets may break and fall apart if sautéed.

Broiling. Cooking under very high heat for a short amount of time; ironically, best for thin fish (which you don't even need to turn) or very meaty, oily fish.

Baking/braising. Cooking at medium temperatures until done, either with or without liquid. This method is best for fillets with seasonings; it is similar in many ways to poaching. Baking can be a wonderful way to cook fish or a horrifying way, depending on the recipe.

Poaching. Cooking in liquid (water or a *court bouillon**) at the simmering point until done. Poaching keeps the fish very moist and is great for fish "steaks" and thick fillets, as well as thinner fillets. Poaching is my favorite way of cooking fish, and the leanest.

Grilling. Cooking over coals or high heat with smoke. Grilling is much like broiling, and is equally difficult for thin fish fillets. There is some negative debate over the healthiness of grilling—that the high heat and smoke of grilling causes carcinogens to be formed in the meat or fish.

Boiling. This ancient method of cooking fish is best forgotten.

Think of cooking fish as you would a fresh vegetable; you don't want to overcook it and make it mushy, but it needs sufficient cooking to make it delectable. Fresh fish should not smell "fishy"—although some fish do indeed have a smell, it should ideally remind you of the open and breezy seas, clean and inviting, not the stagnant algae-covered mire under a low-ebb dock. Oftentimes I have bought a wonderful fillet of salmon and put my nose directly over it and smelled absolutely nothing—the hallmark of a truly fresh fish.

When Is Fish Done?

Fish should never flake; fish should be moist and luscious. Fish is done when it has lost its translucent quality and has become opaque: remember, fish will continue to cook *after* it has been removed from the oven or stovetop, so a good rule of thumb is to remove the fish just *before* it has finished cooking. The point at which fish is done to the point to when it is overdone is usually very short—when cooking fish you must have such a passion for perfection that you are willing to watch it like a hawk. This probably means that you are hovering near the stove awaiting the moment the fish is just done, which should take no more than 3 to 5 minutes near the end of the estimated cooking time. If you estimate that the fish steak will take 20 minutes to cook, go about your business until 17 minutes or so have passed—then take a look at the fish and stand by it until it is done. In fish cookery, the penultimate moment is the most important one; the final moment is too late.

There are many "scientific" methods of cooking fish, but all methods are as valid or invalid as *you* make them. If one method helps you cook fish perfectly almost every time, so be it—that is the method for you. Find what works and stick with it—but there is never a method that will substitute for experience and practice. The more you cook fish the better you will become at it.

*A *court bouillon* is the liquid the fish is poached in; it can be simple salted water, wine with aromatic vegetables (carrots, onions, celery), wine and vegetables and herbs (as in a bouquet garni), sometimes wine with allspice berries, garlic, thyme, and onion—the possibilities go on and on. Sometimes a *court bouillon* is erroneously referred to as a fish fumet, although a fish fumet (or *fumet de poissons*) is more properly thought of as a flavorful fish stock, not merely a poaching liquid.

Delicately Braised Fish ✓

SERVES 4

Subtle and delicate, this recipe is soothing and very French.

1½	**pounds lean fish fillet, such as salmon, tilapia, snapper, or sole**
	salt & pepper
½ to 1	**teaspoon dried tarragon, thyme, or herbes de Provence**
1	**cup finely diced celery**
⅔ to ¾	**cup finely diced onion**
1	**cup finely diced mushrooms**
1	**cup finely diced carrots**
1	**cup dry white vermouth or dry white wine**
½	**cup defatted chicken stock**
1	**teaspoon arrowroot mixed with 2 tablespoons water, wine, or more chicken stock**
¼	**cup nonfat sour cream (optional)**
1	**tablespoon finely chopped parsley**
1	**shallow baking dish sprayed with Pam® (round, oval, oblong, or square—a 9-inch × 12-inch dish is usually more than enough)**

Per serving without optional sour cream:

Calories: 181
Carbohydrates: 6.4 g
Protein: 21.7 g
Fat Total: 3.9 g
Fat Saturated: .6 g

Per serving with optional sour cream:

Calories: 241
Carbohydrates: 10.4 g
Protein: 28.1 g
Fat Total: 4.9 g
Fat Saturated: .75 g

Remove any internal bones from the fish fillet with tweezers or a pair of long-nosed pliers. Season the fillet with salt, pepper, and dried herbs, then place it in the baking dish, cover, and refrigerate.

Place a large sauté pan over a medium flame until hot, then spray the pan with Pam® and add the celery, onion, mushrooms, and carrots. Reduce heat to medium-low and sauté for 5 minutes or so, stirring often, until the vegetables are just cooked. Add the wine and chicken stock, then bring the mixture to a simmer. Taste for seasoning; add salt and (perhaps) a pinch of thyme or tarragon if desired. Add the arrowroot and liquid mixture, stirring well and incorporating thoroughly into the vegetable mixture. Allow the vegetables to come to a simmer again, stirring until the arrowroot has thickened. Add the optional sour cream, stirring well. Let the mixture cool.

Pour the cooled vegetable mixture over the seasoned fish. Sprinkle the chopped parsley on top, then cover until ready to bake. (The fish may stay in the refrigerator for a maximum of 24 hours in this manner without any harm.)

Allow the fish to sit out of the refrigerator for 20 minutes before baking. Depending on the thickness of the fish fillets, bake covered at 350° for 25 to 35 minutes, with a thick salmon fillet taking longer, a thin tilapia fillet a shorter time. Test the fillets for doneness before serving by either pressing gently with your finger on the thickest part of the fish (if it is gently springy but not mushy, it is probably done), or insert a small knife into the fillet and look at the fish. If the fillet is *nearly* done but not quite, I would simply remove the fish and allow it to stand covered for 5 minutes before serving, since the fish will continue to cook gently after it has been removed from the oven.

Serve immediately.

Sword-Fish Swordfish

SERVES 4

Chunks of fish on a miniature sword. Sword-Fish Swordfish, get it?

FOR THE MARINADE:

	juice of one lemon
1 to 2	*tablespoons finely minced or grated onion*
½	*teaspoon finely minced garlic (optional)*
2	*teaspoons fragrant paprika*
¼ to 1	*teaspoon cayenne, as desired*
1	*teaspoon ground cumin*
	sprinkling of salt
2	*tablespoons chopped fresh parsley, mint, cilantro, or basil*
¼	*cup nonfat sour cream or nonfat yogurt*
1 to 1½	*pounds of swordfish, outer skin removed, cut into pieces (approximately 1 × 1 × 2 inches)*
8 to 10	*bay leaves, broken in half*
	cherry tomatoes or Roma tomatoes
8	*metal or bamboo skewers*

Combine the first nine ingredients in a bowl; add the swordfish to the marinade. Set the fish aside. Meanwhile, assemble the skewers, lemon slices, bay leaves, and tomatoes (if using cherry tomatoes, leave whole; if Roma tomatoes, cut into 1-inch pieces).

To assemble, skewer a piece of fish, then a tomato, next a piece of bay leaf, then a piece of fish, then another piece of bay leaf; repeat procedure from beginning. Continue in this manner until all of the fish is used up. Place skewers on platter and pour any remaining marinade over the fish brochettes; let the fish marinate for several hours in the refrigerator.

Simply grill or broil until done, approximately 5 to 8 minutes each side, basting with any leftover marinade. Serve with a rice pilaf and a bright green vegetable, such as broccoli, green beans, or new peas.

Per serving:

Calories: 215
Carbohydrates: 9 g
Protein: 31.8 g
Fat Total: 4.6 g
Fat Saturated: .88 g

Sole Florentine

SERVES 4

2	green onions, minced
1	clove garlic, minced or put through a garlic press (optional)
2	teaspoons butter or oil and Pam®
1	16-ounce package chopped frozen spinach, thawed and squeezed, or 16 ounces fresh spinach, cleaned and blanched
¼	cup dry vermouth
3	tablespoons Parmesan cheese
2	tablespoons chopped parsley
¼	teaspoon ground nutmeg
½	cup nonfat cream cheese
¼ to ⅓	cup nonfat sour cream
3 to 4	tablespoons chopped fresh basil
½ to 1	teaspoon thyme
4	sole (or another mild whitefish) fillets (around 1½ pounds) salt & pepper
4	whole, large basil leaves additional dry vermouth or brandy
1	shallow baking dish large enough to hold 4 fillets (around 8 × 8 inches), sprayed with Pam®

In a large sauté pan, heat the butter over a moderate flame; when the butter has melted, spray the pan with Pam® and add the green onions and garlic. Reduce the flame to medium-low and cook for a minute or so, until the green onions are barely soft and bright green; next add the spinach. Continue cooking and stirring, eliminating some of the excess water from the spinach. When the spinach is hot, add the vermouth and continue cooking for another 2 minutes, reducing some of the liquid in the pan. The spinach should be moist but not standing in liquid. Remove the spinach from heat.

In a medium bowl combine the Parmesan cheese, parsley, nutmeg, cream cheese, nonfat sour cream, chopped fresh basil, and thyme; stir and blend well. When the spinach mixture has cooled somewhat, combine it with the cheese-basil mixture. Blend well and taste the spinach-cheese mixture for seasoning; add salt, pepper, and herbs as desired. Divide the mixture into four equal portions.

Prepare a baking dish with Pam®.

Lightly salt and pepper each fillet. In one corner of the baking dish make a "mound" of one-quarter of the spinach mixture, pressing it into the shape of the fillet; then place one fillet on top, arranging it neatly so that it looks like a nice, compact package. Place one whole basil leaf on

Per serving:

Calories: 215
Carbohydrates: 9 g
Protein: 31.8 g
Fat Total: 4.6 g
Fat Saturated: .88 g

8 5

top of the fillet. Continue with other fillets; sprinkle the fish with a few tablespoons of vermouth or brandy. Cover the dish with foil. (The fish may stay in the refrigerator for a maximum of 24 hours in this manner without any harm.)

Bake the fish covered at 350° for 25 to 35 minutes until just done. Sprinkle the top of each fillet with a tiny bit of paprika for color, if desired.

Tuna Casserole
with Fusilli

SERVES 4

Here we have a more sophisticated version of the mundane tuna casserole. It will make you rethink the way you feel about tuna casserole!

Per serving:

Calories: 398
Carbohydrates: 41.3 g
Protein: 36 g
Fat Total: 7.5 g
Fat Saturated: .95 g

2	**tablespoons flour**
1	**cup skim milk, hot**
4 to 6	**green onions, minced**
½	**cup mushrooms, sliced**
½ to ⅔	**cup celery, finely diced**
⅓	**cup peas, fresh or frozen**
½ to 1	**teaspoon salt**
¼	**teaspoon black pepper**
¼	**teaspoon nutmeg**
⅛	**teaspoon cayenne pepper**
½	**teaspoon basil**
1	**teaspoon thyme or ½ teaspoon thyme and ½ teaspoon tarragon**
½	**cup nonfat sour cream**
1	**cup fusilli springs or macaroni**
2	**tablespoons chopped parsley**
2	**tablespoons Parmesan cheese**
½ to ¾	**cup nonfat cottage cheese**
½	**cup reduced-fat cheddar cheese**
1	**6-ounce can of water-packed tuna, drained**
⅓ to ½	**cup liquid—additional milk or soy milk**
1	**2-quart soufflé dish sprayed with Pam®**

Mix the flour thoroughly in a saucepan with ¼ cup of the milk until there are no lumps. Add the remaining ¾ cup of milk and stir well. Place the saucepan over a medium flame and bring to a boil, stirring with a whisk until the sauce is smooth. Continue to cook for 30 seconds until the sauce thickens and there are no lumps. Reduce the heat to medium-low and add the green onion, mushrooms, celery, peas, salt, pepper, nutmeg, cayenne, basil, and thyme. Stir and cook the sauce for another minute. Remove the sauce from the heat and blend in the nonfat sour cream, getting out any lumps.

Fill a stockpot with water (around 2 quarts to 1 gallon) and bring the water to a boil; add the fusilli springs or macaroni and cook until nearly (but not quite) done, around 3 to 5 minutes. Drain the pasta in a sieve or colander and rinse in cool water.

In a large bowl combine parsley, Parmesan cheese, cottage cheese, cheddar cheese, and tuna. When the sauce mixture is cool enough not to melt the cheese, add the sauce to the tuna /cheese bowl and stir. If mixture seems very thick, add liquid to thin it out some. Fold in the fusilli or macaroni and blend. Place mixture in prepared dish and cover.

(The casserole may stay in the refrigerator for a maximum of 24 hours in this manner without any harm, but the longer it sits the more liquid the pasta may absorb; so if you're not cooking it immediately you may wish to add some more milk or a combination of milk and sour cream.)

Cook the covered casserole in a preheated 350° oven for 45 minutes; remove the cover and cook another 15 minutes or so until bubbling hot and lightly browned on top.

Fish Fingers

SERVES 4

Fish Fingers. What an image that name conjures . . .

These embarrassingly simple things are great for kids—they freeze perfectly and can be popped into the toaster oven to cook. They are mildly flavored, so if you (or your child) prefers a more "seasoned" fish stick, add a tablespoon of your favorite herb mixture to the breading mixture—fine herbes, herbes de Provence, an Italian herb blend, a Cajun mix, or simply chili powder.

1 to 1½	**pounds filleted whitefish, such as snapper, bluefish, tilapia, or roughy (see note below)**
½	**cup all-purpose flour for dusting**
1	**teaspoon salt**
½	**teaspoon lemon-pepper seasoning**
¼	**teaspoon garlic powder**
½	**teaspoon onion powder**

Per serving:

*Calories: 320
Carbohydrates: 35.6 g
Protein: 35.9 g
Fat Total: 3.4 g
Fat Saturated: .56 g*

87

Breading mixture:

3 *tablespoons fresh parsley, chopped finely*
2 *cups breadcrumbs, fresh, store-bought, or a mixture of fresh and store-bought, seasoned or plain*
(see introductory note above about extra seasonings)

⅔ *cup buttermilk*
1 *baking sheet*
Pam®

Note: If, for whatever reason, when you get home from the market and find that the fish smells particularly gamy, you may wish to: a) soak the fish in a bowl of milk for 30 minutes, or b) (my favorite choice) return to the market and buy another piece of fish entirely, complaining bitterly to your fish dealer about the quality of the fish they sell, swearing to tell everyone you know that the standard of fish they sell is rapidly going downhill and everyone had better find another fishmonger pronto. This latter method usually gets results.

Check the fish fillets for any bones by feeling the fish along the central portion of its length; remove any bones you find with tweezers or long-nosed pliers. Remove the skin from the fish, if any. Next, slice the fish into finger-sized strips, approximately 1 × 3 inches. Refrigerate the strips until needed.

In preparation for the breading procedure, place the flour in a plastic bag, add the salt, lemon-pepper seasoning, and garlic and onion powders, shaking the bag to distribute the seasonings evenly. Next combine the breading mixture in a large bowl or plate. Then place the buttermilk in a small bowl. Finally, spray the baking sheet with Pam®.

Remove the fish pieces from refrigerator and place a few pieces in the flour mixture (that is, the plastic bag). Shake the pieces briefly, then remove each piece from the bag, shaking off any excess, then dip the flour-coated fish finger in buttermilk. Place the wet fish piece into the breading mixture and make sure that all sides are coated evenly. Put the breaded fish piece onto the prepared baking sheet. Continue until all the fish pieces are breaded. Cover and refrigerate the fish fingers for 30 minutes or freeze.

To cook, place thawed, uncovered fish in the upper portion of a preheated 375° oven until the fish is done, approximately 20 minutes. If desired, you may briefly broil the fish sticks to lightly brown the top. Serve immediately with ketchup, mustard, BBQ sauce, or malt vinegar.

Indian Fish with Yogurt Sauce

SERVES 4

THE FISH:

	juice of one lemon
	a sprinkling of salt
2	*cloves garlic, minced or put through a garlic press*
1	*teaspoon finely minced gingerroot*
1	*tablespoon chopped cilantro*
1	*teaspoon garam masala, or ½ teaspoon ground cumin, ¼ teaspoon ground coriander, and ¼ teaspoon curry powder*
	a sprinkling of cayenne pepper
1¼	*pounds of lean whitefish fillet (grouper, tilapia, sole, halibut, snapper, or bluefish)*

THE SAUCE:

1	*cup nonfat plain yogurt*
1	*teaspoon cornstarch or arrowroot*
	salt to taste
1	*clove of garlic, minced or put through a garlic press*
1	*teaspoon flavorless oil*
1	*teaspoon mustard seeds (black or yellow)*
½	*teaspoon ground cumin*
1	*teaspoon chopped cilantro*
¼	*cup peeled, seeded, chopped, fresh tomato*
1	*shallow baking dish, around 9 × 12 inches*

Per serving:

Calories: 251
Carbohydrates: 8.1 g
Protein: 43.1 g
Fat Total: 4.2 g
Fat Saturated: .77 g

Combine the first seven ingredients in a baking dish and mix well. Add the fish fillets and turn them in the marinade, coating evenly. Allow the fish to marinate for 20 minutes.

Just before you're ready to bake/broil/grill the fish, make the yogurt sauce.

Place the cornstarch and ¼ cup of yogurt into a small saucepan and stir with a whisk until smooth. Add the remaining yogurt and place pan over a medium-low flame, stirring with the whisk until it is hot but not steaming. (**Note:** Yogurt that reaches the boiling point can "break"; that is, it will separate into curds and whey, resulting in a watery, lumpy sauce. The addition of arrowroot or cornstarch is a preventative measure against this occurrence, but it is important to get the sauce hot enough to cook the starch, but not so hot that it breaks the yogurt. It sounds terribly complicated and difficult, but it's not—just watch the sauce carefully and when it's hot and thick, remove it from the heat!) Set the warmed yogurt aside and keep warm. In a small sauté pan, heat the oil over a medium flame until hot; add the mustard seeds. When they have begun to pop and sizzle, immediately remove the pan from heat and add the garlic and cumin. Let the garlic cook in the hot pan for 30 seconds, stirring a bit. Next pour the cooked spices and garlic into the warmed yogurt; season the sauce with salt, cilantro, and tomato.

Either bake the fish covered at 350° for approximately 25 to 30 minutes, broil for 5 to 8 minutes, or grill outdoors for 5 to 10 minutes.

Serve the fish hot with a squeeze of fresh lemon and the yogurt sauce on the side.

Orange Roughy with Orange-Ginger Flavor

SERVES 4

Per serving:

Calories: 270
Carbohydrates: 24.8 g
Protein: 23 g
Fat Total: 9.4 g
Fat Saturated: .19 g

1   **pound orange roughy fillets**
2   **cloves garlic, minced or put through a garlic press**
    salt and pepper
    flour
    Pam®
2   **cups sugar snap peas**
4   **green onions, minced**
1   **tablespoon finely minced gingerroot**
1   **teaspoon freshly grated orange rind**
    juice from one orange
    salt or tamari to taste

1   **shallow baking dish (about 8 × 8 inches)**

Cut the fish into 2- × 4-inch strips. Rub the minced garlic over the fish, then salt and pepper the fish lightly. Dust the fish pieces with flour.

Heat a large sauté pan over a medium-low flame; when the pan is hot, spray it with Pam®. Add as many of the fish pieces as will fit in one layer; sauté gently until the fish has firmed up, around 2 to 3 minutes. Gently turn the pieces over and firm up the other side as well. Carefully remove the fish from the pan and repeat the procedure with any remaining fish. Place the half-cooked fish strips into a shallow baking dish.

When all of the fish has been cooked, spray the same sauté pan with Pam® and add the sugar snap peas, green onions, gingerroot, orange rind, and orange juice. Bring to a simmer and cover, cooking for 3 minutes or so until the snap peas have softened. Taste the sauce for seasoning, adding salt if necessary. Pour the vegetables and sauce over the fish pieces and cover.

Bake the fish at 325° for 25 to 30 minutes until the fish pieces are just done. Serve immediately with hot rice.

"Oven-Fried" Catfish

SERVES 4

Yet another "comfort food" dish that is usually fried and dripping with grease; this version is lean and delightful, though rather mild. Adjust the seasonings to suit your taste. Perhaps you may want to add some Dry BBQ Marinade (see page 211) for a more Cajun-style catfish, or an Italian herb mixture.

1	**cup low-fat buttermilk in a bowl**
2	**cloves garlic, minced or put through a garlic press**
2	**tablespoons finely grated onion**
4	**small or 2 large dressed catfish, or 4 catfish fillets**
½	**cup flour**
1½	**teaspoons lemon-pepper seasoning**
2	**teaspoons salt**
1 to 2	**tablespoons additional seasonings (see introductory note above; optional)**
1½	**cups yellow cornmeal in a plastic bag**
2	**tablespoons very finely minced fresh parsley**
1	**baking sheet sprayed with Pam®**
2	**plastic bags**

Preheat oven to 375° Combine the buttermilk, garlic, and onion in a bowl large enough for the catfish. Set the bowl aside for the moment.

Place the flour, lemon-pepper seasoning, salt, and optional seasonings in a plastic bag, shaking to distribute the seasonings evenly.

Place the cornmeal and parsley in another plastic bag, shaking once again to distribute the seasonings.

With everything in front of you, place a catfish fillet or a whole catfish into the flour mixture and shake, covering evenly. Remove the fish from the bag, shaking off any excess flour. Place the dusted catfish into the buttermilk-garlic mixture, coating evenly, then place the wet catfish into the bag containing the cornmeal and parsley. Shake until the fish is covered evenly. Remove the breaded catfish and place on a baking sheet. Continue until all of the fish have been coated. Refrigerate the dressed catfish or freeze them.

To cook, place the thawed, uncovered fish into the upper portion of a preheated 375° oven for 30 to 45 minutes until they are done (depending of size of fish—whole catfish will take longer.) If desired, broil briefly to brown and crispen the top. Serve with lemon wedges and/or a low-fat tartar sauce.

Per serving:

Calories: 292
Carbohydrates: 32 g
Protein: 25.7 g
Fat Total: 6.3 g
Fat Saturated: .32 g

91

Sautéed Fish with Peppers

SERVES 4

Per serving:

Calories: 220
Carbohydrates: 8.4 g
Protein: 33.4 g
Fat Total: 4.3 g
Fat Saturated: .71 g

Classically Provençale.

1	**1-pound fish fillet, such as roughy, tilapia, grouper, or bluefish**
1	**teaspoon finest herbes de Provence**
	freshly ground black pepper and salt
	flour for dusting (about 2 tablespoons or so)
2	**teaspoons olive oil and Pam®**
2 to 3	**garlic cloves, put through a garlic press or finely minced**
1	**cup thinly sliced onions, yellow or white**
2	**cups sliced peppers (red, green, yellow, or a combination)**
1	**small zucchini, cut into thin half-moons**
¼	**cup dry white vermouth or white wine**
¼	**cup water or defatted chicken stock**
1	**tablespoon lemon juice, approximately**
1	**teaspoon tamari or soy sauce**

Check the fish fillet for any bones or scales; remove as many of the larger bones as you can find with tweezers or long-nosed pliers. Sprinkle each fillet with a bit of black pepper and salt, then sprinkle with the herbes de Provence. Next, dust with a bit of flour—not much, just enough to lightly cover fish. Set aside.

Place a heavy, nonstick sauté pan (one that is large enough to hold the fish easily) over a moderately high flame. When the pan is hot, add the olive oil and spray with Pam®, then add the garlic. Let the garlic cook a few seconds (15 to 20), then put in the fish. Reduce the flame to medium-low and allow the fish to cook until it has browned lightly on the bottom and you can see the edges cooking nicely; gently turn each fillet over onto the other side. Cook until the other side has browned and you can feel that the fish is no longer springy in the center; check for doneness by cutting into the fish if desired. The thickest part should be *just* done; do not overcook! Remove the fish gently and place in a warm oven.

In the same pan, sauté the onions until limp over a moderate flame; add the peppers and zucchini. Stir-fry the vegetables for 30 seconds or so, then add the vermouth, water, lemon juice, and soy or tamari. Continue to stir-fry until peppers are just cooked through but aren't limp. Taste for seasoning, adding herbes de Provence or tamari as needed.

Arrange the cooked, warm fish prettily on a platter and spread the pepper mixture and sauce on top. Garnish with freshly chopped parsley or fresh thyme.

Variations

- Add 1 cup diced tomatoes with pepper mixture.
- Substitute dried basil for herbes de Provence.
- Substitute ground cumin for herbes de Provence and use cayenne pepper instead of black pepper, garnishing with cilantro.

Siamese Salmon

SERVES 4

A very light, unusual salmon treat with a hint from Thailand. This dish highlights the freshness of the salmon without masking its taste and is uncommonly good, despite being so extraordinarily simple to prepare.

1	**teaspoon toasted sesame oil**
1	**tablespoon tamari**
1	**tablespoon gingerroot, finely minced**
2	**tablespoons sherry**
2	**largish salmon fillets (total weight: 1 to 1¼ pounds)**
2	**green onions, finely minced**
	zest of ¼ lime
	lime wedges
1	**teaspoon sesame seeds**
1	**plate that will hold the fish and marinade**

Per serving:

Calories: 212
Carbohydrates: 4.4 g
Protein: 30.4 g
Fat Total: 6.8 g
Fat Saturated: 1.1 g

Note: The best way to prepare this dish is to steam it, so you will need a plate that can fit into a steamer and then be completely covered. The Chinese usually cross two chopsticks in the bottom of a wok and place the plate on top of the chopsticks, then steam the fish (sitting on top of the plate) in the wok.

Combine the first four ingredients in a bowl.

Check the fish fillets for any bones by gently stroking the fish along its length and feeling with your fingers. Remove any bones with tweezers or long-nosed pliers. Place the fish on a plate that will fit into a steamer or wok, then spread the marinade over fish. Marinate the salmon for at least 30 minutes.

Just before cooking, sprinkle the green onions and lime zest over the salmon; place the entire plate in the steamer or wok and cover. Steam the fish for 12 to 15 minutes until they are just done. Serve hot, spooning any juices from the plate onto the cooked fish and garnish with sesame seeds and fresh lime wedges.

If you don't have anything in which to steam the fish, you can also bake the fish covered for 25 to 30 minutes at 350°, or broil the fish for 8 minutes.

Seafood Stir-fry

SERVES 4

Per serving:

Calories: 159
Carbohydrates: 14.9 g
Protein: 15.4 g
Fat Total: 4.2 g
Fat Saturated: .63 g

½ **pound scallops, shrimp (peeled and deveined), or crabmeat**
1 **egg white**
1 **teaspoon soy sauce**
1 **teaspoon sugar**
½ **teaspoon gingerroot, finely grated**
1 **teaspoon sherry**

FOR THE SAUCE:
½ **cup defatted chicken stock**
1 **tablespoon rice wine vinegar**
2 **tablespoons soy sauce**
1 **teaspoon sugar**
1 **teaspoon arrowroot**
½ **teaspoon chili paste with garlic (optional)**

1 **tablespoon vegetable oil**
3 **green onions, diced**
½ to ¾ **cup sliced mushrooms**
1 **cup snow peas**
1 to 1½ **cups shredded napa cabbage or broccoli florets**
½ to ¾ **cup sliced water chestnuts**

In a bowl, beat the egg white until frothy. Add the soy sauce, sugar, gingerroot, and sherry and mix. Fold in the seafood, coating with the egg white, then set aside.

Combine the ingredients for the sauce in a bowl, then set it aside.

Heat the oil in a wok or skillet over a medium-high flame. When the oil is hot, add the seafood and stir-fry until it is cooked, approximately 2 to 3 minutes. Remove the seafood to a small bowl, draining on paper towels if desired to remove any excess oil.

In the same wok or skillet, immediately add the green onions, mushrooms, snow peas, napa cabbage or broccoli florets, and water chestnuts. Stir-fry for 2 minutes or so, until snow peas are bright green and cooked but still crisp. Add cooked seafood and toss, continuing to stir-fry for another minute to heat the seafood through. Next, add the sauce mixture. Stir and cook until the sauce has thickened (around 2 minutes) and everything is hot. Serve the stir-fry immediately over hot rice.

Shrimp Kabobs
with Bay

SERVES 4

Great for cookouts—easy to prepare and they grill in no time. These brochettes are crowd pleasers and a nice counterpoint to grilled hamburgers and sausages.

The best way to skewer shrimp is to pierce both the thick and thin ends so that it won't flop around on the skewer. This step takes a teeny bit more time, but you will be amply rewarded when a simple turn of the wrist flips them over.

	juice of one lemon
2	**teaspoons olive oil**
1	**teaspoon oregano**
⅛	**teaspoon cayenne pepper**
2	**cloves garlic, minced or put through a garlic press**
1	**tablespoon vermouth**
1	**tablespoon parsley**
2	**teaspoons tamari or soy sauce**
12 to 15	**large shrimp, peeled and deveined**
8	**bay leaves, broken in half**
4	**skewers (bamboo or metal)**

Combine first eight ingredients in a bowl, then add the shrimp and toss, making sure all the shrimp have been coated with the marinade. Carefully place a shrimp on a skewer, securing both the large and small ends so that it doesn't flop around when being turned, then skewer half a bay leaf, then another shrimp, then half a bay leaf, continuing until the shrimp are used up. Place the shrimp brochettes on a large piece of foil or a large platter and drizzle them with any remaining marinade. Cover and refrigerate the shrimp, allowing them to marinate for 1 to 3 hours.

To cook, either broil or grill outdoors, 3 to 5 minutes on each side, basting with any leftover marinade. Serve with a rice dish and a bright green vegetable.

Per serving:

Calories: 50
Carbohydrates: 2 g
Protein: 5 g
Fat Total: 2.3 g
Fat Saturated: .35 g

Szechuan Shrimp

SERVES 4

As with any dish that has hot chili peppers in it, you can always adjust the amount of "heat" to your own taste, increasing or lessening it as desired. Note that this does not have a too-thick cornstarch sauce; I much prefer a thin sauce to an unnaturally thick one.

Per serving:

Calories: 193
Carbohydrates: 9.8 g
Protein: 27.6 g
Fat Total: 4.4 g
Fat Saturated: .72 g

¾ to 1	**pound peeled, deveined shrimp**
2	**tablespoons finely grated gingerroot**
3	**large cloves garlic, minced or put through a garlic press**

S A U C E   M I X T U R E :

2	**tablespoons tamari or soy sauce**
½ to 1	**teaspoon honey or sugar**
1 to 2	**tablespoons chili paste with garlic (see Ingredients page 224)**
¾	**cup defatted stock or water**
1	**teaspoon cornstarch (optional)**
6	**green onions, chopped**
1	**cup finely sliced green and/or red bell peppers (you may use hot chili peppers if you so desire, or a mixture of hot and sweet peppers)**
2	**teaspoons oil for stir-frying**

Marinate the shrimp in a bowl with the grated gingerroot and minced garlic for at least 1 hour. Combine the ingredients for the sauce mixture and set aside. Prepare the green onions and peppers.

When ready to cook, heat a skillet or wok over a medium-high flame. When the pan is hot, add 2 teaspoons oil and the marinated shrimp; stir-fry until the shrimp are nearly cooked, around 2 to 3 minutes. Remove the shrimp. Immediately add the green onions and peppers to the same wok, stir-frying until they are nearly done, around 2 minutes. Add the cooked shrimp, stir-frying another minute to make sure they are hot. When entire mixture is hot, add the sauce mixture and bring to a boil, stirring well and evenly. Serve the shrimp immediately, garnishing with cilantro and a sprinkling of toasted sesame seeds if desired.

Serve with hot rice.

Variations

- Use ⅔ cup broccoli florets instead of peppers.
- Add a handful of snow peas.
- Add ½ cup sliced mushrooms to vegetable stir-fry.

Paella Valenciana

SERVES 4 TO 6

Paella accompanied by new Spanish wine and fresh, crusty bread is a quintes-
sential Spanish meal. It is, as with any "national" dish, one in which every family
not only has their own recipe, but insists their version is the tastiest and the most
authentic! While I was in Spain I must have seen dozens of different styles of
paella, one with chicken, one without; one with squid and fish, one without any
seafood at all! This recipe eschews the fat-laden chorizo *(sausage) and is easier*
on the pocketbook than those including fish, seafood, chicken, meat, and co-
pious amounts of olive oil.

6	*mussels, scrubbed and "sanded" (see note below)*
6	*clams, scrubbed and "sanded" (see note below)*
1	*teaspoon olive oil & Pam®*
3	*chicken breast halves, skinless and boneless, chopped into 1-inch to 2-inch cubes*
1	*small onion, finely chopped*
2	*cloves garlic, minced or put through a garlic press*
1	*large pinch saffron, whole or ground*
½ to 1	*teaspoon turmeric (optional)*
1½	*cups rice, preferably Valencia, arborio, or short-grained white rice*
2	*cups stock, preferably a mixture of defatted chicken stock and clam juice*
½	*cup dry vermouth or white wine*
⅓	*cup chopped fresh basil*
2	*large tomatoes, peeled, seeded, and chopped*
½	*cup red bell pepper, chopped*
6	*large shrimp, sliced in half lengthwise*
½	*cup peas, fresh or frozen*
1	*paella dish or a large, open casserole dish (around 9 × 12 × 1½ inches)*

Note: To clean clams and mussels, scrub their shells vigorously under cool running water and remove any "beard" from the side of the shell. Discard any that seem overly light or whose shell has opened. Soak the clams and mussels in clean, cool water for 10 to 20 minutes or so with the hope that they will begin to disgorge any sand. Rinse and soak again in more water, adding 1 tablespoon of flour to the water. Soak another 10 minutes more, then rinse. Soak again in clean, cool water for 10 to 20 minutes.

Clean the clams and/or mussels according to the note above.

    Place a medium-sized, heavy-bottomed pot over moderate heat; when the pan is hot, add the oil and Pam®. Next add the chicken pieces and cook them just long enough to stiffen the meat, around 2 to 3 min-

Per serving:

Calories: 455
Carbohydrates: 51.1 g
Protein: 41.3 g
Fat Total: 6.1 g
Fat Saturated: 1.2 g

utes; the chicken will not be done. Remove the chicken meat to a bowl and set aside, draining on paper towels if desired. In the same pan, add the onion, garlic, and saffron, stirring and sautéing until the onion is tender, around 3 to 5 minutes. (If desired, you may also add the turmeric along with the saffron to ensure a bright yellow color.) Add the rice and continue stirring for about 2 minutes until the rice has taken on an opaque color and each grain is coated lightly with the oil from the pan. Add the stock and wine, bringing the ingredients to the simmering point and covering tightly. Cook on very low heat for 20 to 25 minutes until the rice is barely done. Remove the rice from the heat and allow it to stand undisturbed for 15 minutes before proceeding.

(**Note:** Depending on weather conditions and the age of the rice, the rice may need more or less liquid to cook. If the rice seems quite underdone at the end of the 25 minutes, add ¼ cup more liquid and continue cooking over low heat until it is just done. If the rice seems in danger of becoming gummy, spoon off any excess liquid. Since the rice will be baked later, the perfect consistency for this stage is for the rice to be just slightly underdone.)

Spray a paella dish or a large, open casserole dish with Pam®. Spoon the rice into the dish. Sprinkle in the fresh basil, tomatoes, red bell pepper, partially cooked chicken, shrimp, mussels, clams, and peas; arrange the shellfish and meat attractively on the rice. Cover the pan with foil and bake at 350° for 35 to 45 minutes until the clams and mussels have opened and the paella is steaming.

Variations

- Use lean whitefish chunks (such as tilapia) for the chicken pieces.
- Add ¼ pound of sliced scallops, squid, or any other shellfish.
- Use cooked turkey sausage instead of (or in addition to) the chicken breasts.

Salmon with Herb Dressing

SERVES 4

The herb dressing below is a light, subtle sauce. For a more complex dining experience, I would strongly recommend using one of the variations, either the ones listed below or one of your own!

Per serving:

Calories: 199
Carbohydrates: 9.2 g
Protein: 28.9 g
Fat Total: 4.5 g
Fat Saturated: .76 g

FOR THE HERB DRESSING:

⅛	**teaspoon garlic, mashed**
½	**cup nonfat yogurt**
1	**tablespoon lemon juice**
1	**teaspoon Dijon mustard**
½	**teaspoon sugar**
½	**teaspoon salt**
¼	**teaspoon pepper**
2 to 3	**tablespoons chopped fresh dill**
⅓	**cup nonfat sour cream**
2	**salmon fillets (enough for four servings, approximately 12 to 16 ounces)**
1	**clove garlic**
3	**tablespoons lemon juice**
1	**tablespoon chopped fresh dill**
½ to 1	**teaspoon sugar (optional)**
	sprinkling of salt and pepper

Combine the ingredients for the herb dressing in a bowl. Taste for seasoning and set aside.

Marinate the salmon fillets in the garlic, lemon juice, dill, optional sugar, and salt and pepper.

When ready to cook, broil or grill the salmon until done, approximately 3 to 5 minutes each side. Do not overcook! Remove the fish when it still looks slightly underdone in the center. Remember: The fish will continue to cook after it has been removed from the heat. Serve the salmon hot or warm with the herb dressing on the side, garnishing with a dill sprig. (Serving portion for dressing: approximately 3 tablespoons per person.)

Variations

- Add 1 to 3 tablespoons reduced-fat mayonnaise to dressing.
- Use a mixture of basil and parsley instead of dill.
- Use a mixture of tarragon and marjoram instead of dill.
- Add ¼ cup finely diced celery or grated cucumber (or both) to the dressing.

Ridiculously Simple Japanese Tuna

SERVES 4

Per serving:

Calories: 127
Carbohydrates: .98 g
Protein: 21 g
Fat Total: 3.8 g
Fat Saturated: .95 g

Japanese cuisine is elegantly simple yet complex; it seamlessly and subtly complements any food without covering the inherent taste of the food. If for no other reason than this, Japanese cuisine deserves great respect; the simplest lessons are always the most difficult to learn.

I first had this "recipe" when a dear friend, artist, author, and marvelous cook, Shozo Sato, was visiting me years ago. He had prepared a gorgeous and sumptuous Japanese dinner, and when I asked him what the incredible marinade for the tuna was, he looked at me blankly and answered, "Soy sauce." I had just learned the most important maxim of the Japanese diet; keep it simple.

fresh tuna, cut into individual steaks (approximately 1 inch × 3 inches × 4 inches)
tamari
finely grated gingerroot

(Sample proportions: 1 pound tuna, ¼ cup tamari, and 1 teaspoon gingerroot.)

In a deep dish or a bowl, combine tamari, a sprinkling of finely grated fresh gingerroot, and the tuna. Allow the fish to marinate 30 minutes.

Place a heavy skillet (cast iron is great) or shallow metal pan directly under the broiler and preheat the broiler at the highest temperature for 30 minutes. When the broiler and skillet are unquestionably and unbelievably hot, carefully put tuna steaks into the blazing hot pan and return it to the broiler. When you place the fish on the hot skillet, the tuna will sizzle and "seize"; it will sound like a steak being put on a grill at a steak house. Allow the tuna steaks to cook until nearly done *without turning*; WATCH THE FISH LIKE A HAWK! Fish steaks can go from underdone to overdone within 30 seconds! When the tuna is still a bit pink in the center remove it from the broiler and allow it to cool for 30 to 60 seconds. Serve the tuna immediately. If desired, pour 1 teaspoon of tamari over the cooked tuna.

Important Note: The tuna will continue to cook after it has been removed from the broiler. It is *imperative* that the fish be removed *before* it has been thoroughly cooked; otherwise it will be overcooked and dry by the time it is served. The texture of a properly cooked tuna steak is moist and succulent, with the tissue sections separating upon being prodded with a fork. No fish in the world should be flaky; flakiness indicates that the fish has been cooked beyond the point of eating. (Perhaps it would do for the cat. . . .)

Variations

- Add a clove of garlic to the tamari mixture.
- To lighten the tamari taste, add 2 tablespoons of sake to dilute saltiness.

Additional note: Do not add sugar or any other sweetener to the marinating sauce with the idea of making a pseudo-teriyaki sauce. Because of the very high heat under the broiler, all you'd be doing is caramelizing and then burning the sugar long before the tuna was done. This is experience talking, folks.

Indian Spiced Fish

SERVES 4

Amazingly simple. Amazingly tasty. And amazingly low in fat.

2	**tablespoons lemon juice**
1	**teaspoon sugar or honey (optional)**
2	**cloves garlic, minced**
2	**teaspoons gingerroot, finely minced**
1	**teaspoon garam masala or**
	(if you're in a bind and don't have garam masala), use ½ teaspoon cumin, ½ teaspoon coriander, and ¼ teaspoon curry powder
3	**tablespoons chopped cilantro**
1 to 1¼	**pounds lean whitefish fillets, such as snapper, tilapia, or bluefish salt and pepper**
1	**shallow baking dish, large enough to hold the fish in one layer**

Place first six ingredients into a ceramic dish large enough to hold the fish, mixing well.

Season the fish with salt and pepper, then place the fillets in the marinade, coating both sides evenly. Allow the fish to marinate for 30 minutes or so.

Bake the fish covered at 350° for 25 to 30 minutes until just done, or broil the fish until done (5 to 8 minutes), turning once. Be very careful not to overcook the fish! Remove the fish when it is barely done in the center; remember that the fish will continue to cook after it has been removed from the oven or broiler.

Serve immediately with a hot rice pilaf and a green vegetable or salad.

Per serving:

*Calories: 163
Carbohydrates: 2.9 g
Protein: 32 g
Fat Total: 1.8 g
Fat Saturated: .39 g*

Shrimp Stir-fry

SERVES 4

Quick and tasty—serve with plain white rice for a colorful and nutritious meal.

FOR THE MARINADE:

½   **teaspoon finely grated or minced gingerroot**
2   **cloves garlic, minced or put through a garlic press**
1   **tablespoon chopped cilantro (optional)**
1   **tablespoon sherry or white wine**
1   **tablespoon tamari or soy sauce**
1   **teaspoon toasted sesame oil**
1   **teaspoon rice wine vinegar**
½   **teaspoon sugar**
½   **teaspoon dried red pepper flakes (optional)**
2   **green onions, diced**

¾ to 1   **pound shrimp, peeled and deveined**

½   **cup each chopped green and red bell peppers**
1   **6- to 8-ounce can of water chestnuts, drained and sliced**
½ to ¾   **cup broccoli florets**
1   **cup snow peas**
½ to ¾   **cup defatted chicken stock**
1   **teaspoon cornstarch or arrowroot**
1   **teaspoon oil**
   additional soy sauce to taste

Combine the ingredients for the marinade in a bowl and add the cleaned shrimp. Let the shrimp marinate for 20 minutes or so.

Chop the vegetables and set aside. In a small bowl, dissolve the cornstarch into the chicken stock, blending well so there are no lumps.

Heat a wok or skillet over a medium-high flame until it is hot. Add 1 teaspoon oil, then the marinated shrimp, stir-frying until they are nearly done, around 3 minutes. Remove the shrimp, draining on paper towels if desired. Immediately in the same wok, add the vegetables and continue stir-frying until they are nearly done, around 2 minutes. Add the shrimp, continuing to stir-fry another minute until everything is hot; then add the chicken stock and cornstarch. Stir everything until the sauce is hot and bubbly and has thickened. Serve the shrimp immediately with hot rice.

Variations

- Add 1 teaspoon chili paste with garlic instead of garlic and red pepper flakes.
- Chop 1 whole (2 halved) chicken breasts instead of shrimp.
- Add ½ cup sliced mushrooms to stir-fry.

Per serving:

Calories: 222
Carbohydrates: 14.7 g
Protein: 28.8 g
Fat Total: 4.5 g
Fat Saturated: .72 g

Indian Shrimp
with Tomato Sauce

SERVES 4

I adore Indian food. My first exposure to it was in London while I was staying with my dear friend Constance McNair, who had prepared a delicious eggplant and tomato dish; never before had I had anything with such a complex layering of tastes and sensations. I was hooked. Upon returning stateside, I immediately bought two Indian cookbooks and began a lengthy in-home course teaching myself the various and complex cuisines of that immense and endearing country.

Per serving:

Calories: 109
Carbohydrates: 11.9 g
Protein: 8.9 g
Fat Total: 3.4 g
Fat Saturated: .48 g

1	**small onion, peeled**
2	**cloves garlic, peeled**
1	**1-inch piece of gingerroot, peeled**
½	**cup water**
2	**teaspoons oil**
2	**teaspoons mustard seeds, black or yellow (but preferably black)**
1	**teaspoon red pepper flakes or ¼ teaspoon cayenne pepper**
1	**teaspoon ground cumin seeds or whole cumin seeds**
1	**teaspoon ground coriander**
½	**teaspoon turmeric**
1	**tablespoon tamarind paste or 2 teaspoons lemon juice mixed with 1 teaspoon sugar**
1	**18-ounce can Italian plum tomatoes, drained and chopped**
12	**medium shrimp, peeled and deveined**
½ to ¾	**cup plain, nonfat yogurt or nonfat sour cream**
½	**teaspoon garam masala (optional)**
1	**tablespoon chopped cilantro**

Place the onion, garlic, gingerroot, and water into a blender or food processor and blend until you have an absolutely smooth paste. Set this paste aside in a bowl.

Heat the oil in a large sauté pan over moderate flame. When the oil is hot, add the mustard seeds and red pepper flakes; when the mustard seeds begin to "pop," immediately remove the pan from the heat and add the cumin, coriander, and turmeric, stirring once. Next add the onion-garlic-ginger paste. (The pan will be very hot!! Keep your face averted when adding the paste, as the moisture will splatter and sputter!) Return the pan to the heat and cook over a moderate flame until the onion has cooked and is beginning to brown slightly, around 15 to 20 minutes. Add the tamarind paste and the tomatoes, continuing to cook for another 5 to 8 minutes. Add the shrimp and continue stirring and cooking until the shrimp are just done, around 3 more minutes.

Remove the pan from the heat and allow it to cool for 1 to 2 minutes. Then stir in one tablespoon of yogurt, mixing it well into the tomato mixture; continue adding yogurt one tablespoon at a time until it is all incorporated. Add the optional garam masala and the cilantro, stirring once. Serve immediately with hot basmati rice (*see* page 212).

Cantonese Five-Spice Fish

SERVES 4

This is reminiscent of a wonderful Chinese smoked-fish recipe I used to make in which you must marinate, then smoke, then sauté the whole fish—this recipe is infinitely easier.

Serve with rice and some stir-fried vegetables.

Per serving:

Calories: 201
Carbohydrates: 4.7 g
Protein: 27.6 g
Fat Total: 6.4 g
Fat Saturated: .15 g

2	**cloves garlic, finely minced or put through a garlic press**
1	**tablespoon gingerroot, finely minced**
2	**tablespoons sherry**
½ to 2	**teaspoons Chinese five-spice powder (optional)**
1½ to 2	**pounds whole bass or similar whitefish, such as snapper, or 1 to 1¼ pounds of fillets**
4	**whole star anise**
4	**green onions, finely chopped**
1	**tablespoon tamari**
1	**teaspoon toasted sesame oil**
	Pam®

Combine the garlic, gingerroot, sherry, and optional five-spice powder in a small bowl. (Use the lesser amount if you can only find fish fillets, and use the greater amount if you are able to find a whole fish.) Set the bowl aside.

Clean and wash the fish. Cut two or three slits on each side if you have a whole fish, making a crosshatch design if you wish. Spread the garlic-ginger mixture on each side, making sure you get it into the slits. Let the fish marinate at least one hour.

For fish fillets, prepare the marinade as usual but allow it to sit on the fillets no more than ½ hour before cooking.

Combine the star anise, green onions, tamari, and sesame oil; place this mixture into the cavity of the whole fish. If using fillets, sprinkle these ingredients over the fish and proceed.

Spray a large piece of foil with Pam® and place the fish into it and seal tightly.

Bake the whole fish for 30 to 45 minutes at 375° until just done, noting a time difference because of the size of the fish. Be sure to check the thickest part of the fish for doneness.

Bake the fillets at 400° for 20 to 25 minutes until they are just done. Garnish with cilantro.

La Ramplas Pescado

SERVES 4

La Ramplas is a bustling, eclectic shopping district running for blocks near the still-extant medieval Cathedral of Barcelona. As with Barcelona, one of my favorite cities in the world, this succulent fish dish from Catalonia has many memories for me. It is served cold and is reminiscent of the kind of seasonal delights the Catalans are famous for. My mind's eye pictures an open-air bistro with umbrellaed tables during the afternoon siesta, lively conversations, fresh bread being torn apart by eager hands, delicious new Spanish wine (or cold beer), and this cool treat. Perfect for an elegant lunch or a light summer dinner.

1½	**pounds tilapia or roughy fillets (or similar firm whitefish)**
	defatted chicken stock
	juice of 1 lemon
¼	**cup white wine or dry vermouth**
	a large pinch of saffron
1	**teaspoon salt**
1	**teaspoon olive oil and Pam®**
1	**red bell pepper, thinly sliced**
8	**green onions, finely sliced**
¼	**cup white wine, dry vermouth, stock, or water**
1 to 2	**teaspoons dried thyme, summer savory, or rosemary**
2	**cloves garlic, minced or put through a garlic press**
2 to 3	**tablespoons balsamic vinegar or red wine vinegar**
	salt to taste

Slice the fish into serving-sized portions, 4 to 5 ounces per person.

Per serving:

*Calories: 206
Carbohydrates: 7.9 g
Protein: 36.3 g
Fat Total: 2.8 g
Fat Saturated: .4 g*

Fill a large, deep skillet with enough chicken stock to come 1 inch up the sides. (This pan should be big enough so that the fish can sit in one layer and poach.) Add the lemon juice, wine, saffron, and salt. Bring to a simmer over a medium flame; when the liquid is hot, gently add the fish pieces. Continue to cook over a very low heat until the fish is just done; the *court bouillon* (poaching liquid) should *never* come to a boil. When the fish is done, remove it carefully with a slotted spatula and place on a platter. Refrigerate the fish.

Heat another skillet over a medium-high flame; when it is hot, add the oil and Pam®. Next add the pepper and onions, covering and cooking until the vegetables are beginning to soften, around 3 minutes; add the wine or water and thyme. Stir-fry until the vegetables are just done, another 2 minutes. Remove the pan from the heat and add the garlic and vinegar.

Remove the fish from the refrigerator and drain off any liquid that may have accumulated in the bottom of the platter. Spread the vegetables and pan juices over the cooked, cold fish. Allow the fish and vegetables to macerate for at least 1 hour. Serve cold or at room temperature, with fresh bread.

Quick Pasta with Red Clam Sauce

SERVES 4

One of the greatest assets to making quick and easy dinners is to have the ingredients on hand; in this case, a can of clams, a large can of tomatoes, and some pasta.

	Basic Tomato Sauce (see page 219)
1	**small can of minced clams (6 to 8 ounces), drained**
3	**tablespoons fresh basil, chopped, or 1½ teaspoons dried basil**
	Parmesan cheese for garnish
8 to 12	**ounces linguini, fusilli, vermicelli, or other similar pasta**

Prepare the Basic Tomato Sauce according to directions. (Depending on how much you like tomato sauces, you may wish to double the recipe.)

Boil the pasta in a large stockpot until just done; drain it in a colander.

Immediately add the clams and basil to the hot tomato sauce, stirring once.

Serve the sauce over the hot pasta, garnishing with additional chopped basil or fresh parsley and Parmesan cheese.

Variations

- Add ½ cup chopped zucchini along with clams.
- Use 1 can of drained, water-packed tuna instead of clams.
- For more "zip," add 3 tablespoons chopped pepperocini to sauce.
- Add 3 tablespoons chopped green or black olives to sauce.
- Use 1 tablespoon chopped fresh rosemary instead of fresh basil.

Per serving:

Calories: 397
Carbohydrates: 61.6 g
Protein: 26.4 g
Fat Total: 3.7 g
Fat Saturated: .8 g

Chicken and Turkey

- *On Purchasing Chicken*

Chicken Dijon
Barbecued Chicken
Casablancan Chicken and Beans
Chinese Chicken Breasts
Chicken Cacciatore
Chinese Peanut Chicken
Chicken Enchiladas
Chicken Florentine
Chicken with Fresh Herbs I, II, III, IV,
　and V
Green Chili Chicken
Chicken with Lemon-Caper Sauce
Grilled Chicken with Mango Relish
Middle Eastern Chicken Kabobs
Mexican Rice Casserole
"Oven-Fried" Chicken
Parmesan Chicken Breasts
Chicken with Red Pipèrade
Fresh Turkey or Chicken Sausage
Tandoori Chicken
Chicken Tostadas
Turkey with Cranberry-Orange Sauce
Chicken with Ginger Salsa
Greek Turkey Kabobs

On Purchasing Chicken

A BRIEF NOTE about poultry.

Despite the best intentions of the government department that inspects poultry processing plants, there still remains the possibility of salmonella and other bacteria infecting the chicken and turkey commonly found in the marketplace. Salmonella and poultry flesh (as well as chicken eggs) go hand in hand—as of yet, there is no sure way of completely eliminating this bacteria.

What is the average cook to do? Nothing. As long as you are careful and use a modicum of caution there is no danger. Simply wash the chicken in hot, running water, then dry it, then cook it. Heat (from the cooking, not from the washing) kills the bacteria and subsequently there is no danger of salmonella poisoning. It is not necessary to cook the chicken to the point of dryness; just getting the internal meat temperature to 140° (quite a low temperature, actually, since chicken isn't really "done" until it reaches an internal temperature of 170°) is sufficient to eliminate all danger.

Since bacteria is easily spread between cutting boards, knives, and fingers, it is important to do all of the necessary preparation and cutting of the chicken at one time; then you can place the dressed chicken on a clean plate and thoroughly wash all utensils, cutting boards, and surfaces, as well as your hands. Throw away any paper towels that have come in contact with the chicken and put aside any cloth towels that may have touched the raw poultry. The ease of transmission of bacteria from hands, knives, and cutting boards is great, so just be scrupulously clean when dealing with raw poultry.

Fat Content of Chicken

Ground chicken. Insofar as the fat content is concerned for ground chicken meat, be sure to purchase ground chicken *breast* meat; otherwise you may be buying breast, leg, and thigh, as well as some added fat. The term "ground chicken" is exactly that; the whole thing. For the leanest commercially available meat, purchase ground chicken breast. And if you want extra-lean meat, trim the breasts of any excess fat and grind the breasts yourself.

Chicken breasts. A general rule about chicken breasts: If you're using whole breasts, remove any skin and excess fat. Boneless breasts are slightly lower in fat than breasts with the bone (even if both are skinless) since it is next to impossible to get out all of the fat from between the ribs of the breast. Boneless breasts are more expensive than breasts with the bone; however, boning a breast is quick and simple, and you have the added benefit of having chicken bones to make homemade, delicious chicken stock (*see* How to Make Defatted Chicken Stock, page 29). However, I do realize that many people don't relish the idea of boning chicken breasts, which is exactly why your local market sells them without bones and skin.

Chicken Dijon

SERVES 4

Per serving:

Calories: 302
Carbohydrates: 30.3 g
Protein: 33.6 g
Fat Total: 3.9 g
Fat Saturated: 1 g

Gail 11/14/04.

2 to 3	tablespoons Dijon mustard, either regular or coarse grind
1	clove garlic, minced or put through a garlic press
1	tablespoon vermouth or white wine
1	teaspoon tarragon or thyme, crushed
¾	cup buttermilk
4	chicken breast halves, skinless and boneless
	salt and pepper
1	teaspoon crushed rosemary or basil (optional)
3	cups fresh breadcrumbs (approximately 6 slices of bread), either white or a mixture of white and whole wheat
4	tablespoons chopped fresh parsley
1	shallow baking dish (9 × 12 inches) sprayed with Pam®

Mix the mustard, garlic, vermouth, tarragon, and buttermilk in a bowl and set aside.

Remove any excess fat from the chicken breasts and lightly season each with salt and pepper. Sprinkle the optional rosemary or basil onto the breasts. Set the seasoned breasts aside on a plate.

Next place the fresh bread into a food processor and blend in short spurts until you've got breadcrumbs. Add the parsley and continue blending until the parsley has been chopped into small bits. Place the breadcrumb-parsley mixture on a large plate.

Dip in flour first. →

Dip the chicken breasts one by one into the buttermilk mixture, and then into the breadcrumbs, coating lightly but well. Place the breaded breasts into the shallow baking dish that has been sprayed with Pam®. (The chicken breasts may be covered and refrigerated for up to 2 days, or they may be frozen at this point.)

Bake the chicken uncovered at 350° for 25 to 35 minutes until the breasts are just done and have lightly browned. (If the chicken is done but hasn't browned, place them under the broiler briefly to darken the top.) Serve with a wedge of fresh lemon for added zest.

Barbecued Chicken

SERVES 4

Barbecue sauce can be quickly and easily made with ingredients you probably have in your refrigerator. The added bonus is not only that it is low in fat, but it didn't come from a bottle!

4 skinless chicken breast halves (with or without ribs)

FOR THE SAUCE:

- ½ **cup low-calorie tomato ketchup**
- 2 **tablespoons brown sugar**
- 1 **tablespoon each tamari, lemon juice, and Worcestershire sauce**
- 1 **teaspoon Dijon mustard**
- 2 **cloves garlic, minced**
- ½ **teaspoon ginger or 1 teaspoon grated gingerroot**
- 1 **teaspoon cumin**
- ½ **teaspoon coriander**
- ½ **teaspoon chili powder**
- ¼ **teaspoon cayenne (or to taste)**
- ¼ **teaspoon curry powder (optional)**
- ½ **teaspoon liquid smoke (optional)**

1 shallow dish large enough for the four chicken breasts

Remove the skin from the chicken breasts and remove as much excess fat as you can. Make two or three ⅛-inch slashes across the top of each breast. Set the chicken aside in a shallow dish that is large enough to hold all 4 chicken breasts.

Mix all of the ingredients for the sauce together in a bowl or jar, then pour the marinade over the chicken breasts, allowing it to sit, covered, for at least one hour in the refrigerator.

(The covered chicken breasts can keep for a maximum of 3 days in the refrigerator just in the barbecue marinade.)

Grill the chicken outdoors or broil the breasts indoors, basting with any extra marinade until the chicken is done, approximately 8 to 10 minutes on each side.

If desired, sprinkle a bit of fresh lemon juice over the top just before serving.

Per serving:

Calories: 204
Carbohydrates: 13.8 g
Protein: 28.1 g
Fat Total: 3.7 g
Fat Saturated: .92 g

Casablancan Chicken and Beans

SERVES 4 TO 6

This is one of those time- and sanity-saving casseroles that can be made way ahead of time and is ostensibly a meal in itself; all you might want on the side would be some steamed broccoli or a fresh salad.

1	**cup couscous or bulgur wheat**
2	**cups strong, defatted chicken stock (for dual use) or 1 cup chicken stock and 1 cup spicy tomato juice**
2	**teaspoons olive oil and Pam®**
2 to 3	**cups thinly sliced onions (for dual use)**
3	**cloves garlic, minced or put through a garlic press**
1	**2-inch piece of stick cinnamon**
1	**teaspoon finely minced gingerroot**
¼	**teaspoon turmeric**
⅛	**teaspoon cayenne pepper**
	big pinch of saffron
1½	**cups drained chickpeas, lentils, or white beans**
4	**chicken breast halves, boneless and skinless, cut into 2-inch chunks**
1	**teaspoon salt**
1	**teaspoon lemon-pepper seasoning**
1	**teaspoon bright, fragrant paprika**
	juice from one lemon
1	**casserole dish (1½-quart), preferably a soufflé type, sprayed with Pam®**

Bring one cup of the chicken stock to the boil in a small saucepan; add the couscous or bulgur wheat. Stir once and cover the pan. Turn off the heat, allowing it to stand covered for 20 minutes.

Place a heavy skillet over a medium flame: when the pan is hot, add oil and Pam®, then add the onions, garlic, cinnamon stick, gingerroot, turmeric, cayenne, and saffron. Sauté the vegetables until the onions have become translucent and are soft, around 5 minutes. Place half of the onion mixture in a tall casserole dish (such as a soufflé dish) that has been sprayed with Pam®. Add the drained, cooked chickpeas or beans on top of onions; next place remaining onion mixture on top of beans.

Cut the chicken into 2-inch pieces and sprinkle the chunks with paprika, salt, and lemon-pepper seasoning, coating evenly. Place the seasoned chicken pieces on top of the onions and beans. Next put the hot couscous or bulgur wheat on top of the chicken, spreading evenly. Pour the remaining cup of chicken stock and lemon juice into the casserole, then cover it with foil or a lid.

Bake the chicken casserole covered at 350° for 1 to 1½ hours until the chicken is done. Serve immediately, garnishing with freshly chopped parsley.

Variations

- Use cooked rice instead of bulgur wheat.
- Use fragrant curry powder instead of the lemon-pepper seasoning.

Per serving (if serving six):

Chinese Chicken Breasts

SERVES 4

Yet another find from China; low in fat and tastiest when grilled outdoors.

4 skinless, boneless chicken breast halves

FOR THE MARINADE:

1 to 2	**cloves garlic, minced or put through a garlic press**
2	**teaspoons finely minced gingerroot**
3	**tablespoons tamari or soy sauce**
1	**tablespoon sherry or white wine**
½	**teaspoon toasted sesame oil**
1	**teaspoon sugar or honey**
2	**teaspoons chopped cilantro**
1	**green onion, finely minced**
½	**teaspoon five-spice powder (optional)**
1	**shallow baking dish, approximately 8 × 8 × 2 inches**

Remove any excess fat from the chicken breasts, then set them aside.

Mix all of the marinade ingredients together in a baking dish; add the chicken and marinate in the sauce for at least 2 hours. (The chicken can be refrigerated at this point for up to 2 to 3 days without any harm.)

Either broil or grill the chicken breasts (approximately 5 to 7 minutes each side for grilling and broiling), or bake the chicken uncovered at 350° until done (approximately 25 to 35 minutes for baking). Serve the chicken with a rice dish and stir-fried vegetables.

Variation

- Use 1 tablespoon oyster sauce instead of sugar.

Per serving:

*Calories: 162
Carbohydrates: 4 g
Protein: 28.2 g
Fat Total: 2.5 g
Fat Saturated: .54 g*

Chicken Cacciatore

SERVES 4

4 to 6	**chicken breast halves, skinless and boneless**
	salt and pepper
1	**teaspoon oil and Pam®**
2	**cloves garlic, minced or put through a garlic press**
½	**cup onions, diced or very thinly sliced**
1	**cup each red and green bell peppers, chopped**
2 to 3	**cups tomatoes (canned or fresh), peeled, seeded, and chopped**
2	**tablespoons tomato paste**
½	**cup vermouth**
½	**cup strong defatted chicken stock**
1	**bay leaf**
1	**teaspoon marjoram**
½	**teaspoon thyme**
2	**tablespoons chopped parsley**
	salt and pepper
1	**shallow baking dish, approximately 8 × 8 × 2 inches**

Trim any excess fat off of the chicken breasts, then season them lightly with salt and pepper. Heat a sauté pan over a medium flame; when the pan is hot, add oil and spray with Pam®. Immediately add the chicken breasts, searing them on both sides (around 2 minutes on each side), then remove them to a dish.

While pan is still hot, add the garlic and onions. Stir and fry, scraping anything leftover from the bottom of the pan, until the onions are soft, around 5 minutes. Add the bell peppers, tomatoes, tomato paste, vermouth, and chicken stock. Bring this to the simmering point, again scraping the bottom of the pan. Add the herbs and continue cooking until the peppers are just tender, around 3 minutes. Remove the pan from the heat and taste for seasoning. (If this mixture tastes fine but seems very watery for whatever reason, you may wish to thicken it with a bit of arrowroot.)

Place the seared chicken breasts into a ceramic dish and spoon the tomato-pepper sauce over the chicken. Garnish with another sprinkle of chopped parsley, then cover with a lid or with foil.

Bake the casserole covered at 350° for 25 to 35 minutes until the chicken is done. Serve with hot rice and a green vegetable; garnish the chicken with lemon wedges and, if desired, a sprinkling of Parmesan cheese.

Per serving:

Calories: 196
Carbohydrates: 9.8 g
Protein: 29.3 g
Fat Total: 2.9 g
Fat Saturated: .56 g

Chinese Peanut Chicken

SERVES 4

If you don't eat chicken, make the sauce and toss with cooked and chilled soba (buckwheat) noodles. Delicious!

Per serving:

Calories: 209
Carbohydrates: 8 g
Protein: 30.4 g
Fat Total: 6.1 g
Fat Saturated: 1.3 g

4	**chicken breast halves, skinless and boneless**
3	**cloves garlic, minced or put through a garlic press**
1	**tablespoon gingerroot, minced**
½	**teaspoon red pepper flakes, or more depending on how much spiciness you like**
¼	**cup tamari**
¼	**cup red wine vinegar**
2	**teaspoons sugar (optional but recommended)**
2	**tablespoons peanut butter (or more, depending on how low-fat you wish to eat)**
⅓ to ½	**cup water**
½	**teaspoon toasted sesame oil**
¼	**cup chopped cilantro**
1	**small, shallow baking dish (8 × 8 inches is more than adequate)**

Trim the chicken breasts of any excess fat and place in a saucepan. Cover the breasts with water, adding a bit of salt, then bring the water and chicken to the simmering point; as soon as you've reached the simmer, turn off the heat. Let the chicken stand in the hot water until the breasts are poached, approximately 10 to 15 minutes. (Check the thickest breast for doneness—if it is still pink inside, bring the water back to a simmer and allow the breasts to sit in the hot water for an additional 10 minutes.) After the chicken has poached, remove the breasts from the water, drain them on paper towels, and cut them into bite-sized pieces. Place these pieces in a ceramic dish; cover and set aside, keeping the chicken warm.

Place a sauté pan over medium heat; when it is hot, spray it with Pam® and add the garlic, gingerroot, and red pepper flakes, cooking for 1 minute or so, until the garlic has begun to toast slightly. Next add the tamari, vinegar, and sugar (be sure to avert your face when adding the liquids as they will sputter and sizzle); bring the mixture to a boil, scraping the garlic and ginger off of the bottom of the pan. Reduce the heat to low and add the peanut butter and water, stirring until the peanut butter has blended with the liquid and has formed a thick sauce. Add the sesame oil and taste for seasoning; it should be rather "potent," as it will season the rather bland, poached chicken. Remove the sauce from the heat.

Pour the hot peanut mixture over the cooked chicken and mix carefully until the chicken is entirely enrobed with sauce. Sprinkle chopped cilantro on top.

Serve immediately with rice and stir-fry vegetables.

Variations

- Use toasted sesame butter instead of peanut butter.
- Add 1 hot green chili to sauce.

Chicken Enchiladas

SERVES 4

Per serving:

Calories: 363
Carbohydrates: 33 g
Protein: 39.6 g
Fat Total: 8.8 g
Fat Saturated: .4 g

A favorite.

4	**skinless, boneless chicken breast halves**
1	**ancho chili (a dried, flat poblano pepper)**
1	**tablespoon each lemon juice, Worcestershire sauce, and soy sauce**
2	**cloves garlic, minced or put through a garlic press**
2 to 3	**tablespoons chopped cilantro**
1	**tablespoon ground coriander**
2	**teaspoons ground cumin**
½	**teaspoon chili powder (optional)**
⅛	**teaspoon curry powder (optional)**
¼	**teaspoon cayenne pepper (optional)**
¼	**teaspoon liquid smoke (optional)**
	Pam®
12	**corn tortillas**
	low-fat cheddar or jack cheese, grated (approximately 6 ounces)
	salsa (picante sauce)
1	**shallow baking dish (around 9 × 12 × 2 inches) sprayed with Pam®**

Remove any excess fat from the chicken breasts and slice each breast into very thin strips. (To get the thinnest possible strips, it is helpful if the chicken breasts are partially frozen; this causes the breast to be firmer and allows for less movement of the meat while slicing. However, don't worry if you don't have partially frozen breasts—it's no big deal.) Set the sliced chicken aside.

Using metal tongs, hold the ancho chili by the stem and roast it over an open flame, holding it about 8 to 12 inches from the heat source (or, if using an electric range, hold over the eye after it has been preheated on high) until it is "roasted"—it will blacken and smoke and might expand; it should not, however, be burned. After it has roasted, quickly remove stem and seeds (careful—it will be hot!). Using a very sharp knife, slice the warm chili into thin strips, then chop the strips into smaller bits. Place these bits into a large bowl and pour ⅓ cup of hot water over them. Let the roasted chili stand for a few minutes and then add the remaining seasonings. Add to the sliced chicken and mix well; the chicken may marinate from 20 minutes to an hour or so.

After the chicken has marinated, place a large sauté pan over a moderate flame; when it is hot, spray it with Pam®. Place the marinated chicken and the marinade in the pan and sauté until it is cooked, around 10 to 15 minutes. (You shouldn't need to add any oil—the chicken will exude some juice as it cooks.) Be careful not to overcook the chicken, though, because it will be reheated later. Set the cooked chicken aside until it has cooled. It is normal for there to be ¼ to ½ cup of "juices" left in the pan after the chicken is done.

The tortillas may be: a) microwaved until hot, b) steamed until hot, c) wrapped in foil and baked at 275° until hot. At any rate, they should be heated through before you make the enchiladas because a cold tortilla will split and crack if it is folded without being heated.

Prepare the final baking dish (an oblong pan or ceramic dish) with Pam®.

Gather the cooked chicken mixture, the warm tortillas, and the cheese(s). Take a tortilla in your hand, add a sprinkling of cheese, then add a few strips of cooked chicken. Roll the tortilla around the filling and place the filled enchilada into the prepared baking dish. Continue until all of the chicken and tortillas are used up. Drizzle any remaining liquid from the cooked chicken over the rolled tortillas. If desired, sprinkle with some additional cheese and cilantro as well. Cover the enchiladas with foil. (The enchiladas may be refrigerated for up to 3 days without any harm; the tortillas may get a bit soggy, however.)

Bake the enchiladas covered at 350° for 35 minutes; then remove foil and bake another 10 to 15 minutes. Serve hot with extra salsa on the side and a large salad.

Variations

- Add chopped green onion, chopped tomato, and/or red bell pepper to chicken mixture.
- Add ⅓ cup cooked black beans to chicken mixture.
- Add a chopped jalapeño pepper to chicken mixture for more "heat."

119

Per serving:

Calories: 236
Carbohydrates: 11.7 g
Protein: 36.6 g
Fat Total: 3.3 g
Fat Saturated: 1.2 g

- For even less fat, use low-fat cottage cheese instead of cheddar or jack cheese.
- Make a puree of 1½ cups nonfat ricotta cheese or cottage cheese, 1 cup of cilantro, 1 teaspoon ground cumin, and 3 tomatillos, and salt to taste: use this mixture instead of the grated jack or cheddar cheese inside the enchilada.

Chicken Florentine

SERVES 4

4 to 6	*green onions, minced*
1	*clove garlic, minced or put through a garlic press (optional)*
	Pam®
1	*16-ounce package frozen spinach, thawed and squeezed to remove excess liquid, or 16 ounces blanched, chopped fresh spinach*
¼	*cup dry vermouth*
3	*tablespoons Parmesan cheese*
2	*tablespoons chopped parsley*
¼	*teaspoon ground nutmeg*
½	*cup nonfat cream cheese*
¼	*cup nonfat sour cream*
4	*tablespoons fresh chopped basil*
4	*boneless, skinless chicken breast halves*
	salt and pepper
1	*shallow baking dish (approximately 8 × 8 inches)*
6	*whole, large basil leaves*
	additional dry vermouth or brandy
	sprinkling of paprika

Place a large sauté pan over a moderate flame; when the pan is hot, spray with a bit of Pam® and then add the green onions and optional garlic. Cook and stir for a minute or so, until the green onions are barely soft and bright green; next add blanched, cooked spinach. Continue cooking and stirring for another couple of minutes, eliminating some of the excess water from the spinach. Add the vermouth, cooking for 1 minute. By this point the spinach should be moist but not standing in liquid. Remove the mixture from the heat.

In a bowl combine the Parmesan cheese, parsley, nutmeg, cream cheese, sour cream, and chopped fresh basil; stir and blend well. When the spinach mixture has cooled, combine it with the cheese-basil mixture, mixing well. Taste the spinach for seasoning, adding salt as necessary.

Prepare a shallow baking dish with Pam®.

Remove any excess fat from the chicken breast halves.

Next you will make a pouch in each chicken breast. Holding the breast down flat with your hand and using a very sharp knife, carefully make a horizontal slice parallel to the working surface into the thickest side of the breast, creating a "pocket," trying to make a neat incision midway between top and bottom, leaving the outer edge intact. In other words, you're creating a space to stuff the breast, much in the same way pita bread opens. Slice all breasts similarly, season each breast lightly with salt, and put equal proportions of the spinach mixture into each breast. Place the stuffed breasts into the prepared baking dish and sprinkle with pepper. Place one whole basil leaf on top of each breast and arrange the chicken prettily in the baking dish. Sprinkle the stuffed breasts with a few tablespoons of vermouth or (better yet) brandy. Cover the chicken with foil.

Bake the chicken breasts covered at 350° for 30 to 40 minutes until they are just done and the stuffing is hot. Garnish with a sprinkling of bright paprika or Parmesan cheese.

Chicken with Fresh Herbs
I, II, III, IV, and V

SERVES 4

The possibilities on this theme are endless. The idea here is to have something that subtly enhances the chicken without overpowering it. These are but a few choices.

I.

- **4** *skinless, boneless chicken breast halves*
- **1** *teaspoon olive oil*
- *salt and pepper (you could use 1 tablespoon tamari instead of salt)*
- **2** *teaspoons fresh lemon juice*
- **1** *clove garlic, minced or put through a garlic press*
- **1** *tablespoon fresh rosemary, chopped*
- **1** *tablespoon chopped parsley*

Per serving: Calories: 143; Carbohydrates: .91 g; Protein: 27.4 g; Fat Total: 2.5 g; Fat Saturated: .53 g

II.

- **4** *skinless, boneless chicken breast halves*
- *salt and pepper*
- **2** *tablespoons fresh chopped basil*
- **1** *clove garlic, minced or put through a garlic press*
- *sprinkling of Parmesan cheese*

Per serving: Calories: 138; Carbohydrates: .57 g; Protein: 27.9 g; Fat Total: 1.9 g; Fat Saturated: .63 g

III.

- **4** *skinless, boneless chicken breast halves*
- *salt and pepper*
- **1** *tablespoon fresh, chopped thyme*
- **1** *tablespoon chopped parsley*
- **2** *teaspoons vermouth or brandy*
- **1** *green onion, finely chopped*
- **1** *tablespoon Dijon mustard*

this is very good, add olive oil

Per serving: Calories: 139; Carbohydrates: 1.3 g; Protein: 27.6 g; Fat Total: 1.7 g; Fat Saturated: .42 g

IV.   ✓

4   skinless, boneless chicken breast halves
1   teaspoon olive oil
    salt and pepper
1   tablespoon fresh chopped tarragon
1   tablespoon chopped shallot or green onion
1   tablespoon cognac   *(wine vinegar)*
1   tablespoon dry vermouth

Per serving: Calories: 154; Carbohydrates: .92 g; Protein: 27.5 g; Fat Total: 2.5 g; Fat Saturated: .54 g

V.

4   skinless, boneless chicken breast halves
    black pepper to taste
1   tablespoon chopped capers
½   teaspoon anchovy paste
1   clove garlic, minced or put through a garlic press
1   tablespoon lemon juice
3   tablespoons finely chopped fresh tomato
        or 1 tablespoon tomato paste
2   tablespoons chopped parsley
½   teaspoon sugar

Per serving: Calories: 139; Carbohydrates: 2 g; Protein: 27.7 g; Fat Total: 1.6 g; Fat Saturated: .41 g

Following any one of the above: Trim the chicken breasts of any excess fat. You can either make kabobs or leave the chicken breasts whole; if making kabobs, slice the breasts into 2- to 3-inch chunks. (Hint: kabobs are more fun.)

Combine all of the ingredients and marinate for at least 2 hours. Either bake at 350° for 25 to 30 minutes, or broil or grill the chicken until done, approximately 5 to 8 minutes on each side.

Green Chili Chicken

SERVES 4

This is perfect for a summer barbecue or a pool party.

Per serving:

Calories: 171
Carbohydrates: 9 g
Protein: 29.1 g
Fat Total: 1.8 g
Fat Saturated: .42 g

4	**chicken breast halves, boneless and skinless**
1 to 2	**cloves garlic, peeled**
2	**green onions, roughly chopped**
2	**small tins of green chilis (4 to 6 ounces each, either whole or diced), drained**
½	**cup cilantro**
4 to 6	**tomatillos, without the papery husks**
2	**tablespoons lemon juice**
1	**teaspoon cumin**
½	**teaspoon salt**
¼	**teaspoon cayenne**
1	**teaspoon sugar (optional)**

Trim off any excess fat from the chicken. Make ⅛-inch deep slash marks across the breasts in one direction or in crosshatch marks. Set the chicken aside on a plate.

Place remaining ingredients in a food processor or blender and blend into a smoothish paste. Spread the green chili paste over the chicken, making sure the marinade gets into the slash marks. Let the chicken marinate several hours, covered, in the refrigerator. (The chicken can keep perfectly for up to 48 hours before cooking.)

Being careful not to shake off all of the marinade, broil the chicken indoors, or grill the chicken outdoors until just done, approximately 5 to 8 minutes on each side. Serve the chicken with fresh pico de gallo (*see* page 215), avocado salad, and hot corn or wheat tortillas.

Variation

- Slice the chicken breasts into ½-inch slices and place on bamboo skewers; marinate and grill as above. Use as a filling for tacos, fajitas, or enchiladas.

Chicken with Lemon-Caper Sauce

SERVES 4

This is a variation of a veal recipe I made once or twice many years ago, but veal is higher in fat (and bad for the conscience). If you wish, substitute veal scallopini for chicken breasts.

4	**chicken breast halves, boneless and skinless**
	salt and pepper
	flour
1	**teaspoon olive oil and Pam®**
1	**tablespoon shallot, finely minced**
2	**tablespoons capers, drained and chopped**
2	**teaspoons fresh thyme, chopped**
3	**tablespoons lemon juice**
⅓	**cup white wine or vermouth**
½	**cup defatted strong chicken stock mixed with 1 teaspoon arrowroot**
1	**teaspoon sugar (optional)**
2	**tablespoons chopped parsley**

Remove any excess fat from the chicken breasts. Place each breast between two pieces of waxed paper or cellophane and pound them slightly with a heavy kitchen tool so that they are equally flat, approximately ¼-inch thick. Sprinkle each breast with a bit of salt and pepper, then dust lightly with the flour, shaking off any excess.

Heat a sauté pan over a medium-high flame, then add the oil and spray the pan with Pam®. Immediately add the chicken breasts, searing each side well. Cook until lightly browned on both sides (and not necessarily cooked through), around 3 to 5 minutes, then remove the breasts to a ceramic dish or plate. While pan is still hot add the shallot, stirring and sautéing for a minute or so, then add the capers, thyme, lemon juice, and white wine, deglazing the pan and scraping any cooked-on bits into the "sauce." After this mixture has simmered for 3 minutes and reduced slightly, add the chicken stock/arrowroot mixture and the optional sugar, bringing the sauce to the simmering point. The sauce should be slightly thickened; that is, just thick enough so that it would lightly cling to the back of a spoon. If the sauce appears too thick, add 1 tablespoon of water (or more) to thin it out. Taste the sauce for seasoning. Return the chicken breasts to the sauté pan and cook over low heat, covered, until the breasts are just done, another 5 minutes. Serve immediately and garnish with the chopped parsley and/or additional fresh thyme.

Per serving:

Calories: 185
Carbohydrates: 6.5 g
Protein: 28.2 g
Fat Total: 2.8 g
Fat Saturated: .55 g

125

Grilled Chicken with Mango Relish

SERVES 4

This is a wonderful summertime treat and perfect for outdoor dinner parties or family get-togethers, since the ingredients are readily available and easily pre-pared ahead of time. The only last-minute job is to cook the chicken, a quick and simple task made enjoyable by friends surrounding you with eager eyes and empty stomachs!

This is best accompanied by a green salad and fresh corn on the cob.

4	**chicken breast halves, skinless and boneless**
2	**tablespoons lime juice**
½	**teaspoon salt**
¼	**teaspoon white pepper**
1	**teaspoon cumin**
1	**clove garlic, minced or put through a garlic press**
1	**large ripe mango**
3	**tablespoons lime juice**
1	**green onion, very finely minced**
1	**jalapeño pepper, very finely minced (as much or as little as you want)**
¼	**cup red bell pepper, diced into ⅛-inch squares**
1	**tablespoon cilantro**
½	**teaspoon cumin**
½	**teaspoon salt**
3	**tablespoons nonfat yogurt (optional)**
	bamboo skewers

Per serving:

Calories: 181
Carbohydrates: 13.1 g
Protein: 28.1 g
Fat Total: 1.8 g
Fat Saturated: .43 g

Remove any excess fat from the chicken breasts. Slice the chicken length-wise into long strips (approximately ½ × 6 inches). Combine the lime juice, salt, pepper, cumin, and garlic in a bowl; add the raw chicken strips, mixing well. Marinate the meat for several hours, covered, in the refrigerator.

Peel and seed the mango; this is a bit tricky because ripe mangoes are slippery objects, but carefully remove as much pulp from the pit as possible. Puree the mango flesh with the lime juice in a food processor. (If desired, you may wish to blend in short spurts to keep some of the mango chunks—that way the relish will have more texture.) Place the mango puree in a bowl and add the green onion, jalapeño, red pepper, cilantro, cumin, salt, and optional yogurt. Taste the relish for seasoning and refrigerate, covered.

Place the marinated chicken pieces onto bamboo skewers; refrige-rate the kabobs until you're ready to grill.

Grill the chicken until done, approximately 3 to 5 minutes on each side, depending on how hot the coals are and how thick the chicken is. Remove the cooked chicken as soon as it is done (so that it's still juicy and not overdone). Serve the kabobs hot with a dollop of mango relish on the side, garnishing with a cilantro leaf.

Middle Eastern Chicken Kabobs

SERVES 4

Middle Eastern foods are an interesting crossover point between the complex spices and tastes of Indian cuisine and the more herb-based cookery of Europe. I'm always ready to board my magic carpet and escort Ms. Scheherazade through her kitchen, exploring the tastes of A Thousand and One Nights!

Per serving:

Calories: 151
Carbohydrates: 4.1 g
Protein: 28.6 g
Fat Total: 1.7 g
Fat Saturated: .42 g

4	**chicken breast halves, skinless and boneless, cut into 2-inch cubes**
2 to 3	**cloves garlic, minced or put through a garlic press**
⅓	**cup plain nonfat yogurt**
½	**teaspoon turmeric**
½	**teaspoon ground cardamom**
¼	**teaspoon ground allspice or cloves**
⅛ to ¼	**teaspoon cayenne**
1	**teaspoon ground cumin**
½ to 1	**teaspoon salt**
¼	**cup lemon juice**
1 to 2	**tablespoons chopped mint, cilantro, or parsley**
4 to 8	**skewers, either bamboo or metal**

Remove any excess fat from the chicken breasts; cut the breasts into 2-inch cubes and set them aside.

Blend the next nine ingredients in a large bowl until everything is smooth; add the mint, cilantro or parsley and the chicken. Toss the chicken well in the marinade, coating evenly. Marinate the chicken for several hours in the refrigerator, covered. (The chicken will keep perfectly in the refrigerator for 2 days.)

Place the marinated chicken pieces onto skewers and grill outdoors (or broil indoors), basting with any leftover marinade, for approximately 5 to 8 minutes on each side. When the chicken is just done, serve the hot kabobs with a green vegetable and rice dish on the side.

Variations

- Use 1 to 2 hot green chili peppers instead of cayenne.
- Add 1 tablespoon mustard oil to marinade.

Mexican Rice Casserole

SERVES 4

Per serving:

Calories: 351
Carbohydrates: 32.2 g
Protein: 38.7 g
Fat Total: 5.7 g
Fat Saturated: .55 g

This is not authentic south-of-the-border cuisine, but it is satisfying and uses ingredients common in Tex-Mex kitchens. It is very popular with children—but for adults who like their food spicier, the addition of ¼ to ½ teaspoon of cayenne pepper is suggested.

1	**cup white rice**
1½	**cups defatted chicken stock**
4	**chicken breast halves, skinless and boneless**
2	**teaspoons chili powder**
½	**cup diced onion**
1 to 2	**cloves garlic, minced or put through a garlic press**
1	**teaspoon whole cumin seed**
⅔	**cup peppers (see note below)**
1	**teaspoon oil**
1	**teaspoon ground coriander**
1 to 3	**tablespoons chopped cilantro**
⅔	**cup chopped tomato**
⅔	**cup shredded reduced-fat jack cheese, or any mixture of jack, cheddar, Colby, or cottage cheeses**
1	**baking dish (approximately 8 × 8 × 2 inches) sprayed with Pam®**

Note: Use whatever kind of pepper you wish, keeping the hotness of the pepper in mind. Use ⅔ cup of any mixture of anaheim, poblano, green or red bell pepper, diced canned green chilies, and/or one roasted, rehydrated ancho chile.

Wash the rice in a bowl, swishing it around with your fingers, washing and rinsing until the water rinses clear and not cloudy. Place the clean rice and chicken stock in a saucepan and bring to a boil; cover and reduce the heat to very low, cooking for 15 minutes. Remove the rice from the heat and allow to stand undisturbed for another 15 minutes. After the "sitting period," the rice should be fluffy and done; but if it is slightly underdone, that's fine since it will bake later.

Remove any excess fat from the chicken breasts and dice the meat into bite-sized pieces. Place the chicken pieces in a bowl and toss with the chili powder, then set it aside.

Place a sauté pan over a moderate flame; when the pan is hot, add 1 teaspoon of oil and then the onion, garlic, and cumin seed; cook for 3 to 5 minutes. Next add the peppers and continue to cook for another 2 to 3 minutes, stirring occasionally. Remove the pan from the heat. Place the onion-pepper mixture in a large, clean bowl and set it aside to cool.

Place the same pan that you cooked the peppers in back over a moderate heat; spray the pan with Pam® and put the marinated chicken pieces in, tossing and cooking, cooking the chicken just long enough to firm it up, around 2 minutes. Remove the chicken from the heat and put the "firmed" chicken into the same bowl as the onions and peppers. Add the coriander and cilantro to the same bowl, mixing well.

Spray a 1½ to 2 quart baking dish with Pam®, then set it aside.

When the chicken-pepper mixture has cooled somewhat, add the cooked rice mixture to the bowl and toss everything well. Pour half of the chicken-rice-pepper blend into the prepared baking dish; top with half of the chopped tomato and cheese. Pour the rest of the chicken mixture in the dish (on top of the tomatoes and cheese) and repeat the procedure. Garnish the top with any remaining cilantro, cheese, or tomato. Cover the baking dish. (The chicken casserole will keep for up to 48 hours covered and refrigerated before its final baking.)

Bake the covered casserole at 350° for 40 to 50 minutes until it is hot. Allow the casserole to cool (still covered) for 10 minutes before serving. Serve the casserole with salsa on the side and a fresh salad.

"Oven-Fried" Chicken

SERVES 4 TO 6

4–6 **chicken pieces with the skin removed, roughly 4–6 ounces each, breasts, thighs, drumsticks, etc., enough for 4–6 servings**

DRY MARINADE:

Gail 8/15/04

1	**cup flour**
1½	**teaspoons salt**
2	**teaspoons lemon-pepper seasoning**
1	**teaspoon onion powder**
1	**teaspoon garlic powder**
1	**teaspoon cumin**
1	**teaspoon paprika**
½	**teaspoon allspice**
1	**teaspoon oregano**
1	**teaspoon thyme**
1	**teaspoon basil**
2	**cups low-fat buttermilk**
2 to 3	**cups breadcrumbs, fresh or a mixture of fresh and packaged**
3	**tablespoons finely chopped fresh parsley**
1	**baking sheet and Pam®**

Per serving:

Calories: 285
Carbohydrates: 33.2 g
Protein: 29.1 g
Fat Total: 3.3 g
Fat Saturated: 1 g

Remove any skin and excess fat from the chicken pieces. Set the chicken aside.

Place the ingredients for the dry marinade into a plastic bag and shake to evenly mix the spices. Set this bag aside.

In a large bowl mix the breadcrumbs and the parsley.

Pour the buttermilk into a separate bowl.

Spray the baking sheet with Pam®.

Assemble all of your ingredients: the chicken, the seasoning mix, the buttermilk bowl, the breadcrumb bowl, and the prepared baking sheet.

Place one piece of chicken into the dry marinade bag and shake. Remove the chicken piece and shake off any excess mixture; place the seasoned chicken on a plate and continue with the remaining chicken pieces. When you've finished coating the chicken, place the pieces *again* into the dry marinade mixture and shake once more, then remove the pieces.

Dip the double-coated chicken pieces into the buttermilk, coating well, then place each piece into the bowl of breadcrumbs. Turn the pieces over to coat evenly with the breadcrumbs; place each breaded piece onto the prepared baking sheet. Continue until all of the chicken has been breaded.

Bake the chicken uncovered at 350° for roughly 35 to 45 minutes (thighs and drumsticks may take a bit longer, small breasts may take less time). When the chicken is done, you may wish to place it under the broiler briefly to brown the breading. Serve immediately.

Parmesan Chicken Breasts

SERVES 4

These are a favorite with adults and children alike. And they have the added bonus of freezing perfectly.

4 to 5	**pieces of fresh bread, white or whole wheat, or a combination**
3	**tablespoons fresh parsley**
1½	**teaspoons finest herbes de Provence or ½ teaspoon thyme, ½ teaspoon basil, ½ teaspoon rosemary**
½	**cup finest Parmesan cheese**
	salt and pepper
	herbes de Provence, or additional thyme, basil, and rosemary
4	**skinless, boneless chicken breast halves**
	all-purpose flour
⅔	**cup low-fat buttermilk or 2 egg whites mixed with ½ cup skim milk**

Pam® and a baking dish large enough for 4 chicken breasts

Per serving:

Calories: 338
Carbohydrates: 24.2 g
Protein: 39.4 g
Fat Total: 8.2 g
Fat Saturated: 4.2 g

Place the bread slices in a food processor or blender, processing in a few short spurts until bread is in pea-sized bits. Add the fresh parsley and blend further (another 30 seconds or so), until the parsley is chopped and the breadcrumbs are fine, not coarse. Place the breadcrumbs and parsley on a large plate and add the herbes de Provence and Parmesan cheese; mix the breading thoroughly.

Spray the pan for the 4 chicken breasts with Pam®. Set it aside.

Pour the buttermilk into a bowl large enough in which to dip the chicken breasts.

Next, remove any excess fat from the chicken breasts. Season the chicken with a bit of salt and pepper and an extra sprinkling of herbes de Provence, then dust lightly with flour. Dip each breast into the buttermilk or egg white mixture, then place the wet breast in the seasoned breading. Turn the breast over, patting each side firmly to keep breading in place, then remove the breast gently, placing it in the prepared baking dish. Continue with the other chicken breasts. (The chicken will keep for 48 hours in the refrigerator, covered, or you may freeze them now.)

Bake the chicken uncovered at 350° for 25 to 35 minutes until they are just done—check for doneness by making a small incision in the thickest part of the breast. If desired, you may place the chicken breasts under a broiler briefly to lightly brown and crispen the top. Garnish with fresh lemon wedges.

Variations

- Fresh herbs may be added to the breading instead of dried herbs.

Chicken with Red Pipérade

SERVES 4

tasty!

2/9/99 ~45 to do

4	**boneless, skinless chicken breast halves**
	salt and pepper
2	**tablespoons all-purpose flour**
1	**teaspoon olive oil and Pam®**
1	**small onion, thinly sliced**
1	**clove garlic, minced or put through a garlic press**
1	**bay leaf**
2	**red bell peppers, thinly sliced**
3	**tablespoons chopped fresh basil or 1 teaspoon dried basil**
½	**teaspoon thyme**
¼	**teaspoon pepper**
¼	**cup white wine or vermouth**
⅓	**cup defatted chicken stock**

Remove any excess fat from the chicken breasts and season each with a bit of salt and pepper. Dust the breasts with a bit of flour, shaking off any excess.

Place a sauté pan over a medium flame and allow the pan to get hot. When hot, reduce the flame to medium-low and spray the pan with Pam®; add the chicken breasts, allowing them to brown lightly on each side, around 3 to 4 minutes each side (not cooking the chicken through, however). When the chicken has browned on each side, remove the breasts to a covered plate and set aside, keeping them warm.

In the same sauté pan (don't clean it out—there are tasty pieces left in it!), add the oil. Return the flame back to medium, then spray the pan with Pam® and add onion and garlic and cook for 2 minutes, stirring as you go, until the onions have begun to soften. Next add the bay, red peppers, basil, thyme, pepper, wine, and chicken stock; cook and stir the mixture for 2 minutes until peppers have barely softened. Place the warm chicken breasts back into the pan and cover, turning the heat to low. Continue to cook for 10 to 14 minutes more, turning the breasts once or twice, until the chicken is just done and the vegetables are cooked through. Serve immediately with hot rice and use pan juices as a "sauce" to flavor the rice.

Fresh Turkey or Chicken Sausage

SERVES 4

Poultry sausage patties are a welcome alternative to chicken nuggets or hamburgers. They're light, savory, and make a lovely breakfast meat as well.

½   **cup onion, very finely minced**
1   **clove garlic, minced (optional)**
1   **teaspoon olive oil and Pam®**
1   **teaspoon dried thyme**
¼   **teaspoon ground allspice**
1   **tablespoon fresh, chopped parsley**
1   **bay leaf**
½   **cup white wine or vermouth**
2   **tablespoons brandy or cognac (optional but recommended)**
1   **pound ground turkey or chicken breast**
1   **teaspoon salt**
½   **teaspoon freshly ground black pepper**

Heat a sauté pan over a moderate flame; when the pan is hot, add the oil and spray with Pam®. Immediately add the onion and cook for a few minutes until the onion is translucent and soft, stirring often. Add the optional garlic and stir for 20 seconds or so; then remove the pan from the heat.

In a bowl combine the remaining ingredients and mix well (this will be very sticky!). Add the partially cooled onion mixture and mix again. Clean off the sides of the bowl, making sure all of the meat is in one central blob in the bowl. Take a piece of plastic wrap and put it directly on top of the meat, patting and covering the meat well so that there is little to no air space left. Let the sausage marinate for two to three days in the refrigerator.

To prepare, simply form the sausage into patties (between your lightly wet hands) and sauté on each side (in either a bit of oil or Pam®) or broil until lightly brown and done, but still juicy. Cooking time is approximately 5 minutes per side.

Variation

- For an Italian-style sausage, sauté ½ teaspoon fennel seed with the onions and use basil (or oregano) and red pepper flakes instead of thyme and allspice.

Per serving:

Calories: 80.5
Carbohydrates: 2.5 g
Protein: 4.5 g
Fat Total: 1.6 g
Fat Saturated: .22 g

133

Tandoori Chicken

SERVES 4

Most people have probably had tandoori chicken at an Indian restaurant, but tandoori chicken refers not to a recipe but to the manner in which the chicken is cooked, that is, in a tandoor. A tandoor is a large earthen pot usually sunk into the ground which is heated by charcoal or wood to such extraordinarily high temperatures that a whole skewered chicken will cook in 10 minutes! Obviously very few Americans will have the capability to reproduce this process; nonetheless, simple grilling or broiling at the highest temperature will suffice.

Per serving:

Calories: 165
Carbohydrates: 6.1 g
Protein: 29.96 g
Fat Total: 1.7 g
Fat Saturated: .45 g

4 to 6   boneless, skinless chicken breast halves, with ¼-inch slices cut across the top of each breast
1   small onion
1   1-inch chunk of gingerroot, peeled and chopped
3   cloves garlic, peeled
1   cup nonfat yogurt
juice of 1 lemon or lime
½   teaspoon salt
¼   teaspoon cayenne pepper or a small, hot chili pepper
1   teaspoon garam masala or ¼ teaspoon curry powder, ½ teaspoon ground cumin, ¼ teaspoon ground coriander, and ⅛ teaspoon allspice
1   tablespoon cilantro

Remove any excess fat from the chicken breasts. Take each breast and slice thin (¼-inch) lines across it either in one direction or in crosshatch marks, enabling the marinade to enter the flesh and flavor it thoroughly.

To make the marinade, place the onion, garlic, and gingerroot into a food processor and blend in spurts until the mixture is fairly fine, around 30 to 45 seconds. Add the yogurt, lemon or lime juice, salt, and spices and blend until completely smooth, another 60 seconds. Add the cilantro and turn on processor until it is chopped but not pureed, one or two short bursts.

Next, place the chicken breasts into a baking container (or in a tightly sealed plastic bag) and pour the marinade over it, making sure that the chicken is covered on all sides. Let the breasts marinate, refrigerated, for 24 to 36 hours. (Chicken may be frozen at this point in the marinade and thawed when ready for cooking.)

The chicken should be either broiled indoors or grilled outdoors. If broiling, preheat the broiler to high. When the broiler is really hot, remove the chicken breasts from the marinade (but don't shake off all of the marinade that sticks to the breast) and place on a baking sheet and broil for approximately 8 to 10 minutes on each side until done.

If you are grilling, follow the same procedure by removing the breasts from the marinade and then grill the chicken. Garnish the tandoori chicken with a large wedge of fresh lemon or lime, serving with a rice pilaf and a green vegetable.

Note: Traditional tandoori chicken is an intense bright red color; this is merely food coloring. If you wish to do this, add 1 tablespoon red food coloring and 1½ tablespoons yellow food coloring to the marinade.

Chicken Tostadas

SERVES 4

4	**skinless, boneless chicken breast halves**
1	**small tin (4 to 6 ounces) diced green chilies, drained**
2	**green onions, diced**
1	**tablespoon lemon juice**
1	**tablespoon Worcestershire sauce**
1	**tablespoon soy sauce or tamari**
1	**teaspoon red wine or balsamic vinegar**
2	**cloves garlic, minced or put through a garlic press**
1 to 2	**tablespoons chopped cilantro**
2	**teaspoons ground coriander**
2	**teaspoons ground cumin**
	Pam®
8 to 12	**corn tortillas**
	low-fat cheddar or jack cheese, grated
	salsa (red and/or green)
	julienned lettuce, chopped tomatoes, and chopped green and/or red peppers
1	**baking sheet sprayed with Pam®**

Remove any excess fat from the chicken breasts and slice into thin strips. (This is easier if the chicken is slightly frozen, but if not, it's not a big deal.) In a large bowl, combine the sliced chicken with the green chilies, green onions, lemon juice, Worcestershire sauce, soy sauce, vinegar, garlic, cilantro, coriander, and cumin. Let the chicken stand for 20 minutes or so, covered, at room temperature.

Per serving:

Calories: 377
Carbohydrates: 36.4 g
Protein: 40.5 g
Fat Total: 8.8 g
Fat Saturated: .44 g

135

After the chicken has marinated, place a sauté pan over a medium flame. When it is hot, spray the pan with Pam® and add the marinated chicken. Stir and fry the chicken for 7 to 10 minutes, until the chicken is just cooked through. Set the chicken aside and keep barely warm.

Place your oven rack in the uppermost slot of the oven and preheat your oven to 425°. Gather your sundry ingredients around you (the chicken, tortillas, salsa, and cheese) and spray a baking sheet with Pam®.

When the oven is hot, place as many tortillas on the baking sheet as will fit (usually 4 to 6) and place ⅓ cup of the chicken mixture on top of each tortilla. Pour 1 to 2 tablespoons of red and/or green salsa on top of the chicken, then top with a sprinkling of cheese (2 tablespoons or so). Place the tostadas in the uppermost portion of the oven and cook until the chicken is hot and the cheese has melted and just browned, around 15 to 20 minutes. Remove the tostadas immediately and sprinkle some chopped tomato, lettuce, peppers, and additional salsa on top of each tostada as desired. Eat the tostadas with your fingers!

Variations

- Add a roasted ancho chili to the marinade.
- Add ⅓ cup cooked black beans to the chicken mixture.
- Add a chopped jalapeño pepper to the chicken mixture for more "heat."

Turkey with Cranberry-Orange Sauce

SERVES 4

This recipe is reminiscent of Canard à l'Orange in a strange way—probably the combination of the sweet and savory.

2	*tablespoons lemon juice*
1	*tablespoon fresh orange peel, grated*
	salt and pepper
1	*clove garlic, minced or put through a garlic press*
1	*tablespoon fresh thyme*
2	*tablespoons white wine or vermouth*
½	*turkey breast, boneless and skinless*

3	green onions, finely chopped
1	cup defatted chicken stock
½	cup vermouth
¼	cup orange juice
¼	cup port or Madeira
1 to 2	tablespoons fresh orange peel, grated
1	teaspoon fresh lemon peel, grated
½	teaspoon tarragon
1	teaspoon thyme
1	tablespoon fresh parsley, chopped
½	cup sugar
1	cup cranberries, fresh or frozen
1	teaspoon arrowroot mixed with 1 tablespoon water (perhaps optional) salt to taste
4	metal skewers

Per serving:

Calories: 289
Carbohydrates: 35.5 g
Protein: 25.3 g
Fat Total: .79 g
Fat Saturated: .22 g

Place the lemon juice, orange peel, a sprinkling of salt and pepper, garlic, thyme, and the wine in a medium-sized bowl, mixing briefly. Remove any excess fat from the turkey breast (there probably will be no fat at all). Cut the turkey breast into 2-inch chunks, then place the turkey in the bowl with the marinade, mixing well. Allow the chunks of turkey to marinate, refrigerated, for 3 or more hours.

Place the green onions in a saucepan with the chicken stock and vermouth; bring the mixture to the simmering point and add the port, orange juice, orange and lemon peels, herbs, and sugar. Let the mixture cook for 10 minutes or so just at the simmer, then add the cranberries. After the cranberries have cooked somewhat (5 minutes or so) and have begun to "pop," place the hot orange-cranberry mixture in the food processor and blend in quick spurts until the sauce is chunky and thicker, but so that there are still recognizable pieces of cranberry left. Return the mixture to the pan and bring the sauce back to the simmering point. If the sauce seems watery, add the arrowroot mixture, stirring well and bringing the sauce just to a boil; if the sauce is already slightly thick, do not add the arrowroot. Remove the sauce from the heat and taste it for seasoning.

Place the turkey pieces on skewers and broil or grill until done (approximately 8 to 10 minutes on each side), basting with the cranberry sauce. Serve the hot turkey kabobs with rice and a green vegetable, serving the warmed cranberry sauce on the side.

Chicken with Ginger Salsa

SERVES 4

A perfect do-ahead dish, ideal for outdoor parties, pool parties, or for summer family reunions in the park. Easy, unusual, and delicious.

¼   **cup rice wine vinegar**
1   **tablespoon dry sherry**
2   **tablespoons soy sauce**
1   **clove garlic, minced or put through a garlic press**
4   **boneless, skinless chicken breast halves, pounded to a ¼-inch thickness**

FOR THE SALSA:
12   **ripe tomatoes**
3   **tablespoons gingerroot, grated**
1   **clove garlic, minced or put through a garlic press**
1   **tablespoon red pepper flakes**
4   **green onions**
½   **cup green bell pepper, diced**
3   **tablespoons chopped cilantro**
1   **tablespoon lime juice**
   salt to taste

Combine the rice wine vinegar, sherry, soy sauce, and garlic in a large bowl. Trim the chicken breasts of any excess fat and pound with a heavy spoon or a meat tenderizer to a ¼-inch thickness. (You may pound the chicken between plastic or waxed paper if desired.) Place the flattened chicken in the marinade and allow to sit for 1 hour.

Meanwhile, bring a large pot of water to a boil. When the water is boiling furiously, turn off the heat and add the tomatoes, allowing the tomatoes to sit in the hot water for 45 seconds. Immediately drain the tomatoes into a colander, rinsing them with cold water. The tomatoes will now be very easy to peel and seed. Remove the core, the seeds, and the peel, and chop the tomatoes roughly.

Combine all of the the salsa ingredients in a food processor and blend in quick spurts until you have a chunky sauce. Taste the salsa for seasoning, then remove it from the processor bowl. Refrigerate the ginger salsa until ready to eat.

Remove the chicken from the marinade and broil or grill until just done, approximately 5 to 7 minutes on each side. Serve the chicken breast with the 2 to 3 tablespoons of ginger salsa on top, garnishing with cilantro.

Per serving:

Calories: 233
Carbohydrates: 22.8 g
Protein: 31.6 g
Fat Total: 2.4 g
Fat Saturated: .54 g

Greek Turkey Kabobs

SERVES 4

I recall a lunch overlooking the Aegean Sea just outside the city of Xaniá on the isle of Crete: we were sitting under a large patio umbrella, the sun was blazing down, the air hot but dry, the shade cool and inviting. Since we were on the ocean, the sand reflected the intensity of the sun, and the sound of the ocean beating against the shore was hypnotic. The "lunch special" had, among other things, a tomato salad, that is, a ripe sliced tomato with fresh, green olive oil poured on top, and fried baby okra. Both items were swimming in oil and were utterly delicious. The combination of heat and fresh produce was unbeatable. I'm sure the bottle of wine had nothing to do with it.

Greek cuisine reminds me of Spanish cuisine; not in taste, but in style. Simple, easy, and best served alfresco with a cool glass of wine among friends. But like all "simple" cuisines, it is of utmost priority that the freshest, best ingredients are used, since there is nothing included to mask anything of poor quality!

Per serving:

Calories: 146
Carbohydrates: 2.1 g
Protein: 24.2 g
Fat Total: 4.1 g
Fat Saturated: .68 g

3	**tablespoons lemon juice**
1	**teaspoon grated lemon peel**
1	**tablespoon fruity extra virgin olive oil**
1	**teaspoon oregano (or 1 tablespoon fresh oregano)**
½	**teaspoon thyme (or 2 teaspoons fresh thyme)**
2	**cloves garlic, minced or put through a garlic press**
2	**tablespoons parsley**
½	**teaspoon salt**
1½	**pound turkey breast, cut into 2-inch chunks**
4	**skewers**

Combine the first eight ingredients in a bowl, mixing briefly; add the turkey meat, tossing well, then marinate the turkey several hours covered in the refrigerator. After the turkey has marinated, place the meat onto the skewers.

Broil or grill the kabobs until done, approximately 8 minutes on each side, basting with any leftover marinade or olive oil. Remove the turkey immediately when it is done.

Serve with a rice pilaf, a large salad, and fresh, ripe, sliced tomatoes lightly drizzled with olive oil and sprinkled with fresh basil and pepper. And don't forget a glass of wine!

Meat

- *On Low-Fat Eating and Meat*

  Beef Stir-Fry
  Ginger Beef with Pineapple
  Beef Kabobs I, II, III, and IV
  Lamb with Garlic and Balsamic
  * Vinaigrette*
  Lamb with Rosemary
  Mughlai Lamb
  Butterflied Pork Chops with Green
  * Peppercorn Marinade*
  Pork Tender Sauté

On Low-Fat Eating and Meat

*M*EAT? On a low-fat diet?

Yes, it is possible. The major problem with meat on a low-fat regimen is not the meat itself (since there are an increasingly growing number of "leaner" cuts available), but what Americans perceive as a *portion* of meat. We were raised to believe that a twelve-ounce T-bone was the perfect serving size, and the most often-heard response to a six-ounce filet mignon being "Is that *all*?" Four ounces of beef, lamb, or pork are sufficient for most people's daily protein needs, which is a very small amount juxtaposed to an eighteen-ounce porterhouse steak. So the real change not only needs to be in the meat itself, but in our *perception* of meat as a part of a meal.

On a similar note, several years ago a dear friend of mine, Jerry Williams, received a Fulbright grant and was teaching scene design in Taipei on the island of Taiwan; he tells a story about his time there which typifies this idea. After being in Taipei for several weeks, he began to suffer from culture shock, and subsequently, he took some of his students out to the best "American" restaurant in the city in an effort to succor his own nostalgia for the U.S. as well as to introduce some Asian college students to American cuisine. He ordered a sixteen-ounce steak, a fact which he had up to that point never given much thought. When the meal arrived, the students' eyes became huge—they stared at the enormous steak on his plate and were very quiet. Jerry asked what was wrong, and they replied in broken English, "We're sorry for staring. But you have to realize that that is enough meat to feed a family." Suddenly the travesty of a single person consuming such a large piece of beef became apparent to Jerry; for the students, the idea of one person eating a steak was almost inconceivable.

But we are in America. I'm not advocating the total renunciation of steaks, but we as a society need to look at what the human organism *needs*, rather than what we *want* or what is merely *available*. Just because a thirty-six-ounce steak exists doesn't necessitate that it must be consumed by one person. The point is: analyze what you need to eat to remain healthy and try to stick to that amount. Occasional indulgences are fine and normal, but I beseech all readers to seriously evaluate their own diet and see if they are guilty of being a "meat glutton."

On to the fat content of beef.

Although there are many lean "low-fat" choices of meat on the market, it is still a sticking point for those monitoring their fat intake. Unlike chicken, where the fat is quite visible and easily removed, the inner fat of beef and lamb is entwined within the meat itself; and though you can remove the obvious excess fat, the inner fat (which makes the meat moist and "juicy") is part and parcel of the cut. So how can one approach beef and lamb with a fat-conscious bent?

The best way is to find a good butcher and trust her or him. Make sure you're purchasing the leanest cuts available. To illustrate the importance of purchasing the leanest cuts, see the chart below:

*Four ounces of **LEAN:***

Prime eye of round	= 169 calories, 7.1 g fat total, 2.6 g fat saturated
Short/top loin	= 214 calories, 12.2 g fat total, 4.9 g fat saturated
Porterhouse	= 178 calories, 8.9 g fat total, 3.6 g fat saturated
T-bone	= 180 calories, 9.1 g fat total, 3.7 g fat saturated
Prime tenderloin	= 192 calories, 10 g fat total, 4 g fat saturated
Prime sirloin	= 176 calories, 8 g total fat, 3 g fat saturated

As illustrated, even four ounces of *lean* beef are not created equal.

Reduce your portion of meat to the minimum you need. And most importantly, enjoy every bite you take—don't look upon four ounces of a filet mignon as a scrawny portion, but as twelve bites of a wonderfully prepared treat. Not only will you be eating healthier, but since you will be cutting down the amount of meat consumed, you will be saving money as well, so the cost per pound of the meat becomes less important in the light of the quality of meat bought.

This chapter is noticeably slim (no pun intended). The healthiest diets are rich in vegetables, grains, beans, and fruits, and low in fats. The best way to get your fill of meat and eat "lite" is to couple the meat with vegetables and grains—such as stir-frys, kebobs with rice pilafs, or a minimal amount of meat with pastas.

Beef Stir-Fry

SERVES 4

Almost all of the fat in this dish is from the beef alone; when served with plain rice it becomes a nutritious and healthy dinner.

Per serving:

Calories: 252
Carbohydrates: 19 g
Protein: 20.9 g
Fat Total: 10.6 g
Fat Saturated: 3.8 g

2 to 3	**cloves garlic, minced or put through a garlic press**
2	**teaspoons gingerroot, finely minced**
3	**tablespoons tamari**
2	**tablespoons water**
2	**tablespoons white wine or sherry**
1	**tablespoon sugar or honey**
1	**tablespoon cilantro**
1	**teaspoon toasted sesame oil**
1	**teaspoon red pepper flakes (optional)**
¾-pound	**flank steak, sliced into ¼- × 1- × 2-inch pieces**
1	**teaspoon oil & Pam®**
1	**cup broccoli florets**
4	**green onions, roughly chopped**
½	**red bell pepper, sliced**
1	**cup snow peas**
1	**can (8 ounces) sliced water chestnuts**
⅔	**cup defatted chicken stock mixed with 1 teaspoon cornstarch or arrowroot**

Combine the first 9 ingredients in a bowl; stir and add the sliced beef. Marinate the beef for at least 20 minutes.

Chop up the vegetables and mix the chicken stock and arrowroot in a small bowl.

Heat a wok or large skillet over a moderate flame. When the wok is hot, add 1 teaspoon oil and immediately spray the pan with Pam®. Add the beef mixture and stir-fry until it is nearly done, around 3 to 4 minutes; remove the beef and set it aside, keeping it warm. In the same wok, add the vegetables and stir-fry until they are nearly done, around 3 minutes, then return the cooked beef to the wok. Continue stirring until everything is hot, around 2 additional minutes. Add the chicken-stock mixture, bringing the liquid to a boil; as soon as the sauce has cleared and thickened, remove the stir-fry from the heat and serve with rice.

Variation

- Reduce tamari to 1 tablespoon and add 2 tablespoons of oyster sauce to marinade.

Ginger Beef
with Pineapple

SERVES 4

Per serving without rice:

Calories: 251
Carbohydrates: 22.3 g
Protein: 20.3 g
Fat Total: 9.3 g
Fat Saturated: 3.6 g

Per serving with rice:

Calories: 474
Carbohydrates: 71.9 g
Protein: 24.4 g
Fat Total: 9.5 g
Fat Saturated: 3.6 g

1	¾-pound lean flank steak, sliced into ¼- × 1- × 3-inch strips
1	tablespoon finely minced gingerroot
2	cloves garlic, minced or put through a garlic press
2	tablespoons tamari
2	teaspoons sugar
½	teaspoon toasted sesame oil
1	teaspoon cornstarch
4	teaspoons rice wine vinegar
⅓	cup defatted chicken stock
	Pam®
2	cups pineapple cubes, either fresh or canned
6	green onions, sliced into 2-inch pieces
1	cup snow peas
1	cup mushrooms, sliced
½	red bell pepper, sliced into thin strips
1	cup fresh bean sprouts (optional)
4	cups cooked white rice

Trim off any fat from the flank steak and slice into strips. Combine the gingerroot, garlic, tamari, sugar, and sesame oil in a bowl. Add the beef slices to the bowl and coat well, allowing the beef to marinate at least one hour.

Combine the cornstarch, vinegar, and chicken stock in a small bowl, making sure there are no lumps in the cornstarch. Clean and slice all of the vegetables.

When ready to cook, heat a wok or heavy skillet over a medium-high flame. When the pan is hot, spray it with Pam® and add the marinated beef. Stir-fry for 3 minutes or so, until the beef is almost done. Add the pineapple and the cornstarch mixture, bringing the liquid to a boil, cooking until the mixture has thickened; add the green onions, snow peas, mushrooms, red bell pepper, and optional bean sprouts. Continue stir-frying until the vegetables are just done, another 1 to 2 minutes. Serve immediately with white rice or rice noodles.

Beef Kabobs
I, II, III, and IV

SERVES 4

Here are four easy variations on a theme. These kabobs are designed to be mildly seasoned so that the inherent taste of the beef is not overwhelmed. And of course, they are best when grilled outdoors with friends, sunshine, and wine.

I.

- **1 pound lean beef, cut into 2-inch chunks**
- **2 cloves garlic, minced or put through a garlic press**
- **2 tablespoons tamari**
- **1 tablespoon fresh rosemary (optional)**

Per serving: Calories: 161; Carbohydrates: 1.4 g; Protein: 24.5 g; Fat Total: 5.7 g; Fat Saturated: 2.1 g

II.

- **1 pound lean beef, cut into 2-inch chunks**
- **2 teaspoons minced gingerroot**
- **1 teaspoon toasted sesame oil**
- **1 tablespoon sherry**
- **1 tablespoon tamari**
- **1 clove garlic, minced or put through a garlic press (optional)**

Per serving: Calories: 172; Carbohydrates: 1.2 g; Protein: 24.2 g; Fat Total: 6.7 g; Fat Saturated: 2.3 g

III.

- **1 pound lean beef, cut into 2-inch chunks**
- **2 tablespoons freshly chopped parsley**
- **1 teaspoon thyme**
- **½ teaspoon salt**
- **¼ teaspoon pepper**
- **2 tablespoons lemon juice**
- **1 tablespoon Dijon mustard**
- **2 tablespoons finely minced green onion**

Per serving: Calories: 163; Carbohydrates: 1.9 g; Protein: 24.3 g; Fat Total: 6 g; Fat Saturated: 2.1 g

IV.

1	*pound lean beef, cut into 2-inch chunks*
⅓	*cup plain, nonfat yogurt*
1	*tablespoon chopped cilantro*
½	*teaspoon salt*
1½	*teaspoons garam masala or 1 teaspoon cumin, ¼ teaspoon coriander, and ¼ teaspoon curry powder*
¼	*teaspoon cayenne*

Per serving: Calories: 166; Carbohydrates: 1.9 g; Protein: 25 g; Fat Total: 5.9 g; Fat Saturated: 2.1 g

To prepare any one of the above, combine the ingredients and marinate the beef chunks for 1 to 6 hours. Place the marinated beef on skewers and broil or grill outdoors, basting occasionally until you have reached the desired doneness.

Lamb with Garlic and Balsamic Vinaigrette

SERVES 4

Lamb isn't the leanest of meats, but it is quite delicious when properly prepared and cooked. In my not-so-humble opinion, it is a great sin to cook lamb beyond the medium-rare stage. Rare to medium-rare lamb has a velvety, buttery, melting quality that is lost if it is overcooked even to the medium point.

4	*lamb chops, very lean*
2	*tablespoons Dijon mustard*
2	*cloves garlic, minced or put through a garlic press*
3	*tablespoons balsamic vinegar*
1	*tablespoon lemon juice*
1	*tablespoon sugar (optional)*
1	*teaspoon oregano or thyme (optional)*
¼	*teaspoon pepper*
1	*tablespoon tamari*

Per chop:

Calories: 120
Carbohydrates: 5.6 g
Protein: 14.4 g
Fat Total: 4.4 g
Fat Saturated: 1.5 g

Trim off excess fat from lamb chops. Combine all ingredients in a dish and marinate, covered, for 3 to 6 hours.

Grill the chops outdoors or broil indoors until done, around 5 minutes on each side, basting with any leftover marinade. Garnish the lamb with freshly chopped parsley.

Lamb with Rosemary

SERVES 4

This lamb is quite stunningly delicious and remarkably easy to make. Although lamb served with potatoes is a classic and perhaps hackneyed combination, I never think twice about serving this duo. They complement each other so perfectly the phrase comes to mind: "If it ain't broke, don't fix it!"

4	**lean lamb chops**
2	**cloves garlic, minced or put through a garlic press**
1	**tablespoon fresh lemon peel, finely grated**
2	**tablespoons lemon juice**
2	**tablespoons tamari**
1	**tablespoon fresh rosemary, chopped**
1	**teaspoon olive oil**

FOR AN OPTIONAL SAUCE:

1	**cup defatted beef broth**
¼	**cup port**
	any remaining marinade
1 to 2	**teaspoons arrowroot dissolved in 1 tablespoon water**
	freshly chopped parsley

Remove any excess fat from the lamb and combine it with the next 6 ingredients in a baking dish and marinate, covered, for 4 to 6 hours.

Broil or grill the lamb until it is rare to medium-rare, around 4 to 5 minutes on each side, basting with a bit of marinade. Do not overcook the lamb! It will continue to cook after it is removed from the grill or broiler, so watch it carefully.

If you desire a gravy with the lamb, bring the beef broth and port to a boil in a small saucepan. Add any remaining marinade from the lamb, then slowly add the arrowroot, stirring briskly with a whisk, until the sauce has come to a boil and has thickened slightly. Remove, taste for seasoning, and add the parsley.

Serve the lamb immediately, accompanied by the sauce in a gravy boat.

Note: I dislike thick, cornstarchy sauces; the real culprit here is not cornstarch itself, but too much cornstarch. I find it infinitely preferable to have a sauce thickened just so that it has gone from being watery to smooth; it is not necessary for any sauce or gravy to stick to a plate if turned upside down.

Per serving without sauce:

Calories: 89.3
Carbohydrates: 1.3 g
Protein: 11.4 g
Fat Total: 3.9 g
Fat Saturated: 1.2 g

Per serving with sauce:

Calories: 154
Carbohydrates: 6.1 g
Protein: 16.9 g
Fat Total: 4.9 g
Fat Saturated: 1.5 g

Mughlai Lamb

SERVES 4

Per serving:

Calories: 258
Carbohydrates: 19.1 g
Protein: 27.7 g
Fat Total: 7.9 g
Fat Saturated: 2.5 g

Ages ago, natives to the region of Asia that we now call Mongolia storm-trooped their way across the Indian subcontinent, occasionally stopping long enough to pillage and pick up a few cooking tips. These people from Mongolia were known as Tartars, Mongols, or Moghuls, and were discovered to be particularly fond of the region, culture, and cuisine of Persia. Even though the Moghuls like Persia, being the nomads they were, they had ants in their pants about staying put in any one place: so they pulled up stakes and eventually worked their riotous way up to India, finally settling down in the north central provinces.

While in India, the Moghuls introduced their favorite Persian cooking style to the Indians. Mother India, though, was not about to sit still for such impertinence! It was unthinkable that the Moghuls could succeed in their bloodless coup upon Indian cuisine! What we commonly call Moghulai or Mughlai cooking is the hybrid flower bred from this fusion of native and alien influences, resulting in a lovely, fragrant blend of savory Persian temperament with spicy Indian inventiveness.

2	**small onions, peeled**
4	**cloves garlic, peeled**
1	**1-inch square piece of gingerroot, peeled**
1	**cup water**
1	**teaspoon oil and Pam®**
1	**2-inch stick of cinnamon**
6	**allspice berries or ¼ teaspoon ground allspice**
6	**whole cardamom seeds**
	or ⅓ teaspoon ground cardamom
1	**teaspoon cumin**
1	**teaspoon ground coriander**
¼	**teaspoon ground nutmeg**
¼	**teaspoon cayenne**
1	**pound lean lamb, diced into 1 to 2-inch pieces**
¼	**cup raisins**
½	**teaspoon salt**
1	**cup nonfat yogurt**
1	**tablespoon chopped cilantro**

Place the onions, garlic, and gingerroot in a blender or food processor along with ⅓ cup water and blend into a fine paste, around 60 seconds. Set aside until needed.

Heat a deep-sided skillet or large pot over a medium flame; when it is hot, add the oil and spray it with Pam®. Add the whole (or ground) spices and stir until they are fragrant but not overcooked, around 15 to 20 seconds or so. Add the lamb pieces and continue to stir and fry, until the lamb is lightly browned on all sides, around 3 to 5 minutes. Add the raisins and cook for another minute until they have expanded and are plump. Remove as much of the lamb mixture as possible into a bowl. Next add the garlic-onion mixture to the pan, keeping your face averted from the pan as you add the paste. Stir and fry the garlic-onion paste over a medium-high flame until the garlic-onion mixture browns lightly, around 15 minutes. Return the lamb mixture to the pan along with ⅔ cup water and ½ teaspoon salt, bringing it to a simmer, then cover and cook over low heat for 45 minutes. Check and stir lamb periodically, adding a bit of water if the mixture is becoming dry.

When lamb is very tender, remove the pan from heat. Just before serving, add the yogurt 1 tablespoon at a time, stirring well with each addition. The lamb should have a thick sauce coating it; if it seems a bit dry, add more yogurt or a bit of water.

Eat immediately with rice, garnishing with chopped cilantro.

Note: This recipe contains whole spices. Either remove the spices before serving the lamb or warn your guests that they're there. There's no danger in eating a whole spice, it's just unusual for most Americans to chomp down on a clove or cardamom pod—even if someone should bite into a whole allspice berry (for example), there is no real harm; they will just receive an intense allspice taste. Since the spices have been cooking with the lamb, they have softened and aren't hard enough to break a tooth.

Butterflied Pork Chops with Green Peppercorn Marinade

SERVES 4

Try this next time you have a cookout—your guests will be thrilled!

4	**butterflied lean pork chops or pork tenderloin slices**
2	**tablespoons green peppercorns packed in brine**
2	**tablespoons lemon juice**
1	**tablespoon fresh lemon rind, grated**
¼	**cup orange juice**
2	**tablespoons lime juice**
1	**teaspoon thyme**
1 to 2	**cloves garlic, minced or put through a garlic press**
1	**tablespoon tamari**
2	**tablespoons chopped parsley**
1½	**teaspoons Dijon mustard**
1	**green onion, finely chopped (optional)**
1	**8-inch × 8-inch baking dish**

Trim off any excess fat from the pork chops and set aside.

Place the green peppercorns in a mortar and grind them with a pestle until they are mushy. Place the mashed peppercorns in a 8-inch × 8-inch baking dish, then combine them with the remaining ingredients, mixing well. Marinate the pork chops in this mixture for 4 to 6 hours, refrigerated and covered.

Grill the pork chops outdoors, basting with the marinade until done, around 10 to 12 minutes on each side.

Per serving:

Calories: 188
Carbohydrates: 5.3 g
Protein: 20 g
Fat Total: 9.6 g
Fat Saturated: 3.3 g

Pork Tender Sauté

SERVES 4

This is a very simple way to cook pork; it isn't really "sauced" in the traditional sense, but has a light wine-flavored garnish to create a more complex finished product.

1 to 1¼	**pounds lean pork tender, cut into 4 equal pieces**
3 to 4	**tablespoons tamari or soy sauce**
1	**clove garlic, sliced lengthwise into 2 or 3 pieces**
1	**teaspoon Dijon mustard (optional)**
¼	**cup fine tawny port**
	Pam®

Per serving:

Calories: 218
Carbohydrates: 2.1 g
Protein: 33.2 g
Fat Total: 5.8 g
Fat Saturated: 1.9 g

Place the tamari and garlic in a shallow bowl and mix in the optional mustard; add the pork pieces. Turn the meat to coat well with the marinade, then pierce each piece 5 to 10 times with a knife so that some of the marinade can get into the center. Allow the pork to sit for 30 minutes. When you're ready to cook, remove and discard the garlic.

Place a heavy skillet over medium-high heat and allow the pan to get *very* hot. (If you put a drop of water in the pan, the droplet should "dance" and hop about like a ball rather than sit and sizzle and then evaporate.) The next step is to sear and "seize" the outside of the meat so that it will seal in the juices. Spray the hot pan with Pam®, then immediately place the pork into the skillet; it will sizzle and smoke. Turn the pieces when each side has browned, then reduce the heat to very low. Cover and cook the meat for 10 minutes or so, turning often, adding 2 to 3 tablespoons of water occasionally if the meat looks dry. You will be able to tell when the pork is nearly done by the feel of the meat; if it is still soft and "squishy," it may need to cook longer. The best method is to either use a meat thermometer (internal temperature of 145° to 150°) or cut into the center of 1 piece and see if it is thoroughly cooked. When the meat is done, remove it and keep it warm. Deglaze the pan by pouring ¼ cup of port into it, return the pan to the heat and boil the wine, scraping any bits that have stuck to the bottom of the pan into the sauce.

To serve, slice each portion of cooked pork tender into ½-inch medallions and arrange prettily in a row on a warmed plate; pour a tablespoon of the wine sauce over the medallions just before serving. Garnish with our kitchen friend, the ubiquitous Mr. Parsley, or a sprig of fresh thyme.

Variation

- Double and mince the garlic; add 1 tablespoon chopped fresh rosemary and cracked black peppercorns to the marinade: proceed as directed, substituting ¼ cup fine red wine instead of the port.

Vegetables, Salads, and Side Dishes

Chi Mei's Green Beans (Almost)

Baked Onions

Broccoli with Garlic

Hunan Eggplant

Navy Beans with Fresh Fennel

Roasted Peppers

Ratatouille

Cucumber-Cilantro Raita

Rice Pilaf

Risotto

Spaghetti Squash with Rosemary

Spinach with Garlic, Cardamom,
    and Yogurt Sauce

Squash-Tomato Casserole

Summer Squash and Onion Bake

Stir-Fry Greens

Tabbouleh

Szechuan Eggplant

Wild Rice Pilaf

Zucchini-Tomato Curry

SALADS

Chickpea Salad

Dijon Potato Salad

Dilled Potato Salad

Five-Bean Salad

Chinese Chicken Salad

Lentil Salad

Navy Bean Salad with Vinaigrette

Pasta Salad

Spinach Fusilli Salad

Spaghetti Squash Salad

Shrimp and Spinach Salad

Chicken Salad with Fresh Herbs

Summer Tuna Salad

Tropical Chicken Salad

Tortellini Salad

SALAD DRESSINGS

Blue Cheese Dressing

Celery Seed Dressing

Ginger-Miso Dressing

Ranch Dressing

Zippy Poppy Seed Dressing

Creamy Cucumber Dressing

Sweet Ginger Dressing

Chi Mei's Green Beans (Almost)

SERVES 4

Per serving:

Calories: 68.4
Carbohydrates: 14.4 g
Protein: 3.2 g
Fat Total: .78 g
Fat Saturated: .12 g

I first had this dish when my friend Wang Chi Mei from Taipei was visiting, and we spent an afternoon in the kitchen (with me watching her every move like a hawk to pick up any secrets!). As I watched her cleaning some cilantro, pulling off each leaf individually, I showed her a quicker method, wherein you hold the top end of the cilantro stem and pull off all of the leaves at once. She said, "But sometimes you get threads from the stem when you do that." I replied, "I know, but it's so much quicker." She said that on Taiwan the process of preparing meals was considered a time to talk and relax, not to rush around madly attempting to dash out a meal by 6 P.M. So we talked, relaxed, and enjoyed standing around picking cilantro leaf by leaf, washing vegetables, and sipping occasionally from our cups of tea, luxuriating in the sense that there was no hurry and the joy was the company, the conversation, and doing the job well, existing "in the moment."

This particular dish was a labor of love for Chi Mei, since the beans were fried in quite a bit of oil and turned individually to ensure proper cooking. By the time each bean was cooked most of the color had disappeared; I was naturally dubious about how this vegetable dish was going to turn out! I said nothing and watched as she finished preparing the dish, sautéing the seasonings and adding the already limp beans. Needless to say, they were exquisite. Sweet, salty, hot, garlicky, and absolutely wonderful. The following variation doesn't require you to fry each bean individually and uses a fraction of the oil. Not a bad compromise, if I do say so myself.

1	**pound fresh green beans**
½	**teaspoon toasted sesame oil**
2 to 3	**cloves garlic, minced or put through a garlic press**
1 to 2	**teaspoons shredded or minced gingerroot**
2	**green onions, very finely minced**
1 to 2	**teaspoons sugar**
½	**teaspoon red pepper flakes**
3	**tablespoons tamari or soy sauce**
2	**tablespoons water**

Wash and trim the ends from the green beans. If desired, slice the beans into 1-inch pieces, then set them aside. Prepare remaining ingredients.

Place a large skillet or wok over medium-high flame and heat it thoroughly. When it is hot, add the sesame oil, garlic, gingerroot, green onions, and green beans. Cover the wok and stir-fry every 30 seconds or so, until the green beans are three-quarters cooked, around 5 to 7 minutes. Add the sugar, red pepper flakes, tamari, and water, bringing the heat to high. Stir and fry until the green beans are thoroughly cooked and the sugar and tamari have combined to form a "sauce" that sticks slightly to the beans in smallish brown globs. If the sauce is runny, continue to cook until it has reduced sufficiently. Remove the beans and serve hot.

Baked Onions

SERVES 4

This sounds like an unlikely dish, but is in fact quite delicious. Baked onions work perfectly as a side dish for any dinner, or as a take-along for a picnic.

4 to 6 **medium to large onions, white or yellow**
1 **tablespoon olive oil (optional)**
¼ **cup balsamic vinegar**
salt and cracked black pepper
1 **baking sheet**

Preheat the oven to 375°.

Place the whole, unpeeled onions on a baking sheet and lightly coat them with the optional olive oil. Bake them for approximately 45 to 60 minutes, or until they are soft and have oozed some juices. Gently squeeze them to test for doneness. If they are firm, let them cook for another 10 minutes. Remove the onions from the oven and from the baking sheet, setting them aside on a plate.

Deglaze the baking sheet by placing it over medium-high heat and pouring in the balsamic vinegar, scraping where the onions have left cooked-on juices, reducing the vinegar a bit. Pour the vinegar reduction into a small bowl.

When the onions have cooled somewhat, cut each in half lengthwise (that is, from the end where the roots are to where the sprout would be) and spoon some of the balsamic vinegar glaze into the cut halves. Sprinkle each half with salt and pepper, serving either warm or cold.

Variations

- When deglazing pan, add 1 teaspoon fresh chopped rosemary or fresh thyme.
- Add 2 or 3 whole unpeeled cloves of garlic midway through the baking of the onions; after removing the onions, peel and mash the garlic on the pan before deglazing. Deglaze as usual, scraping and mashing the garlic into the vinegar sauce.

**Per serving
without olive oil:**

Calories: 84.4
Carbohydrates: 18.6 g
Protein: 2.9 g
Fat Total: .63 g
Fat Saturated: .11 g

**Per serving
with olive oil:**

Calories: 114
Carbohydrates: 18.6 g
Protein: 2.8 g
Fat Total: 4 g
Fat Saturated: .56 g

Broccoli with Garlic

SERVES 4

Steamed broccoli is so simple that we frequently forget that there is any other way to prepare it; and besides a heavy cream-and-cheese laden sauce (another popular favorite), here's a quick, light, and delicious alternative.

1	**large bunch broccoli**
2 to 3	**cloves garlic, minced or put through a garlic press**
2	**teaspoons olive oil or butter**
¼	**cup defatted stock or water**
	salt and pepper to taste

Per serving:

Calories: 64.9
Carbohydrates: 8.8 g
Protein: 4.8 g
Fat Total: 2.6 g
Fat Saturated: .36 g

Wash and trim the broccoli, peeling the stalk to remove the tough outer skin. Cut the broccoli head into small florets, then chop the peeled stalk into ¼-inch cubes.

Heat a large sauté pan over a medium flame and add olive oil and garlic; sauté until the garlic just begins to brown (around 1 minute), then add the broccoli. Stir the broccoli and garlic once, then add the stock and cover, turning the flame a notch lower. Allow the broccoli to steam for 2 minutes or so until the broccoli is just done, stirring once or twice. Remove the pan from the heat and add salt and pepper to taste.

Variation

- Add 1 teaspoon finely grated gingerroot, ½ teaspoon toasted sesame oil, and season with tamari instead of salt.

Hunan Eggplant

SERVES 4

Eggplant is wonderfully versatile and an indispensable part of anyone's summer meals. If you have a garden, in addition to the regular eggplant, try planting some long Japanese varieties or some pink or white Persian eggplants. Though they're all related, the textures differ between the varieties and you may discover a new favorite!

This eggplant dish is simple yet quite satisfying, a lovely accompaniment to any meal.

6	**small firm Japanese eggplants, or 1 large regular eggplant**
1	**teaspoon vegetable oil**
1	**teaspoon grated gingerroot**
2	**cloves garlic, minced or put through a garlic press**
	juice of ½ lemon
1	**tablespoon soy sauce**
1	**teaspoon sugar**
¼	**teaspoon toasted sesame oil**
	a steamer basket
1	**large Dutch oven with lid**

Wash the eggplants and trim off the stem ends. Cut each eggplant into ¼-inch half-moon shapes. Place the eggplant pieces in a steamer basket and steam covered until done, approximately 8 minutes. Cool the eggplant.

Heat a wok or skillet over a medium flame and add the oil, gingerroot, and garlic. When the garlic has lost its translucent color and is beginning to toast lightly, add the remaining ingredients (except the cooked eggplant) and heat, stir-frying. Next add the eggplant and toss to coat it in the sauce; cook for 1 minute to heat the eggplant through. Add a tablespoon or two of water if the mixture seems too dry. Serve immediately.

Per serving:

Calories: 35.9
Carbohydrates: 5.8 g
Protein: .96 g
Fat Total: 1.4 g
Fat Saturated: .19 g

Navy Beans
with Fresh Fennel

SERVES 4

This dish can be served either hot or cold, as a side dish or as a salad.

1	**bulb fresh fennel (or fresh anise)**
1	**teaspoon olive oil and Pam®**
1	**clove minced garlic (optional)**
1	**tablespoon Dijon mustard**
¼	**cup red or white wine vinegar**
2	**tablespoons lemon juice**
⅓	**cup chopped fresh parsley**
¼	**cup sugar**
½	**cup red bell pepper, finely diced**
2	**green onions, diced**
2 to 2½	**cups cooked navy beans**
	salt and pepper to taste

Separate the fennel bulb and wash the pieces thoroughly under cool running water. If the stalks seem unduly woody, use only the whitish bottoms. Slice the fennel into thin strips until you have approximately 2 cups of sliced fennel, including some of the feathery leaves if desired. Sauté the fennel and optional garlic in the olive oil and Pam® over medium heat, until the fennel has barely softened and still retains its crunch, around 1 minute of stir-frying. Set the fennel aside to cool.

In a large bowl, combine the Dijon mustard, vinegar, lemon juice, parsley, and sugar, stirring well. Add the bell pepper, onions, and beans; mix well. Add the cooled fennel and stir again, tasting for seasoning. This dish is best after it has marinated several hours. Serve hot, room temperature, or cold.

Variations

- Add 1 teaspoon herbes de Provence.
- Add ½ cup diced, peeled, and seeded tomatoes.

Per serving:

Calories: 270
Carbohydrates: 51.4 g
Protein: 13.5 g
Fat Total: 2.5 g
Fat Saturated: .37 g

Roasted Peppers

SERVES 4

No matter how often I have these they always remind me of the sunny Mediterranean. Sweet and slightly smoky, the peppers are an exquisite accompaniment for a light meal alfresco, with pasta, or in a salad. Serve with a bottle of wine, a fresh baguette, some fresh fruit, cheese, olives . . . mmm-m-m-m-m!

2 to 3   **red, green, or yellow bell peppers**
       olive oil (optional)
       balsamic vinegar
1   **clove garlic, peeled and sliced in half**
       salt and pepper to taste
       freshly chopped basil

Per serving:

Calories: 18.1
Carbohydrates: 4.1 g
Protein: .64 g
Fat Total: .28 g
Fat Saturated: .039 g

Place the whole bell peppers over (and sitting in, if possible) an open flame and cook, turning periodically, until they are completely black and charred on the outside. (If you don't have a gas flame, roast the peppers under the broiler of an electric oven.) Remove the peppers and wrap them in a paper towel, then wrap the paper towel in a cloth towel. (You could also place the roasted peppers in a paper or plastic bag, sealing well.) Let the hot peppers sit on the counter and steam for at least 20 minutes.

Place a small amount of olive oil (1 to 2 tablespoons) and balsamic vinegar (3 to 4 tablespoons) in a small bowl; add the garlic and allow to marinate while peppers are cooling.

After the peppers have cooled at least 20 minutes, remove them from their wrappings and rinse the peppers under cool water, removing the blackened, charred outer skin. Some spots of black should remain; this gives a nice, smoky flavor. When all of the skin has been removed, core and seed the peppers, then slice them thinly, arranging them attractively on a plate. Pour the oil (optional)–vinegar mixture over the peppers, sprinkling them with salt and pepper, and finally sprinkle the chopped fresh basil on top. Eat immediately, or allow the peppers to marinate a few hours.

Variations

- Add 1 teaspoon finely chopped fresh rosemary instead of basil.
- Add 1 tablespoon finely chopped fresh oregano or marjoram instead of basil.
- Add 2 tablespoons chopped Kalamata olives.

Ratatouille

SERVES 4

There are as many recipes for ratatouille as there are cooks. Some people may wish to use concentrated chicken stock instead of vermouth; some people may wish to use tamari instead of salt. Some like a drier ratatouille (which this recipe would probably be catagorized as); others prefer a wet, stewlike one. For those wishing a wetter ratatouille, add some additional defatted stock and/or tomatoes.

At any rate, here is a basic guideline for this famous eggplant dish, and experimentation is encouraged!

Per serving:

Calories: 181
Carbohydrates: 25.3 g
Protein: 4.4 g
Fat Total: 5.2 g
Fat Saturated: .28 g

3	**small (or 2 medium) eggplants**
	olive oil or Pam®
1	**tablespoon olive oil**
½	**teaspoon fennel seed**
1	**medium onion, thinly sliced**
2	**cloves garlic, minced or put through a garlic press**
1	**cup sliced red bell pepper, or a mixture of red and green**
1	**bay leaf**
1	**teaspoon thyme**
½	**teaspoon oregano (optional)**
½	**teaspoon black pepper**
3	**cups tomatoes (canned, fresh, crushed, or any combination), chopped and seeded, including any juice from the tomatoes**
3	**tablespoons tomato paste**
1 to 2	**teaspoons sugar (optional)**
3	**tablespoons fresh chopped basil**
2	**tablespoons chopped parsley**
¾ to 1	**cup vermouth or defatted stock, or a mixture of both**
	salt to taste
1	**baking sheet**
1	**pastry brush (optional)**

Preheat the broiler to high. Spray a baking sheet with Pam®.

Peel the eggplants and slice into ¼-inch rounds. Place as many eggplant slices as will fit onto the prepared baking sheet. Now you have two options on how to cook the eggplants.

Option 1:
Pour ¼ cup or so of olive oil into a small bowl. Dipping your pastry brush lightly into the olive oil, brush each side of the eggplants with a small amount of the oil. Broil the eggplants until they are reddish brown on each side, turning once. Continue until all slices are cooked. Set the slices aside to cool.

Option 2:
Spritz each side of the eggplants with nonaerosol Pam®. Broil the eggplants until they are reddish brown on each side, turning once.

Continue until all slices are cooked. Set the slices aside to cool. (This option raises many eyebrows; but the ingredients of non-aerosol Pam® are oil, grain alcohol (a preservative that evaporates during cooking), and lecithin, a natural soybean by-product which, it has been suggested, helps in reducing cholesterol. Nothing artificial!)

While the eggplant slices are cooling, heat a large sauté pan over a moderate flame; when the pan is hot, add 1 tablespoon olive oil. Add the fennel seeds, sliced onion, and the garlic. Stir and cook until the onion is tender, around 4 to 5 minutes. Reduce the heat to medium-low, and add the bell peppers, bay leaf, thyme, pepper, tomatoes, and tomato paste; cook for another 3 to 5 minutes until the peppers soften. Add the remaining ingredients and stir. Reduce the flame to low.

Cut the cooked eggplant pieces into 1-inch chunks. Add the eggplant pieces to the onion-tomato mixture and cook for 15 to 20 minutes until the entire mixture is hot and all of the vegetables are done. Taste for seasoning.

Eat immediately or refrigerate, reheating gently before serving.

Cucumber-Cilantro Raita

SERVES 4

Raitas, or Indian yogurt salads, are tiny side dishes (like chutneys) and are bright, cooling additions to spicy meals. There are as many raita variations as there are cooks, and substitutions are not only acceptable but actively encouraged. This raita is savory, but you can easily make a sweet one with ripe bananas, coconut, yogurt, garlic (yes, garlic!), and spices.

2	**cups nonfat yogurt**
1	**teaspoon salt (or to taste)**
1	**cup finely chopped or grated cucumber**
¼	**cup tomatoes, chopped, seeded, and peeled**
3 to 4	**tablespoons chopped cilantro or fresh mint, or a combination of the two**
¼	**teaspoon cayenne pepper (optional)**
1 to 2	**tablespoons lemon juice**
½	**teaspoon garam masala or ½ teaspoon ground cumin**
¼	**teaspoon black or cayenne pepper**

Per serving:

Calories: 73.9
Carbohydrates: 11.2 g
Protein: 6.9 g
Fat Total: .41 g
Fat Saturated: .16 g

Combine all of the ingredients in a bowl. Taste the raita for seasoning and refrigerate. I would serve the raita within 2 hours of preparation, as the salt will pull water from the cucumbers and tomatoes, causing a thinner raita.

Serve the raita chilled with an Indian meal, or have as a summer between-meal snack.

Rice Pilaf

SERVES 4

Pilaf, pilau, and pulau are all generic terms for a "rice dish cooked with stock" and/ or vegetables and meats. They are sometimes eaten as the main part of a dinner or lunch, but in America, pilafs are more frequently seen as a side dish. They are incomparable additions to buffet tables and necessities for dinner parties since they can be made ahead of time and reheated easily as you are taking care of guests. As with rice in general, pilafs are excellent with gravy-laden dishes.

Per serving:

Calories: 242
Carbohydrates: 47.3 g
Protein: 7.3 g
Fat Total: 2.7 g
Fat Saturated: .33 g

1½	**cups white or brown rice (see note below)**
2½ to 3	**cups defatted chicken, beef, or vegetable stock**
1	**teaspoon fragrant curry powder or ¼ teaspoon cumin, ¼ teaspoon coriander, ¼ teaspoon ground fenugreek, ¼ teaspoon turmeric, and a 2-inch cinnamon stick**
1	**teaspoon salt**
2	**teaspoons oil**
1 to 2	**teaspoons cumin seeds**
3	**green onions, finely chopped**
1	**clove garlic, minced or put through a garlic press**
1	**cup mushrooms, sliced**
½	**green and/or red bell pepper, sliced or chopped**
1	**cup broccoli florets (approximately 1-inch pieces)**
½	**cup celery, chopped**
¼	**cup peas, fresh or frozen**
2	**tablespoons chopped cilantro**
1	**cup tomatoes, peeled, seeded, and chopped**
1	**baking dish sprayed with Pam® (8 × 8 inches or 9 × 12 inches)**

Note: If you are using white rice, use 1½ cups rice and 2½ cups liquid. If making brown rice, use 1½ cups rice and 3 cups liquid. In either case, use defatted chicken, beef, or vegetable stock for the liquid.

Wash the rice in a bowl (if using white rice, rinse several times to remove cloudy residue) and allow the rice to soak in the water for 15 minutes. After soaking, drain the rice in a sieve.

In a heavy pot with a tight-fitting lid, bring the chicken stock and spices to a boil over a medium-high flame. Add the drained rice and return to the simmering point; cover and reduce the heat to low. Cook the rice until done, approximately 20 minutes for white rice, 35 to 40 minutes for brown rice. After the liquid has been absorbed, allow the pot to stand covered and off of the heat for 15 minutes or longer.

Next, heat the oil in a large sauté pan over a medium flame; when it is hot, add the cumin seeds and let cook for 30 seconds until it is fragrant and bubbling. Add the onions, garlic, and mushrooms; stir-fry the vegetables for 30 seconds. Next add the bell pepper, broccoli, celery, and peas, stir-frying for another 30 to 45 seconds. Remove the pan from the heat.

Put the cooked rice into the sauté pan and toss with the vegetables. Add the cilantro and tomatoes and toss briefly; taste the pilaf for seasoning. Place the pilaf in a baking dish sprayed with Pam® and cover it with foil. (If you wish, you may refrigerate the pilaf at this point; it may stay refrigerated for up to 48 hours without any harm.)

Bake the covered pilaf at 350° for 30 to 40 minutes until it is steaming and hot. (If you are reheating a cold pilaf, cooking time will increase by 20 to 30 minutes.)

Variations

- Use 2 tablespoons soy sauce and 1 teaspoon grated gingerroot instead of the curry powder and salt. Omit the cumin seeds. In addition, use ¾ cup snow peas instead of regular peas. Season with additional soy sauce at the end.
- Use herbes de Provence instead of curry powder. Omit the cumin seeds. Use parsley or a combination of fresh herbs instead of cilantro.
- In the main recipe or the variations, add 1 cup cooked, shredded chicken.

Risotto

SERVES 4

Risotto (French-style, not Italian) is just as easy to make as regular rice and is certain to be a favorite with family and guests. It is best served immediately after it is done, so timing is important!

Per serving:

Calories: 263
Carbohydrates: 34.2 g
Protein: 12.9 g
Fat Total: 7.8 g
Fat Saturated: 4.6 g

⅓	**cup onion, finely minced**
1	**teaspoon butter or oil plus some Pam®**
1¼	**cups arborio rice**
2¼	**cups simmering liquid (any combination of defatted chicken stock, meat stock, and/or wine)**
⅓	**cup finest quality grated Parmesan cheese**
2	**tablespoons chopped parsley**
	freshly ground black pepper

Note: This is not traditional Italian risotto where you must stand over a hot pot stirring for 20 to 30 minutes while adding the simmering stock dribble by dribble.

In a heavy pot with a tight-fitting lid, sauté the onion in butter and Pam® over medium-low heat until the onion is soft and translucent, around 3 to 5 minutes. Add the rice and stir, coating all of the grains of rice with a bit of butter. Cook and stir the rice for one minute. Add the hot stock and stir, covering when the mixture returns to the boil. Reduce the heat to low. Let the rice cook undisturbed for 20 minutes; then check for doneness. The rice should be cooked but not gummy, and there should not be much (if any) liquid remaining in the bottom of the pot. To test the rice, take a few grains from the pot and carefully chew them; the rice should have the consistency of pasta al dente, (firm but not undercooked). If the rice seems like it is chalky and hard in the very center, add ¼ cup more liquid and cook for another 5 minutes. Remove the rice from the heat. Allow the rice to stand, undisturbed and covered, for 5 to 8 minutes. Finally, stir in the Parmesan cheese and parsley. Garnish with freshly ground pepper and parsley sprigs and serve.

Variations

- Add 3 tablespoons fresh basil and ½ cup chopped sun-dried tomatoes at the end.
- While cooking the onions add ½ cup sliced mushrooms, and add 1 tablespoon chopped fresh thyme at the end.
- Add ¼ cup chopped, toasted walnuts and ¼ cup chopped Kalamata olives.

Spaghetti Squash
with Rosemary

SERVES 4

I am a founding father of the Society to Promote Spaghetti Squash. It's a much-neglected vegetable that deserves more recognition! Tasty, colorful, crunchy, and high in fiber with no inherent fat, you'll be surprised how delicious this is for being so simple to prepare. Surprise your guests the next time you have a party—serve them spaghetti squash and give outdoor prizes to those guests who have never had it before!

1	**medium spaghetti squash, about 8 inches in length**
1 to 3	**tablespoons fruity olive oil, or 1 teaspoon olive oil and Pam®**
2 to 3	**cloves garlic, minced or put through a garlic press**
1 to 2	**tablespoons finely chopped fresh rosemary (do not use dried!)**
	copious grinds of fresh black pepper
	salt to taste (probably about 2 teaspoons)
2 to 4	**tablespoons Parmesan cheese (optional but recommended)**
2	**tablespoons chopped parsley**

Slice squash in half lengthwise and scrape out the seeds with a spoon. Place the squash in a steamer (it may be necessary to cut the squash halves into quarters) and steam, covered, for 20 to 30 minutes until the squash is done. Spaghetti squash is done when a knife enters the inside flesh easily and the color goes from whitish yellow to deep yellow. (Be careful not to overcook, though.)

When the squash is done, remove it from the steamer and allow it to cool for 10 to 15 minutes, or until you can handle it easily. First, turn it upside down to allow any excess liquid to drain off. Next, using a fork, scrape the inside flesh into a large bowl; the squash will form strands not unlike spaghetti (Surprise!).

In a large sauté pan, heat the olive oil over a medium-high flame. When the oil is hot, add the garlic and rosemary, stirring until garlic has cooked thoroughly, about 30 to 45 seconds. Remove the pan from the heat and add the squash; toss the strands in the garlic oil, then season the squash with salt and pepper.

Serve immediately with parsley and Parmesan cheese as garnish, if desired.

Per serving (based on 1 tablespoon olive oil):

Calories: 62.4
Carbohydrates: 8.9 g
Protein: 2 g
Fat Total: 2.4 g
Fat Saturated: .69 g

Spinach with Garlic, Cardamom, and Yogurt Sauce

SERVES 4

A creamy and smooth side dish straight from India. Exquisite!

1	**pound fresh, washed, and stemmed spinach**
⅔	**cup nonfat yogurt**
½	**cup nonfat sour cream**
½ to 1	**teaspoon salt**
1	**teaspoon vegetable oil**
2	**cloves garlic, minced or put through a garlic press**
¼	**teaspoon ground cardamom**
½ to 1	**teaspoon finely minced gingerroot**
⅛ to ½	**teaspoon cayenne (optional)**
¼ to ½	**teaspoon curry powder, garam masala, or ground cumin**

Wash and remove the stems from the spinach. Place the clean spinach in a large colander or sieve in the sink.

Bring a large pot of water or kettle to the boil; when it is boiling, pour the hot water over the spinach, wilting it, turning the spinach over with a spoon once or twice. When all of the spinach has become dark green and limp, rinse immediately with cool water. When the spinach is cool, squeeze out any excess liquid and leave the wilted greens in the colander until needed. If desired, you may chop the spinach.

Place the yogurt and sour cream in a small bowl and add the salt. Stir with a fork until it is completely smooth.

Heat a large skillet over a medium flame; when the skillet is hot, add the oil, garlic, cardamom, gingerroot, optional cayenne, and cumin, curry, or garam masala. When the garlic has cooked lightly (approximately 20 to 30 seconds), add the blanched spinach and cover, reducing the heat to low, cooking only long enough for the spinach to heat through, around 1 to 2 minutes. Add the yogurt-sour cream mixture by tablespoonfuls, mixing well between spoonfuls. When all of the yogurt-sour cream mixture has been incorporated into the pan, remove the spinach from the heat. (If the yogurt remains over a flame and becomes too hot it will "break"—and instead of having a smooth, creamy appearance, the dish will have speckles of curds and watery spinach. Not very attractive.) Taste the creamy spinach for seasoning and serve immediately.

Although this dish can technically be reheated (by reheating quite gently over low heat in order not to break the yogurt), it's so quick and simple to prepare I can't think of any reason why you would want to prepare it ahead of time.

Per serving:

Calories: 88.8
Carbohydrates: 12.8 g
Protein: 7.4 g
Fat Total: 1.6 g
Fat Saturated: .25 g

Squash-Tomato Casserole

SERVES 4

Got those "Summer's Here and I-Got-Too-Many-Zucchini Blues"? Try this!

Pam®
1   **cup thinly sliced onions**
3   **small to medium yellow crookneck squashes, sliced into ¼-inch rounds**
3   **small zucchini, sliced into ¼-inch rounds**
2   **cloves garlic, minced or put through a garlic press**
2   **cups chopped tomatoes, fresh or canned**
¼   **cup defatted stock, white wine, or water**
1   **teaspoon basil**
¼   **teaspoon herbes de Provence**
¼ to ½   **teaspoon lemon-pepper seasoning**
    salt to taste
½   **cup low-fat or nonfat cottage cheese**
½   **cup low-fat buttermilk**
½   **cup nonfat sour cream (optional)**
½   **cup breadcrumbs**
4   **ounces low-fat sharp cheddar cheese**
1   **8- × 8-inch baking dish, coated lightly with Pam**®

Place a large skillet over a medium to medium-low flame. When the skillet is hot, spray it with Pam® and add the onions. Cover and cook until the onions have softened and may have browned lightly, around 10 to 12 minutes. Add the squashes, zucchini, garlic, tomatoes, stock, and herbs. Bring the mixture to a simmer and cook until the squashes are just soft, around 4 minutes. Remove the pan from the heat.

Spray an 8- × 8-inch baking pan with Pam®.

When the vegetables have cooled somewhat, mix in the cottage cheese and optional sour cream with the vegetables. Place the squashes in the prepared baking dish. Drizzle the buttermilk over the vegetable mixture, then sprinkle the cheese and breadcrumbs on top.

Bake uncovered at 350° for 30 to 40 minutes until hot.

Per serving:

Calories: 256
Carbohydrates: 29.3 g
Protein: 18.6 g
Fat Total: 6.7 g
Fat Saturated: .42 g

Summer Squash and Onion Bake

SERVES 4

This lightly herbed, savory, and mildly cheesy vegetable casserole is a perfect accompaniment to many entrées since it doesn't overpower other foods with its taste. Another way to beat those "Summer's Here and I-Got-Too-Many-Zucchini Blues"!

Per serving:

Calories: 235
Carbohydrates: 25 g
Protein: 17.6 g
Fat Total: 6.6 g
Fat Saturated: .4 g

2	**cups very thinly sliced onions**
5	**summer squashes (a mixture of medium yellow crookneck squashes and small zucchini)**
1	**clove garlic, minced or put through a garlic press**
1	**teaspoon thyme**
½ to 1	**teaspoon marjoram**
½	**teaspoon lemon-pepper seasoning**
¼	**cup defatted stock, white wine, or water**
	salt to taste
½	**cup low-fat buttermilk**
4	**ounces reduced-fat sharp cheddar cheese**
4	**ounces nonfat cottage cheese (optional)**
½	**cup breadcrumbs, either store-bought or fresh**
	Pam®
1	**8- × 8-inch baking dish sprayed with Pam®**

Heat a large skillet over a medium flame; when it is hot, spray it with Pam® and add the onions. Cover and cook until the onions have softened and may have browned lightly, around 10 to 12 minutes. Add the squashes, garlic, herbs, and stock. Cover and cook until the squashes are barely soft, around 2 minutes.

Remove the pan from the heat and place the cooked vegetables in a prepared 8- × 8-inch baking dish; sprinkle the cheese on top and briefly mix the cheese with the vegetables using a fork or spatula. Drizzle the buttermilk over the vegetables, then place the breadcrumbs on the top and cover the pan with a lid or foil.

Bake the squashes covered at 350° for 20 to 25 minutes, then remove the foil and bake an additional 10 minutes until the casserole is hot and has lightly browned on top. Serve immediately.

Stir-fry Greens

SERVES 4

Greens are a "comfort food"; they aren't fancy, are quite nutritious, and are a much-neglected alternative to broccoli or green beans. Most southern cooks will be shocked at how little time it takes to prepare this recipe, for in the South, greens are usually cooked for hours; this is not only excessive but reduces a vegetable high in fiber and vitamin A to a soft, gray, nutritionless mush. If you've never had greens that were vibrant in color and firm in texture, try this—you'll be more than pleasantly surprised!

2	**large bunches greens (either collards or kale—preferably small-leaved greens, not large, tough greens)**
½	**teaspoon toasted sesame oil**
1 to 2	**teaspoons finely grated gingerroot**
1 to 2	**cloves garlic, minced**
4 to 5	**tablespoons tamari**

Wash and trim the greens, removing the stems and any parts that seem excessively tough or browned. Slice the greens into ¼-inch strips. Fill a large soup pot with water and bring it to a boil; remove the pot from the heat and add the sliced greens; allow the greens to stand in the hot water for 20 to 30 seconds (or until they are bright green), then drain them in a large colander and immediately rinse them in cold water. When they are cool, shake the colander well to remove any excess liquid.

In a wok or sauté pan, heat the sesame oil over a medium-high flame; when it is hot, add the garlic and gingerroot, cooking for 20 seconds. Add the blanched greens and toss with the garlic and gingerroot. Add 2 tablespoons tamari and continue stirring until the greens are hot, tender, and moist, around 1 to 2 minutes. Taste the greens for seasoning and add additional tamari as needed. Serve immediately.

Variations

- Follow the directions above except eliminate the garlic and sesame oil.
- Add ½ cup sliced mushrooms or water chestnuts while cooking greens.
- Add ¼ cup imitation bacon bits just before serving.
- Use teriyaki sauce instead of tamari.

Per serving:

Calories: 85.2
Carbohydrates: 15.9 g
Protein: 5.5 g
Fat Total: 1.5 g
Fat Saturated: .2 g

Tabbouleh

SERVES 4

The first question asked when the uninitiated tastes tabbouleh is, "What is it?" Bulgur wheat, cracked wheat, or tabbouleh wheat stems from the Caucasus / Middle Eastern regions of Asia. Cooked wheat kernels are first dried, cracked, then sorted by size (fine, medium, coarse). Some people insist on cooking bulgur wheat before using it, others say merely soaking it in warm water is sufficient. My experience has shown that it has never been necessary to actually cook bulgur, but bulgur will differ in its soaking time depending on how old it is and what size it is; the older it is, the longer it needs. Of course, the easiest way to tell if it is ready to use is to take a teaspoon of bulgur from the soaking water and eat it; if it's crunchy and hard, it obviously needs to soak some more!

1	cup bulgur wheat
1	teaspoon olive oil
½	teaspoon fennel seeds
½	teaspoon red pepper flakes
4 to 5	green onions, chopped
2	cloves garlic, minced or put through a garlic press
1 to 2	teaspoons ground cumin
1	teaspoon ground coriander
1½	cups tomatoes, peeled, seeded, and chopped
½	cup each red and green bell peppers
½ to 1	teaspoon garam masala (optional but recommended)
1	tablespoon tamari
2	tablespoons to ¼ cup lemon juice, to taste
¾	cup fresh parsley, chopped

Place the bulgur wheat into a bowl and add 3 to 4 cups of hot or boiling water. Set the bowl aside for 45 minutes.

Place a sauté pan over a moderate flame and add the olive oil. When the oil is hot, add the fennel seeds and the red pepper flakes; as soon as the fennel seeds begins to fry and go from dull green to mild tan in color, add the green onions and garlic. Stir for a minute or so, then add the cumin, coriander, tomatoes, peppers, and garam masala. Continue cooking until the tomatoes have reduced somewhat and are soft, around 2 minutes, then add the tamari and 2 tablespoons of the lemon juice. Set this mixture aside to cool.

After the bulgur wheat has soaked for 45 to 60 minutes, take a teaspoon of the bulgur (draining off the water) and taste it to make sure it has soaked long enough. Bulgur should be chewy but not hard; some people think it has the texture of brown rice, but I think it is firmer than that. If the wheat isn't "done" and seems hard rather than chewy, soak the wheat some more, draining off the cooled water from the bowl and replacing it with more hot water, allowing the bulgur to soak until it is soft, perhaps another 30 minutes. When you're satisfied that the bulgur is "done," take

Per serving:

Calories: 211
Carbohydrates: 43.3 g
Protein: 6.9 g
Fat Total: 2.4 g
Fat Saturated: .19 g

the bowl with the bulgur to the sink along with another large, empty, clean bowl. First, carefully drain off any excess liquid from the soaked wheat. Next, take a handful of the bulgur and squeeze out any liquid, placing this handful of "dry" wheat in the large, empty bowl. Continue in this manner until all of the bulgur has been squeezed and you've got a separate bowlful of "dry" wheat.

Add the parsley and the tomato mixture from the sauté pan to the bulgur, mixing it thoroughly. Taste the tabbouleh for seasoning, adding salt and lemon juice as desired. Serve at room temperature.

Szechuan Eggplant

SERVES 4

Simple and delicious, quick and easy—the trademarks of fine Chinese cuisine!

4 firm Japanese eggplants, or one large regular eggplant
1 teaspoon dried red pepper flakes
3 large cloves garlic, minced or put through a garlic press
4 to 6 green onions, sliced into 1-inch pieces

SAUCE MIXTURE:
3 tablespoons tamari or soy sauce
¼ cup water
¼ teaspoon ground white pepper
1 teaspoon sugar
½ teaspoon vinegar, preferably rice vinegar
1 teaspoon cornstarch
1 teaspoon vegetable oil and Pam®

Wash the eggplants and cut off the stem end. Slice eggplants into 1½- × ½- × ½-inch oblong pieces. Place the eggplant pieces in a large bowl and cover them with water. Allow the eggplant pieces to sit in the water for 20 to 30 minutes.

While the eggplant pieces are soaking, peel the garlic; clean and trim the green onions, chopping them into one-inch pieces. Combine the sauce mixture in a small bowl.

When you're ready to cook, drain the eggplant pieces thoroughly in a colander or sieve, shaking off any excess water. Heat a wok or skillet over a medium-high flame; when the pan is hot, add the oil and spray it with Pam®. Immediately add the eggplant pieces, red pepper flakes, minced garlic, and green onions. Stir-fry until the eggplant pieces are softened and nearly done, around 5 to 7 minutes. Add the sauce mixture and bring everything to a boil. When the sauce has thickened, remove the eggplant pieces and serve immediately.

Per serving:

Calories: 57.1
Carbohydrates: 10.5 g
Protein: 1.8 g
Fat Total: 1.4 g
Fat Saturated: .15 g

175

Wild Rice Pilaf

SERVES 4

Wild rice isn't actually rice but the seed of a grass plant; regardless of its classification, it's quite delicious! Luckily for everyone, the prices of wild rice have gone down in the last ten years, making it a much more reasonable alternative to plain rice. Also, this is a perfect ahead-of-time dish to make the day before and reheat for a dinner or buffet.

Note the two methods of finishing off this dish.

Per serving:

Calories: 250
Carbohydrates: 40.9 g
Protein: 9.3 g
Fat Total: .9 g
Fat Saturated: .035 g

1	**tablespoon salt (for water)**
1	**cup wild rice**
	Pam®
¼	**cup onion, finely diced**
¼	**cup celery, finely diced**
¼	**cup mushrooms, finely diced**
¼	**cup carrot, finely diced**
1	**small clove garlic, minced or put through a garlic press**
1	**teaspoon tamari**
1	**bay leaf**
1 to 2	**teaspoons herbes de Provence or ½ teaspoon thyme, ½ teaspoon basil, ½ teaspoon marjoram, and ½ teaspoon rosemary**
1¼	**cup strong, defatted beef or chicken broth (or both)**
¼	**cup white wine or vermouth**
¼	**cup port or Madeira**
2	**tablespoons parsley**

Fill a large saucepan with water, add the salt, and bring the water to a boil. When it is boiling, add the wild rice and continue to boil for 6 to 8 minutes. Drain the wild rice in a colander or sieve. Set the parboiled rice aside.

Place a heavy pan with a tight-fitting lid over medium heat; spray the pan with Pam® and add the onion, celery, mushrooms, carrot, and garlic. Stir and cook until the onion is tender, around 5 minutes, then add the tamari, bay leaf, herbs, stock, and wines. Bring the stock to the simmering point and add the drained wild rice. Return the rice to the simmering point.

Range-top method. Cover and cook over very low heat until the liquid has been absorbed, anywhere from 20 to 40 minutes. The cooking time will vary depending upon the age of the rice, the weather conditions, and the quality and tightness of the pan. It's fine to check the rice occasionally—and it may even be necessary to add more liquid if the rice isn't done when the liquid has evaporated. After the rice is done and the liquid has been absorbed, remove the covered pan from the heat and allow the rice to sit, undisturbed and covered, for 15 minutes. Finally, add the parsley and serve immediately, or cool and refrigerate.

Oven method. Cover and place in a preheated 350° oven for 45 minutes or more, until the rice has absorbed the liquid and has cooked through. After the rice is done and the liquid has been absorbed, remove the covered pan from the heat and allow the rice to sit, undisturbed and covered, for 15 minutes. At the last moment add the parsley and serve immediately, or cool and refrigerate.

Zucchini-Tomato Curry

SERVES 4

This is an excellent accompaniment to your favorite basic main course. The mild spices create a wonderful counterpoint to anything savory, such as roasted chicken or simple poached fish.

1	**teaspoon oil and Pam®**
1	**teaspoon cumin seeds, crushed but not ground to a powder**
½	**teaspoon ground coriander**
¼	**teaspoon fragrant curry powder or garam masala**
⅛	**teaspoon cayenne pepper (optional)**
1	**small onion, sliced very thinly and cut into half-moons**
1	**clove garlic, minced or put through a garlic press**
	juice of one lemon
4	**small zucchini, sliced into ¼-inch rounds**
1½ to 2	**cups fresh tomato pieces, seeded and peeled, or 1 18-ounce can Italian plum tomatoes, chopped, with ½ cup of the juice**
1	**teaspoon sugar or honey**
	salt (or tamari) to taste

Heat a heavy skillet over a moderate flame; when the skillet is hot, add the oil and the cumin seeds. Allow the cumin to sizzle and cook for 30 seconds or so, until it has emitted a fragrant smell. Spray the hot skillet with Pam® and add the remaining spices and the onion and garlic. Cover the pan and reduce the heat to medium-low; allow it to cook until the onion has softened and may have browned lightly, around 10 minutes. Add the lemon juice, zucchini, tomatoes, and sugar. Toss the vegetables and cover again, cooking until the zucchini has softened and is just done, approximately 3 to 4 minutes. Uncover the pan and salt to taste, correcting the seasoning as desired. Serve immediately.

Per serving:

Calories: 75.1
Carbohydrates: 13.7 g
Protein: 3.3 g
Fat Total: 2 g
Fat Saturated: .23 g

Chickpea Salad

SERVES 4

This refreshing and delicately spiced salad is perfect for a picnic or a hot summer's day. AND it is a complete source of vegetarian protein.

2	**ears of corn, yellow or white**
	Pam®
½	**teaspoon vegetable oil**
2	**cloves garlic, minced or put through a garlic press**
1½	**teaspoons cumin**
1	**teaspoon chili powder**
1	**vegetable bouillon cube (such as Morga) or ⅓ cup very flavorful, defatted chicken stock**
⅓	**cup water (see directions)**
2½ to 3	**cups cooked chickpeas, drained**
1	**large or 2 small ripe tomatoes, chopped**
½	**green or red bell pepper, diced**
1	**small cucumber, peeled, seeded, and diced**
¼	**cup chopped cilantro**
2	**teaspoons Dijon mustard**
3 to 4	**tablespoons balsamic vinegar**
	juice of 1 lemon
½	**teaspoon salt**
½ to 2	**teaspoons sugar**

Husk the corn, then take each ear and scrub it under cool, running water to remove any of the corn silk. Either with a knife or with one of those "corn-ing gadgets," remove the kernels from the cob and place the kernels into a bowl. Set them aside.

Heat a skillet over a medium flame; when the pan is hot, spray it with Pam® and add the oil and the garlic. Stir and cook the garlic for about 30 seconds or so, then add the corn kernels and cumin, chili powder, vegetable bouillon cube, and water. (If using chicken stock, omit the water.) Bring the mixture to a simmer, reduce the flame to medium-low, and cook the corn for 5 minutes until it is just done. Remove the skillet from the heat and let it cool a bit.

Place the chickpeas in a large bowl. Add the fresh green or red bell pepper, cucumber, tomatoes, and cilantro, mixing briefly. In a separate small bowl combine the Dijon mustard, vinegar, lemon juice, salt, and sugar, mixing well so that you have a smooth vinaigrette. Pour the vinaigrette over the chickpeas, stirring briefly. Next pour the cooled corn mixture into the chickpea bowl and stir. Taste the salad for seasoning.

Serve the salad cold or at room temperature. To serve, simply stir to redistribute the vinaigrette and place ½ to ⅔ cup or so on a large lettuce leaf. Garnish with a whole cilantro leaf.

Per serving:

Calories: 258
Carbohydrates: 50.8 g
Protein: 10.2 g
Fat Total: 3.4 g
Fat Saturated: .4 g

178

Dijon Potato Salad

SERVES 4

This recipe has a creamy, velvety dressing, unlike Grandma's thick-as-glue potato salad! Delicious and mustardy, this is great for a picnic or with a light lunch. The amount of mustard can be reduced if you think it is too intense.

6	small new red potatoes
	salt and pepper
⅓	cup dry vermouth, white wine, or water

FOR THE DRESSING:

2	tablespoons Dijon mustard
½ to 1	teaspoon sugar
½	cup nonfat yogurt
2	tablespoons reduced-fat mayonnaise
2	tablespoons nonfat sour cream (optional)
1	teaspoon fresh tarragon, chopped
3	tablespoons finely chopped fresh parsley
2	green onions, finely chopped
	juice of 1 lemon
	salt to taste

Per serving:

Calories: 184
Carbohydrates: 36 g
Protein: 5.2 g
Fat Total: 2.2 g
Fat Saturated: .1 g

Wash the potatoes, then slice them into ¼-inch rounds. Place the potato rounds in a steamer basket and steam, covered, for 10 to 15 minutes, until the potatoes are just cooked through. (Insert a small knife into the center of a potato slice; if the knife goes in easily, it is done.) When the potatoes are done, turn off heat and allow the potatoes to stand covered for an additional 10 minutes.

As the potatoes are cooking, prepare the dressing by mixing the remaining dressing ingredients in a bowl.

When the potatoes have cooled somewhat, place them carefully in a large bowl. Sprinkle the warm potato slices with the vermouth, salt, and pepper; toss them gently, being careful not to break the slices up into small pieces. Allow the potatoes to absorb the wine and seasonings until they are cool, gently turning once or twice during the cooling process to evenly distribute the seasonings.

When potatoes have completely cooled, pour the dressing into the bowl and toss the salad gently. Taste the potatoes for seasoning and refrigerate. (**Note:** Foods eaten cold usually need additional salt. If you're in doubt, season with salt until you're satisfied and then refrigerate the salad; after the salad is cold, reseason if necessary. Also, potato salad that is freshly made will be creamier and smoother than day-old salad, as the potatoes will absorb some of the dressing.)

Dilled Potato Salad

SERVES 4

Spiked with dill, this salad is colorful, healthy, and quite good. The taste is much perkier than your average garden-variety potato salad, a fact which I think is unquestionably in its favor!

6	**small new red potatoes**
	salt and pepper
⅓	**cup water**

THE DRESSING:

¼	**cup chopped fresh dill**
½	**cup nonfat yogurt**
2	**tablespoons reduced-fat mayonnaise**
2	**tablespoons nonfat sour cream**
1 to 2	**teaspoons Dijon mustard or horseradish mustard**
1	**tablespoon lemon juice**
½ to 1	**teaspoon sugar**
⅓	**cup celery, chopped into ¼-inch cubes**
½	**cup red bell pepper, chopped into ¼-inch cubes**
2	**green onions, finely chopped**
	salt and pepper to taste

Wash the potatoes and slice them into ¼-inch rounds. Place the potato slices in a steamer basket and steam, covered, for 10 to 15 minutes, until the potatoes are just cooked through. (Insert a small knife into the center of a potato slice; if the knife goes in easily, it is done.) When they are done, turn off heat and allow the potatoes to stand covered for 10 more minutes.

As the potatoes are cooking, prepare the dressing by mixing the remaining dressing ingredients in a bowl or jar.

When the potatoes have cooled somewhat, place them carefully in a large bowl. Sprinkle the warm potato slices with the water, salt, and pepper; toss them gently, being careful not to break the slices up into small pieces. Allow the potatoes to absorb the water and seasonings until they are cool, gently turning once or twice during the cooling process to evenly distribute the seasonings.

Fold the dressing into the potatoes when they have sufficiently cooled; taste for seasoning, adding salt as necessary. Refrigerate the salad until ready to serve. (**Note:** Foods eaten cold usually need additional salt. If you're in doubt, season with salt until you're satisfied and then refrigerate the salad; after the salad is cold, reseason if necessary. Also, potato salad that is freshly made will be creamier and smoother than day-old salad, as the potatoes will absorb some of the dressing.)

Per serving:

Calories: 176
Carbohydrates: 36.6 g
Protein: 5.1 g
Fat Total: 2 g
Fat Saturated: .073 g

Five-Bean Salad

SERVES 10 TO 12

Nothing brings back instant memories of summer barbecues and family re-unions like cold bean salads. Most common would be a three-bean salad, but my mother had a recipe for five-bean salad, which I thought infinitely superior because it had more beans! This salad should be filed under EMBARRASSINGLY EASY TO MAKE and quite tasty too. I make no apologies for the canned beans—as far as I'm concerned, canned beans are part and parcel of bean salads, and old-fashioned bean salads wouldn't taste the same if you used fresh beans!

1	15-ounce can each red beans, navy beans, and garbanzo beans (chickpeas)
1	15-ounce can wax beans (or 1½ cups fresh steamed wax beans, cut into 2-inch pieces)
1	15-ounce can green beans (or 1½ cups fresh steamed green beans, cut into 2-inch pieces)
2 to 3	green onions, sliced very thinly
1	red bell pepper, diced into ¼-inch cubes

Per serving (for 10):

Calories: 170
Carbohydrates: 31.5 g
Protein: 7.7 g
Fat Total: 2.2 g
Fat Saturated: .33 g

VINAIGRETTE:

2 to 5	tablespoons sugar (depending on how sweet you like bean salad)
½	cup cider vinegar
1	clove garlic, finely minced or put through a garlic press
1	tablespoon Dijon mustard
⅓	cup finely chopped fresh parsley
1	teaspoon dried basil
1	tablespoon olive oil
	salt and pepper to taste

Drain the canned beans in a large colander, rinsing them under cold water to remove any excess salt. Place the rinsed beans in a large bowl. Add the green onions and the red bell pepper.

In a small bowl or jar, mix the vinaigrette ingredients until smooth, then pour the vinaigrette over the beans: stir the salad and allow to marinate for at least 2 hours. Garnish with fresh parsley or fresh basil.

Chinese Chicken Salad

SERVES 4

In the mid-'80s it seemed every trendy restaurant had Chinese chicken salad on their menu; some were decidedly better than others in taste, but this one is unquestionably the lowest in fat and the tastiest to boot.

2	**whole chicken breasts, boneless and skinless, with any excess fat removed**
4	**cups washed, shredded greens (such as lettuce or spinach)**
2	**cups washed, shredded Chinese cabbage (napa cabbage)**
1	**red bell pepper, sliced into thin strips**
½	**cucumber, peeled, sliced, and seeded**
2	**cups bean sprouts**
2	**tablespoons toasted sesame seeds (see note below)**

VINAIGRETTE:

1	**teaspoon toasted sesame oil**
1	**1-inch piece of gingerroot, peeled and chopped**
¼	**cup rice wine vinegar**
¼	**cup water**
2	**tablespoons oyster sauce (see Ingredients page 226)**
1	**tablespoon sugar**
¼	**cup cilantro**
1	**teaspoon red pepper flakes**
½	**teaspoon salt**
1	**tablespoon poppy seeds**

Note: To toast sesame seeds, place the sesame seeds in a small sauté pan over a moderate flame. Constantly stir the seeds until they just get hot and begin to emit a roasted, toasty smell, around 3 minutes. Remove them immediately—remember, sesame seeds will continue to roast after they've been removed from the heat, so it's better to undertoast them than overtoast them.

Per serving:

Calories: 256
Carbohydrates: 16.5 g
Protein: 32.5 g
Total Fat: 7.4 g
Fat Saturated: 1.2 g

Remove any excess fat from the chicken breasts and slice them into 4 equal portions. Place the chicken breasts in a saucepan filled with salted water and bring to a simmer over a moderate flame; reduce the heat to low and continue to simmer the chicken until it is just done (around 8 minutes). Remove the chicken from the hot water and drain it on paper towels, allowing it to cool.

Chop the vegetables and the greens, and set them aside. Blanch the bean sprouts briefly by dropping them in boiling water for 15 seconds, then immediately drain them in a colander and rinse them in cold water. Toast the sesame seeds (*see note above*).

For the vinaigrette, place the sesame oil, gingerroot, rice wine vinegar, water, oyster sauce, and sugar in a blender or food processor and blend until you have a smooth mixture, around 1 minute's worth of processing, pushing the ginger down with a spatula as necessary. Add the cilantro and blend in 1 or 2 quick bursts, briefly chopping the cilantro. Remove the vinaigrette from the blender or processor and add the remaining ingredients and stir. Refrigerate the vinaigrette until needed.

When chicken has cooled, slice the breasts into bite-sized pieces or into strips.

To assemble, arrange the greens and cabbage prettily on a plate or in a wide, shallow bowl; artistically top the shredded greens with the sprouts, chicken, red bell pepper, and cucumber. Sprinkle some sesame seeds over the top and garnish with a sprig of cilantro. When ready to serve, spoon the vinaigrette over the salad and serve cold or cool.

Variation

- If you prefer a thicker vinaigrette, blend 1 teaspoon of arrowroot with the ¼ cup water and bring the mixture to a boil. Add the thickened water to the vinaigrette.

Lentil Salad

SERVES 4

Per serving:

Calories: 206
Carbohydrates: 33 g
Protein: 12 g
Fat Total: 4.3 g
Fat Saturated: .57 g

Bean salads are wonderfully nutritious and tasty as well—and a nice change of pace from the more mundane lettuce-tomato-cucumber salad.

1	**cup lentils, soaked for 4 hours or more**
3	**cups water**
3	**tablespoons tamari**

VINAIGRETTE:

¼	**teaspoon garlic, mashed or put through a garlic press**
1 to 2	**teaspoons Dijon mustard**
1 to 2	**teaspoons sugar**
1	**teaspoon basil**
3	**tablespoons chopped parsley**
2	**tablespoons lemon juice**
2 to 3	**tablespoons red wine vinegar**
1	**tablespoon olive oil**
¼	**cup water**
1	**cup chopped fresh tomato**
½ to ¾	**cup diced celery**
2	**green onions, finely minced (optional)**
½	**red bell pepper, diced**
½ to 1	**cup sliced snow peas**
½ to 1	**cup blanched broccoli florets**

Pick over the lentils to see if there is any debris, picking out any matter such as dirt or tiny pebbles. Place the lentils in a bowl and add enough cool water to come at least 1 inch above the lentils. Allow the lentils to soak for 4 hours.

After soaking, drain the soaked lentils and rinse them thoroughly in cool water. Place the lentils in a heavy pot and add 3 cups water and the tamari. Bring the lentils to the simmering point and cover. Depending on the lentils, they could cook for anywhere from 15 minutes to 45 minutes until done. Periodically check the lentils, and when they're soft but not mushy, remove them from the heat, allowing them to cool. When they have cooled, drain them in a sieve or colander.

Combine the ingredients for the vinaigrette in a large bowl, mixing well. Add the drained lentils, tossing gently in the vinaigrette. Taste for seasoning, adding salt, sugar, and additional vinegar as desired. Add the remaining ingredients and again toss gently. Cover the salad and refrigerate until needed. (I think this salad is best served at room temperature, so you may wish to remove the salad from the refrigerator for an hour, covered, before serving.)

To serve, place ½ to ⅔ cup of the drained lentil salad on a large lettuce leaf.

Navy Bean Salad
with Vinaigrette

SERVES 4

I love navy beans—and I've never discovered exactly why they're called navy beans! Were they a popular food with sea-bound voyagers? Were they a standard with early navy cooks? They are unquestionably one of the most versatile and appealing of beans, with their small, pea-shaped size, their gentle, creamy color, and mild taste.

FOR THE VINAIGRETTE:

½	**teaspoon thyme**
⅓	**cup red wine vinegar**
1	**tablespoon lemon juice**
1	**tablespoon water**
1	**tablespoon sugar**
1	**tablespoon Dijon mustard**
¼	**cup fresh basil or tarragon, finely chopped**
1	**clove garlic, minced or put through a garlic press**
1	**tablespoon olive oil**
2	**cups cooked navy beans (if canned, rinse well)**
1	**cup blanched green beans or sugar snap peas (see note below)**
½	**each red and green bell pepper, chopped**
4	**green onions, finely chopped**
½	**cup chopped parsley**
	salt and pepper to taste

Note: To blanch beans or snap peas, bring a large saucepan of water to a boil; add the cleaned beans or peas, and allow them to cook for 30 to 60 seconds until they are bright green and are lightly cooked, still retaining their crispness. Drain the beans or peas into a colander or sieve, rinsing well with cold water until the vegetables are cool.

Combine the ingredients for the vinaigrette in a large bowl, mixing well.

Add remaining ingredients in the same bowl with the vinaigrette; fold gently until everything is coated with the vinaigrette. Serve the salad at room temperature.

Variations

- Use Ginger-Miso (*see* page 195) dressing instead of vinaigrette.
- Add 1 to 2 tablespoons grated Parmesan cheese to vinaigrette. (This adds fat, but it also adds taste. The choice is yours.)

Per serving:

*Calories: 223
Carbohydrates: 37.5 g
Protein: 11.2 g
Fat Total: 4.3 g
Fat Saturated: .67 g*

Pasta Salad

SERVES 4

Per serving:

Calories: 348
Carbohydrates: 53.6 g
Protein: 14.5 g
Fat Total: 8.7 g
Fat Saturated: 3.2 g

1	tablespoon olive oil
1	clove garlic, minced or put through a garlic press
8	ounces pasta, preferably fusilli or rotini

FOR THE VINAIGRETTE:

⅓	cup red wine vinegar
2	tablespoons lemon juice
2	teaspoons Dijon mustard
1	teaspoon sugar
1	teaspoon oregano
¼	teaspoon black pepper
1	clove garlic, minced (optional)

½	small zucchini, julienned and blanched (see note below)
½	cup carrots, julienned and blanched (see note below)
½	each red and green bell pepper, finely sliced and blanched (see note below)
¼	cup pepperocini, diced
½ to ¾	cup tomatoes, peeled, seeded, and chopped
¼	cup Parmesan cheese
⅓	cup fresh basil, chopped
¼	cup parsley, chopped
2	green onions, finely minced
	salt and pepper to taste

Note: To blanch vegetables, bring a large saucepan of water to the boil; add the cleaned vegetables and allow them to cook for 30 to 60 seconds until they are lightly cooked, but still retain their crispness. Drain the vegetables into a colander or sieve, rinsing well with cold water until the vegetables are cool.

Combine the garlic and 1 tablespoon of olive oil in a small bowl. Set it aside.

Bring a large pot of water to a boil (add 1 tablespoon of salt if desired). Add the pasta and continue to boil until it is *almost* done; it should still be on the underdone side. Drain the pasta in a colander and rinse under cold water until it is no longer hot. When the pasta is cool, shake off any excess water, then place the cooked, drained pasta in a large bowl. Add the olive oil-garlic mixture to the pasta and toss gently.

Combine the ingredients for the vinaigrette in a bowl or jar, mixing well, then set it aside.

Individually blanch the zucchini, carrots, and bell peppers in boiling water until they are bright in color and slightly tender, yet retain their crispness. (You don't want to add them all at once, since they will have different cooking times.) Drain them in a colander and rinse under cold water until they are cool. Combine the vegetables with the pasta, adding the pepperocini, tomatoes, cheese, and green onions; toss the vegetables with the pasta. Add the vinaigrette and toss again, tasting for seasoning, adding salt as desired. Refrigerate until ready to eat.

I think this pasta is best served cool, not cold.

Variations

- Add 1 cup cooked, chopped chicken breast.
- Substitute any vegetable in season: sugar snap peas, snow peas, mushrooms, artichoke hearts, fresh fennel, or celery.

Spinach Fusilli Salad

SERVES 4

	Zippy Poppy Seed Dressing (see page 197)
12	*ounces spinach fusilli, cooked until just tender*
¼ to ⅓	*pound snow peas, raw or blanched*
1	*cup finely sliced or torn radicchio*
2	*oranges, peeled with the sections removed*
4	*green onions, chopped into ¼-inch pieces (optional)*
½	*yellow bell pepper, sliced into thin strips*

Prepare the Zippy Poppy Seed Dressing according to directions.

Bring a large pot of water to the boil. Add 1 tablespoon salt (if desired) and then the spinach fusilli. Boil the pasta for 5 to 8 minutes until the pasta is barely done and not mushy. Drain the pasta in a colander and rinse with cold water until it is cool. Set it aside to drain.

Clean the snow peas and trim any untidy ends. (If desired, you may blanch the snow peas by putting them in boiling water for 20 seconds, then draining and rinsing in cold water.) Wash the radicchio and tear it into bite-sized pieces. Peel the oranges completely and remove the sections from the inner membrane by cutting down toward the center, much the same as you would section a grapefruit, except in this case you're dealing with the entire fruit and not a halved fruit. Set aside the sectioned orange pieces. Wash and slice the yellow bell pepper.

Combine the cooked fusilli, vegetables, and fruit. Toss gently and pour on the salad dressing to taste. Serve the salad immediately with additional dressing on the side, if desired. (**Note:** If the salad sits in the refrigerator for a day or two, it may be necessary to reseason it with more salad dressing since pasta tends to absorb liquids—in this case, the dressing.)

Per serving:

Calories: 415
Carbohydrates: 84.8 g
Protein: 13.5 g
Fat Total: 2.8 g
Fat Saturated: .2 g

Spaghetti Squash Salad

SERVES 4

1 small to medium spaghetti squash
2 tablespoons sesame seeds, toasted lightly
   salt to taste

SALAD DRESSING:

¼ rice wine vinegar
¼ cup water
1 tablespoon finely grated gingerroot
1 teaspoon hot Chinese mustard, wasabi (or horseradish), or Dijon
     mustard
½ teaspoon toasted sesame oil (optional)
   salt to taste
1 clove garlic, finely minced or put through a garlic press
1 teaspoon red pepper flakes
2 to 4 teaspoons sugar

1 each red and green bell peppers

Slice the spaghetti squash in half lengthwise and scoop out the seeds and stringy matter.

Place the squash in a steamer (it may be necessary to slice it into quarters to fit the pot), with 1 to 2 inches of water in the bottom. Bring the water to a boil over high heat, covering the steamer once the boil has been reached. Reduce the heat to medium and steam until the squash is tender, around 15 to 25 minutes. Meanwhile, lightly toast the sesame seeds by placing them in a small sauté pan and tossing them over medium heat until they are just tan and have a pleasant toasted aroma. Remove the seeds from the hot pan and set them aside in a small bowl, keeping in mind that sesame seeds will continue to toast *after* they've been removed from the heat; it's better to err on the side of undercooking them than overcooking them.

Combine the salad dressing ingredients in a blender or food processor and blend until thoroughly mixed, around 45 seconds. Set the salad dressing aside.

Remove the squash from the steamer when it is done; spaghetti squash is done when a knife enters the inside flesh easily and the color goes from whitish yellow to deep yellow. Allow it to cool for 10 minutes. After cooling, use a fork and scrape the "spaghetti" from the inside of the warm squash, placing the yellow squash in a bowl, a casserole dish, or on 4 salad plates.

Wash, core, and slice bell peppers into thin strips. Place the pepper slices in the same steamer and steam, covered, over moderate heat, until the pepper strips are brightly colored and just tender, approximately 1

Per serving:

Calories: 103
Carbohydrates: 16.6 g
Protein: 2.5 g
Fat Total: 3.9 g
Fat Saturated: .57 g

minute. Remove the peppers from the steamer. The cooked squash and peppers may be placed artistically on a plate, in bowls, or in a festive casserole dish.

Allow the squash to cool some more until it is just barely warm. Drain off any liquid that may have accumulated in the bowl or plate. Pour the dressing over squash and peppers, sprinkling the top with the toasted sesame seeds. Serve the salad at room temperature or cover and refrigerate until needed. Garnish the squash attractively with cilantro leaves.

Shrimp and Spinach Salad

SERVES 4

24   medium, peeled, deveined shrimp

Celery Seed Dressing (see page 194) or Zippy Poppy Seed Dressing (see page 197)

16   ounces fresh spinach, washed and torn into bite-sized pieces, or a mixture of fresh greens
1   tablespoon lemon juice
a sprinkling of salt
2   ruby red grapefruit, peeled and sectioned
2   navel oranges, peeled and sectioned
½   red onion, cut into very thin half-rings (optional)
garlic croutons (optional but recommended)

Per serving (with Celery Seed Dressing):

Calories: 118
Carbohydrates: 28.1 g
Protein: 13.64 g
Fat Total: 1.9 g
Fat Saturated: .29 g

Per serving (with Zippy Poppy Seed Dressing):

Calories: 179.1
Carbohydrates: 28.9 g
Protein: 13.8 g
Fat Total: 2.8 g
Fat Saturated: .41 g

Peel the shells off the shrimp, then devein each shrimp by drawing a sharp knife along the upper center portion down the length of the tail, cutting ¼-inch deep. Inside the cut you may (or may not) see a brownish, grayish "vein"; this is easily removed if you hold the shrimp under cool, running water. Continue until all of the shrimp are cleaned and deveined. Toss the shrimp with the lemon juice and salt in a bowl. Either broil or grill the shrimp until just done, about 1 to 2 minutes on each side. Let them cool.

Prepare the salad dressing of your choice. (The Celery Seed Dressing is milder; the Zippy Poppy Seed Dressing is livelier.)

Place the washed spinach or salad greens on 4 plates. Peel and section the grapefruit and oranges, arranging them prettily over the salad greens. Add the optional red onion on top of the fruits.

Attractively arrange 6 cooked shrimp on each plate, garnishing with the optional croutons.

Pour the salad dressing over each salad before serving. Eat immediately.

189

Chicken Salad
with Fresh Herbs

SERVES 4

Who says chicken salad is always full of mayonnaise?

Per serving:

Calories: 203
Carbohydrates: 10.4 g
Protein: 30.9 g
Fat Total: 3.4 g
Fat Saturated: .48 g

4	**chicken breast halves, boneless and skinless**
2	**tablespoons reduced-fat mayonnaise**
⅓	**cup nonfat yogurt**
⅓	**cup nonfat sour cream**
1	**tablespoon Dijon mustard**
1	**tablespoon tamari**
½ to 1	**teaspoon sugar**
1	**cup celery, chopped into ¼-inch pieces**
3	**tablespoons freshly chopped parsley**
1	**teaspoon fresh thyme, chopped or ½ teaspoon dried thyme**
1 to 2	**tablespoons chopped fresh Mexican marigold mint or tarragon, or ½ teaspoon dried tarragon**
3	**tablespoons fresh chives or the green part of 2 green onions, chopped**
¼	**cup sweet pickle relish (optional)**
	cracked black pepper to taste

Remove any excess fat from the chicken breasts.

Place the trimmed chicken breasts in a large pan and fill with water; place the pan over medium heat and bring it to a simmer. Reduce the flame to low, simmering (not boiling!) until the breasts are just done, approximately 7 to 10 minutes. (Check by inserting a knife into the thickest portion of the breast; it should be just done with perhaps a tiniest bit of pink.) Remove the breasts from the pan and rinse under cold water. Place the cooked chicken on a plate, covering and refrigerating until it is cold.

When the chicken has cooled completely, either chop it into small pieces (¼-inch cubes) or chop the chicken roughly, then place it in a food processor and process in short, quick spurts until the chicken is chopped but not a paste. Set aside.

Combine the remaining ingredients in a large bowl.

Scoop the chicken out of the processor and place it in the large bowl with the dressing, coating it with the mixture evenly. Taste for seasoning, adding salt, mustard, or more nonfat sour cream and yogurt as desired. (Remember: Foods served chilled usually require more salt than foods served warm.) Refrigerate the salad until needed, serving it on toasted whole wheat bread with lettuce, or in a large, ripe tomato.

Variations

- Substitute 2 teaspoons curry powder instead of tarragon and thyme.
- Substitute 1 tablespoon finely grated gingerroot for herbs and add ½ teaspoon toasted sesame oil, 3 tablespoons chopped cilantro, and season to taste with tamari instead of salt.

Summer Tuna Salad

SERVES 4

There's no real reason to have tuna salad swimming in high-fat mayonnaise, other than the usual, "But that's the way my mother always made it. . . ."! Try this and you'll never miss the calories or fat.

2	6½-ounce cans of solid white tuna packed in water
⅔	cup finely chopped celery
3	tablespoons finely chopped parsley
2	green onions, finely chopped
½	teaspoon thyme
1	tablespoon finely chopped fresh basil or ½ teaspoon dried basil
1	tablespoon tamari
1 to 2	teaspoons Dijon mustard
⅓	cup nonfat yogurt
⅓	cup nonfat sour cream
2	tablespoons reduced-fat mayonnaise
1	tablespoon lemon juice or white wine vinegar
	dash of cayenne pepper
½	cup chopped apple (optional)
	salt and pepper to taste

Open the cans of tuna and squeeze out as much liquid as possible, then place the tuna in a bowl. Break up the tuna somewhat, leaving some largish chunks.

Add all of the remaining ingredients to the same bowl with the tuna and mix thoroughly. Taste it for seasoning, adding salt or whatever tickles your fancy. Keep the salad refrigerated until needed.

Per serving:

Calories: 160
Carbohydrates: 9.6 g
Protein: 23.4 g
Fat Total: 2.6 g
Fat Saturated: .28 g

Tropical Chicken Salad

SERVES 4

This is one of those salad-as-a-meal dishes. It is brimming with tastes, both sweet and sour, and is quite enlivening on a hot summer's eve. As with all fruit, freshness and ripeness is paramount.

1½	teaspoons arrowroot
½	cup water
⅓	cup raspberry vinegar
1½	tablespoons Dijon mustard
1 to 2	tablespoons fresh sage, finely chopped
1	teaspoon salt
½	teaspoon sugar
4	boneless, skinless chicken breast halves, broiled or grilled
	salt and pepper
1	ripe papaya, peeled and cut into bite-sized pieces
1	ripe mango, peeled and cut into bite-sized pieces
2	cups fresh pineapple pieces, or canned pineapple pieces packed in juice
2	tablespoons lemon juice and/or pineapple juice
1	cup raspberries
16	ounces mixed salad greens, such as spinach, lettuce, and escarole, torn into bite-sized pieces
½	cup mint leaves, chopped
¼	cup walnuts (optional)

**Per serving
(without walnuts):**

*Calories: 285
Carbohydrates: 37.1 g
Protein: 32.1 g
Fat Total: 2.8 g
Fat Saturated: .57 g*

**Per serving
(with walnuts):**

*Calories: 333
Carbohydrates: 38.5 g
Protein: 33.2 g
Fat Total: 7.4 g
Fat Saturated: .99 g*

Combine the arrowroot and water in a small saucepan and mix thoroughly. Place the pan over medium heat and stir until the mixture comes to a boil, thickens, and turns from milky in appearance to clear. Remove immediately from the heat and add the vinegar, mustard, sage, salt, and sugar. Stir well and set aside.

Remove any excess fat from the chicken breasts. Lightly season the chicken breasts with salt and pepper and broil or grill until just done, about 4 to 5 minutes on each side. Remove the breasts from the heat and cool.

Combine the papaya, mango, pineapple, and lemon juice in a bowl. Be sure to coat the papaya and mango with lemon since they discolor easily. (Or you could substitute pineapple juice for the lemon, since pineapple juice is high in ascorbic acid, the ingredient in lemon juice that helps prevent discoloration.)

Place the washed and trimmed salad greens on 4 plates and arrange the fruits on top. Slice the chicken breasts into long, thin pieces and arrange 1 breast on each plate prettily on top of the fruit; garnish with fresh, chopped mint leaves, raspberries, and optional walnuts. Pour raspberry vinaigrette on top and eat immediately.

Tortellini Salad

SERVES 4

2	9-ounce packages of fresh tortellini, such as spinach or egg filled with chicken or cheese
½	cup rice wine vinegar
½	teaspoon toasted sesame oil
1	tablespoon tamari
3	tablespoons chopped cilantro
1	clove garlic, minced or put through a garlic press
2	teaspoons freshly grated gingerroot
¼ to ½	teaspoon red pepper flakes
1	cup snow peas, blanched and sliced on the diagonal into ½-inch pieces
1	red bell pepper, chopped into ¼-inch cubes
2	chopped green onions

Per serving:

Calories: 283
Carbohydrates: 46.3 g
Protein: 15.2 g
Fat Total: 4.3 g
Fat Saturated: .05 g

Bring a large pan of water to a boil; add the tortellini and cook for 3 to 5 minutes, or until they are just done. Drain immediately in a colander and rinse them in cold water until they have cooled somewhat, shaking off any excess water. Allow the tortellini to continue to drain as you proceed.

In a bowl or jar, combine the vinegar, sesame oil, tamari, cilantro, garlic, gingerroot, and red pepper flakes; mix well or shake until thoroughly blended.

Blanch the snow peas by bringing a large saucepan of water to a boil and adding the cleaned peas, allowing them to cook for 30 seconds until they are lightly cooked and have turned bright green, still retaining their crispness. Drain the snow peas into a colander or sieve, rinsing well with cold water until they are cool. Slice the snow peas on the diagonal into ½-inch pieces, forming a rhombus. (I can hear it now . . . : "Rhombus? What's a *rhombus*?" Get out your dictionary and look it up!)

Place the drained tortellini, bell pepper, onions, and snow peas in a bowl; toss gently. Pour the vinaigrette mixture on top and toss gently, coating evenly. Serve immediately or refrigerate until needed.

Blue Cheese Dressing

I love blue cheese dressing. It's a pungent yet creamy contrast to the fresh green taste of a spring salad. Makes my mouth water just thinking about it . . . !

Per ounce:

Calories: 28.2
Carbohydrates: 2.3 g
Protein: 2 g
Fat Total: 1.2 g
Fat Saturated: .76 g

1	**cup nonfat yogurt**
½	**cup nonfat buttermilk**
¼	**cup nonfat sour cream**
½	**cup crumbled blue cheese**
1 to 2	**teaspoons Dijon mustard**
1	**tablespoon lemon juice**
⅛	**teaspoon minced garlic**
2 to 3	**tablespoons freshly chopped parsley or basil**
½ to 1	**teaspoon sugar**
½ to 1	**teaspoon salt**
	freshly ground pepper to taste
2	**tablespoons reduced-fat mayonnaise (optional)**

Combine all of the ingredients in a bowl and mix well. Taste for seasoning and refrigerate until needed.

Celery Seed Dressing

Per ounce with olive oil:

Calories: 36.9
Carbohydrates: 5.8 g
Protein: .44 g
Fat Total: 1.7 g
Fat Saturated: .21 g

Per ounce without olive oil:

Calories: 26.7
Carbohydrates: 5.8 g
Protein: .44 g
Fat Total: .57 g
Fat Saturated: .057 g

This mild dressing is best for truly "mixed" salads, that is, salads that are not just mixed greens. Since it is so simple and mild, it enhances any salad made with a variety of ingredients, such as avocados, oranges, apples, steamed broccoli, blanched green beans, and so on.

1½ to 2	**teaspoons arrowroot (the lesser amount for a thinner dressing)**
½	**cup water**
2	**tablespoons sugar**
1	**teaspoon salt**
2	**teaspoons Dijon mustard**
2	**tablespoons finely minced green onion or chives**
½	**cup mild white or rice wine vinegar**
1	**tablespoon balsamic vinegar**
2	**teaspoons olive oil (optional)**
2	**tablespoons celery seed**

Mix the arrowroot, water, sugar, and salt thoroughly in a small saucepan. Place the pan over moderate heat and stir continuously until the mixture has come to a boil and has changed from milky in appearance to clear and is thick. Remove from heat.

Place the thick arrowroot mixture in a bowl. Add the remaining ingredients and mix with a whisk until thoroughly blended. Refrigerate the dressing until needed.

Variation

- For a creamier taste, add ¼ cup nonfat sour cream to the dressing.

Ginger-Miso Dressing

Miso is a fermented soy product from Japan. It can be found at health-food stores either in plastic tubs in the refrigerated section or in aseptically sealed pouches in the macrobiotic section. Miso is like yogurt; it contains active cultures, and some people say that the aseptic packaging kills the beneficial cultures—thus, those who want miso's health benefits are left with only the refrigerated product. Miso stored in the refrigerator will last practically indefinitely, so once you purchase it, you won't have to worry about it spoiling.

1	**1-inch square piece of gingerroot, peeled and roughly chopped**
2	**tablespoons miso (mugi miso recommended; i.e., barley miso)**
¼	**cup rice wine vinegar**
¼	**cup water**
1 to 2	**teaspoons honey, to taste**
	juice of ½ lemon
½	**teaspoon toasted sesame oil**

Per ounce:

Calories: 33.5
Carbohydrates: 5.9 g
Protein: .96 g
Fat Total: .98 g
Fat Saturated: .15 g

Place all of the ingredients into a blender and blend until smooth, around 1 minute. Keep the dressing refrigerated for up to 5 days.

Variations

- Add 1 tablespoon chopped cilantro to the dressing.
- Add ½ teaspoon chili (hot) oil or Tabasco® for a spicier taste.
- Add 1 tablespoon toasted sesame seeds at the end for texture.
- Add 1 tablespoon poppy seeds for a more traditional dressing.
- Add ¼ cup plain yogurt or buttermilk for a creamier dressing.
- Use orange juice instead of lemon juice.

Ranch Dressing

1	**cup nonfat buttermilk**
⅓	**cup nonfat sour cream**
2	**tablespoons reduced-fat mayonnaise**
1	**tablespoon freshly grated Parmesan cheese**
2	**tablespoons finely chopped green onions or chives**
⅛	**teaspoon finely minced garlic**
½	**teaspoon salt**
¼	**teaspoon pepper**
1	**tablespoon poppy seeds**
¼ to ½	**teaspoon sugar, to taste (optional)**

Combine all of the ingredients in a bowl. Taste for seasoning and refrigerate until needed.

Per ounce:

Calories: 23.9
Carbohydrates: 2 g
Protein: 1.2 g
Fat Total: 1.2 g
Fat Saturated: .25 g

Zippy Poppy Seed Dressing

This delicious dressing is delightful and exciting. And it's amazing that it only has 1 teaspoon of oil!

1 to 1½	**teaspoons arrowroot**
½	**cup water**
1	**teaspoon toasted sesame oil**
1	**tablespoon finely grated gingerroot**
½	**cup rice wine vinegar**
4	**tablespoons oyster sauce (see *Ingredients* page 226)**
2	**tablespoons sugar**
1	**teaspoon salt**
½	**cup cilantro leaves, not packed**
1 to 2	**teaspoons red pepper flakes**
1 to 2	**tablespoons poppy seeds**

Combine the arrowroot and water in a small saucepan, dissolving the arrowroot well. Place the pan over a medium flame, stirring constantly, until the mixture comes to a boil, changes from milky in appearance to clear, and has thickened. Remove the mixture from the heat.

Place the arrowroot mixture in a food processor. Add the sesame oil, gingerroot, rice wine vinegar, oyster sauce, sugar, salt, and cilantro leaves. Process the mixture until the cilantro is finely chopped, around 30 seconds. Add the red pepper flakes and poppy seeds; process once briefly to mix.

Remove dressing from the processor and refrigerate until needed.

Per ounce:

Calories: 39.1
Carbohydrates: 6.6 g
Protein: .57 g
Fat Total: 1.5 g
Fat Saturated: .18 g

Creamy Cucumber Dressing

1	cup nonfat yogurt
2	tablespoons reduced-fat mayonnaise
3	tablespoons nonfat sour cream
1 to 2	tablespoons lemon juice
⅓	cup peeled, seeded, and grated cucumber
2	tablespoons finely chopped green onions
2 to 3	tablespoons finely chopped fresh dill
½ to 1	teaspoon sugar
½	teaspoon salt
⅛	teaspoon white pepper
1	teaspoon Dijon mustard (optional)

Combine all of the ingredients in a bowl. Taste for seasoning and refrigerate until needed.

Per ounce:

Calories: 20.6
Carbohydrates: 2.9 g
Protein: 1.2 g
Fat Total: .47 g
Fat Saturated: .02 g

Sweet Ginger Dressing

This dressing is great for fruit salads or for a morning brunch featuring the freshest melons or berries.

1	cup plain nonfat yogurt
⅓	cup nonfat sour cream
3 to 4	tablespoons concentrated orange or orange-pineapple juice (undiluted frozen orange or orange-pinapple juice)
½ to 1	teaspoon freshly grated orange rind
1	tablespoon finely grated gingerroot
1	teaspoon lemon juice
½	teaspoon vanilla
	honey to taste (approximately 2 to 3 tablespoons)
½	teaspoon ground cinnamon

Combine all of the ingredients in a bowl. Taste for seasoning and refrigerate until needed.

Per ounce:

Calories: 25.6
Carbohydrates: 5.2 g
Protein: 1.3 g
Fat Total: .038 g
Fat Saturated: .02 g

Desserts and Miscellaneous

- *A Dessert Editorial*

  Apple Crisp
  Berry Cobbler
  Ginger-Honey Custard
  Muffins
  Shannon's Banana-Nut Muffins
  Baba Ganoush
  Dry BBQ Marinade
  Basmati Rice and Variations
  Perky Corn Bread
  Pico de Gallo
  Salsa Rojo (Picante Sauce)
  Salsa Verde
  Cucumber Dip
  Spinach Dip
  Basic Tomato Sauce

A Dessert Editorial

*I*T IS MY VIEW that desserts serve a function beyond merely satisfying a sweet tooth; they are an inexplicable sensory experience that resonate on many levels. The primary level is that of taste, whether it be chocolate, vanilla, or praline; the secondary level is that of texture—crunchy, light, heavy, smooth—the physical realities of dessert making and eating. But the third level is the level of experience, the existential level if you will, wherein the body and mind have a joint reaction to the totality of the dessert. This level is felt; this is the level of emotion; this level cannot be deceived! Scientists worked for years to discover that chocolate triggered a response in the brain akin to the feeling of being in love; food unquestionably has an emotional charge which cannot be ignored.

Many times guests have taken their first mouthfuls of an incredibly dark chocolate mousse and reacted as if in ecstasy, in awe of the moment. They were totally concentrated and focused on the reality of chocolate mousse. Once a guest said, after taking her first taste, "Don't anyone dare speak!" For her, silence was the only way to show obeisance to the myriad of feelings shooting through her mind and body. Her brow eased, her eyes closed in sympathetic reaction to the sultry smoothness of experiencing this truly wonderful sensory input. Her face showed the closest approximation to epiphany I shall probably ever witness. Food and desserts are more than nutritional counts to be monitored, they equal our overall acceptance of ourselves. Food, like life, comes around only once—enjoying and savoring the moment is all we can ask. A friend once said, "Preparing dinner is the ultimate existential experience—all of that work and then it's over. All that energy spent on the moment of consumption." And after the dessert is gone—poof! What are we left with but memories?

So what does all this have to do with a skimpy dessert chapter? In all honesty I've never had a low-fat dessert that triggered the same emotional response to that of standard, high-fat desserts. (And I'm certainly not talking about store-bought cake mixes! I mean real, honest-to-goodness, homemade desserts!) It is my belief that if you want a dessert, have a dessert, fat and all. Low-fat desserts fill only the first two levels of the "dessert experience," leaving the participant hungry and void of the third experiential level. For me, without satisfaction on the third level there is no point or reason to have a dessert at all! Without the soul-shaking resonance of a truly fine dessert, all that remains is taste and texture. May as well have a piece of toast with jam. Just ask anyone, "Would you rather have a bowl of ice cream or a bran muffin?", and witness their reaction.

However, for those who are monitoring their fat intake for health reasons, I have enclosed a few items that are simple and low-fat. But at other times when you're out in a restaurant or at a friend's house, perhaps a compromise can be reached. Still have a high-fat dessert, but only have half or a third the amount you would ordinarily have. Use a modicum of common sense and keep a sense of humor. Eating three or four bites of a fabulous crème brûlée isn't going to be the end of the world. And perhaps the action of allowing yourself to have something that's normally off-limits will brighten your outlook—after all, if *you* don't deserve to have a special treat occasionally, who does?

Apple Crisp

SERVES 4 TO 6

This is a lovely, simple apple dessert. Nothing fancy, just the taste of fresh apples and subtle spices.

2	**tablespoons lemon juice**
1	**teaspoon finely grated fresh lemon rind**
½	**cup raisins or currants (or if in season, blueberries, cranberries, straw-berries, or blackberries)**
1	**teaspoon cinnamon**
⅓	**cup maple syrup or honey, depending on how tart the apples are**
½	**cup apple juice**
1	**tablespoon cornstarch**
6	**baking apples, such as Granny Smith or McIntosh**
1	**cup rolled oats, quick or long-cooking**
⅓	**cup flour**
⅓	**cup brown sugar**
½	**teaspoon ground allspice or cloves**
¼	**cup buttermilk (approximately)**
1	**8-inch square baking dish sprayed with Pam®**

Preheat the oven to 350°.

In a large bowl, combine the lemon juice, lemon rind, currants or raisins, cinnamon, maple syrup, apple juice, and cornstarch. Make sure the cornstarch is thoroughly mixed and is not lumpy. Peel and slice the apples into ¼-inch slices, adding them to the bowl and coating them with the lemon-syrup mixture as you go, until you have used up all of the apples. Pour the apple mixture into the prepared baking dish.

In another bowl, combine the oats, flour, brown sugar, and allspice. Add the buttermilk gradually, until you've reached a crumbly but moist consistency; the mixture should not be soggy clumps, but have the texture of granola. Sprinkle the oatmeal mixture on top of the apples. Bake at 350° for 45 to 60 minutes until the apples are tender, the top has lightly browned, and the juices are slightly thick and bubbly. This is best served warm with frozen vanilla yogurt or ice cream.

Variations

- Delete 1 apple and add 1 cup of fresh rhubarb; this will mean increasing the sweetener to taste.
- If fat isn't a major concern, dot the top with 3 to 4 tablespoons of butter before sprinkling on the topping.
- For a richer taste but no additional fat, add ¾ cup nonfat sour cream to the apple mixture before baking.

Per serving for six:

Calories: 255
Carbohydrates: 60.1 g
Protein: 3.6 g
Fat Total: 1.5 g
Fat Saturated: .3 g

Berry Cobbler

SERVES 6 TO 8

I'll never forget going to the river one hot, HOT summer's morning with my father; the sun was bouncing off the gently dancing water when we spied a fruit-laden mulberry tree by the shore. I, being only 5 or 6 at the time, had never before seen a mulberry tree. We opened a newspaper and picked a seemingly endless amount of mulberries with the intention (hope?) of having my mother make a cobbler with them when we arrived home. She did, and it was delicious. The image of a neglected tree by the river producing wonderful, sweet berries haunts me to this day; I felt as if we'd stumbled upon the magic kingdom of Mother Nature where surprises lay everywhere—if you just knew where to look.

Since the best berries are usually only available in the summer, this is a special hot-weather treat. You can prepare it in the morning while the day is cool, and have a wonderful, home-baked dessert waiting at the end of a long day's gardening or tennis playing.

2	**tablespoons cornstarch**
¼	**cup liquid (preferably a mixture of brandy and water, or just plain water)**
⅔	**cup sugar (more or less, depending on the sweetness of the berries)**
1	**tablespoon lemon juice**
1	**teaspoon grated lemon rind**
4	**cups blackberries, raspberries, strawberries, mulberries, boysenberries, gooseberries, or huckleberries, or a mixture of berries**
½	**cup flour**
¾	**cup oatmeal, quick or long-cooking**
⅓	**cup brown sugar**
1	**teaspoon baking powder**
1	**teaspoon cinnamon**
¼	**teaspoon ground cloves (optional)**
½	**teaspoon salt**
¼	**cup buttermilk**
1	**8-inch square baking dish sprayed with Pam®**

Per serving for 6:

Calories: 246
Carbohydrates: 57.4 g
Protein: 3.8 g
Fat Total: 1.2 g
Fat Saturated: .18 g

Preheat the oven to 375°.

Combine the cornstarch and water (or a mixture of water and brandy) in a large bowl; mix thoroughly to be sure there are no lumps. Add the sugar, lemon juice, lemon rind, and berries; stir gently to coat the berries, trying not to mash them in the process. Gently pour berries into the prepared baking dish.

In another bowl, combine the flour, oatmeal, brown sugar, baking powder, cinnamon, optional cloves, and salt. Gradually add the buttermilk, mixing until you have reached a crumbly but moist texture; it should not be heavy, soggy clumps but dryish and light. Sprinkle the topping evenly over the berry mixture and place the baking dish on a foil-lined baking sheet. Bake the cobbler uncovered in the middle of the pre-heated oven for 45 to 55 minutes until the mixture is bubbling throughout and the top has lightly browned. Remove and serve warm with ice cream or frozen yogurt.

Variations

- If fat isn't a problem, dot the top with 3 to 5 tablespoons of butter before sprinkling on topping.
- For an unusual spice combination, add ¼ teaspoon ground all-spice, ¼ teaspoon freshly ground cardamom, ½ teaspoon ground cinnamon, and ½ teaspoon finely grated gingerroot to the berry mixture.
- For a creamier, richer taste, add ¾ cup nonfat sour cream to the berry mixture.

Ginger-Honey Custard

MAKES 6 CUSTARDS

I love custards. This particular recipe is not comparable to a high-fat crème cara-mel or crème brûlée; it is exactly what it should be—a perfect finish to a light meal, bright and refreshing.

Per serving:

*Calories: 111
Carbohydrates: 13 g
Protein: 5.3 g
Fat Total: 4.3 g
Fat Saturated: 1.4 g*

2	**cups skim milk**
2 to 4	**tablespoons honey or maple syrup (depending on how sweet you like custards)**
3	**large egg yolks (or 4 medium egg yolks)**
1	**whole egg**
1½	**teaspoons finely grated fresh gingerroot**
1½	**teaspoons vanilla or ½ teaspoon fresh vanilla bean seeds (see note below)**
6	**small (½-cup) ramekin dishes**
	a bain-marie, or at least a 3-inch tall roasting pan in which all of the ramekins will fit

Note: To get vanilla seeds, cut off a 1-inch piece of fresh vanilla bean, then slice the piece in half. Scrape the flat side of a knife along the inside of the halved bean, scooping out all of the practically microscopic seeds. Add these seeds instead of the vanilla extract.

Preheat the oven to 325°. Bring a large kettle of water to a boil on top of the stove and maintain it at a simmer.

Heat the milk and honey or maple syrup in a saucepan over moderate heat until it is quite hot but not simmering.

Beat the egg yolks, whole egg, gingerroot, and vanilla in a large bowl with a whisk until the ingredients are thoroughly mixed but *not* frothy. Slowly add the hot milk and honey, mixing gently, until you have a hot milky custard base. Don't beat it briskly with the whisk—you want to avoid having the custard get frothy and bubbly.

Place the six ramekins into the roasting pan; pour equal amounts of the custard through a handheld sieve into the ramekin dishes. Pour the simmering water from the kettle into the roasting pan until it comes at least half way up the sides of the ramekins. Place the entire roasting pan into the preheated oven and bake for 25 to 30 minutes until the custard has just set, but looks slightly liquidy in the center. (To test, insert a clean knife in the center; if it comes out clean the custard is overdone! If the knife looks as if it has just been stuck into milk, it is not done. If the knife has tiny custardy globules clinging to it with a liquidy film, it is done!) Remove the pan carefully from the oven and allow it to cool in the water for 10 minutes. After the initial cooling, remove the ramekins from the roasting pan and allow them to cool completely. When the custards are cool, cover them and refrigerate; serve the custard either room temperature or chilled with fresh fruit and a cookie.

Variation

- Add ½ teaspoon cinnamon to the custard.

Muffins

MAKES 12 MUFFINS

Muffins are extraordinarily easy to make, but for some reason people think of them as being time-consuming and difficult. Perhaps this misunderstanding should be attributed to the popular notion that "Anything That Is Baked Must Be Difficult to Make"! Who knows? This recipe can be whipped up in less than 20 minutes, if you know what you're doing!

DRY INGREDIENTS:

¾	cup all-purpose flour
¾	cup whole wheat flour
⅓	cup wheat bran or wheat germ
1	teaspoon baking soda
1	tablespoon baking powder
½ to 1	teaspoon ground cinnamon (see note below)
¼	teaspoon ground allspice
¼	teaspoon ground nutmeg
¼	teaspoon ground cloves (optional)
¼	teaspoon ground cardamom (optional)
¼	teaspoon ground ginger (optional)

½ c chopped walnuts

WET INGREDIENTS:

2	teaspoons lemon juice
1	very ripe banana (optional)
3	egg whites
1	teaspoon vanilla
⅓	cup brown or white sugar
1	cup liquid (buttermilk, milk, soybean milk, nonfat yogurt with milk, etc.)

½ cup maple syrup

yogurt / juice

FRUITS AND VEGETABLES:

1	cup fruit or vegetables (blueberries, shredded carrots, shredded zucchini, cranberries, raisins, etc., perhaps a teaspoon of grated orange rind)

1 sm grated carrot

Note: This recipe allows you to change types of muffins quite easily by varying the options available; so you can make blueberry-banana muffins, or carrot-raisin muffins, or plain zucchini muffins—and you can also vary the spices so that you don't always have the same cinnamon-based muffins for everything.

Preheat the oven to 400° and spray a muffin tin with Pam®.

Blend all of the dry ingredients in a medium-sized bowl. In a large bowl, combine the wet ingredients. Keep the fruit or vegetables in a separate bowl.

Per muffin:

Calories: 104
Carbohydrates: 20.9 g
Protein: 4.2 g
Fat Total: .78 g
Fat Saturated: .19 g

Now, one of the prime tricks of making good muffins is to act quickly and *not to overmix the batter*. The procedure is to pour the dry mixture into the wet, mix a bit, add the fruit or vegetables, mix again until just blended, then spoon the batter into the prepared muffin tin.

So, pour the dry ingredients into the wet ingredients, folding quickly (and it's fine if there are floury streaks running through the batter, as long as they are merely streaks and not great portions of the dry mixture), add the fruit or vegetables, mix a bit more, then spoon the mixture evenly into the prepared muffin tin. The batter should fill each compartment of the tin ⅔ of the way to the top. Set the filled tin in the middle of the preheated oven. The cooking time will vary depending on what kind of muffins you're making; but generally they should bake from 12 to 15 minutes, until they have risen, are lightly browned on top, and gently firm if you touch them. After they are done, remove them from the oven, then take each muffin out of the tin and cool on a rack.

Makes approximately 12 muffins.

Shannon's Banana-Nut Muffins

MAKES ABOUT 12 MUFFINS

My friend Shannon Rankin generously gave me her "famous" muffin recipe, and here it is. This recipe works for sweet bread loaf as well—great for afternoon tea or lightly toasted for breakfast. Enjoy!

Per muffin:

Calories: 126
Carbohydrates: 27.1 g
Protein: 3.7 g
Fat Total: .85 g
Fat Saturated: .18 g

DRY INGREDIENTS:

1	**cup white flour**
½	**cup whole wheat flour**
½	**cup bran (wheat or oat)**
1	**teaspoon baking soda**
½	**teaspoon salt**
½	**cup chopped nuts (optional)**
¼	**cup currants (optional)**
½	**teaspoon vanilla**
¼	**teaspoon nutmeg**
1	**teaspoon cinnamon**

WET INGREDIENTS:

- ½   cup maple syrup or ¾ cup brown sugar
- 1   cup very ripe banana, mashed
- 1   egg white
- ½   cup liquid (fruit juice, skim milk, or buttermilk)

- 1   muffin tin or 1 bread loaf pan

Preheat the oven to 350°. Spray a loaf pan or muffin tin with Pam®.

Mix the dry ingredients together in a medium-sized bowl. Mix the wet ingredients together in a large bowl. Combine the two quickly by adding the dry mixture to the wet, folding until the batter is nearly incorporated, but not overblended.

Pour the batter into the prepared loaf pan or spoon it equally into the prepared muffin tin. If making muffins, the batter should come ⅔ of the way up the side of the tin.

Bake a loaf for 50 to 60 minutes at 350° until done, or bake the muffins for 18 to 20 minutes. Let the cooked muffins or bread rest in the pan or tin for 2 to 3 minutes before removing. Cool both on a rack.

Variation

- Add 1 cup grated zucchini or ½ cup grated carrot. (Note: If adding carrot or zucchini, add the grated vegetable to the *dry* ingredients and stir well before folding into the wet ingredients. By coating the vegetables with flour you will help suspend them in the batter, keeping them from settling to the bottom.)

Baba Ganoush

MAKES 6 1-OUNCE SERVINGS

Per 1-ounce serving:

Calories: 30.3
Carbohydrates: 2.7 g
Protein: .97 g
Fat Total: 2.1 g
Fat Saturated: .29 g

This is a great party dip. Serve with crudités or crackers and chips. This doesn't make a terribly large amount, so you may wish to double the recipe.

1	**medium to large eggplant**
1 to 2	**cloves garlic, minced**
2	**tablespoons tahini**
	juice of 1 lemon
	salt and pepper to taste
¼	**cup parsley, minced**
½	**teaspoon cumin (optional)**
1	**baking sheet**

Place the eggplant on a baking sheet and bake at 375° until it is done (approximately 30 to 40 minutes). The baked eggplant will have "deflated" somewhat, will have exuded some juices, and will be quite soft. Alternatively, you could add a slight smokiness to this dip by placing the eggplant on a baking sheet and broiling it, turning it frequently, until the outside skin is blackened and the inside is soft.

Slice the cooked eggplant in half. Scoop out the inside flesh with a spoon and place it into a bowl. Mash the eggplant with a fork until it is practically smooth. Add the remaining ingredients, mixing well, and allow it to stand for at least an hour before serving.

Variations

- Add ½ cup peeled, seeded, and chopped fresh tomato.
- Use 1 tablespoon olive oil instead of tahini and substitute fresh basil for parsley.

Dry BBQ Marinade

This is one of those spicy mixtures which turns an ordinary chicken breast or butterflied shrimp into something wonderful. It keeps for months tightly sealed, so there's no reason not to always have some on hand! Just "marinate" the meat or fish for 30 minutes or so, then grill, broil, or sauté. Easy and satisfying, particularly after a hard day's work when you don't want to think about cooking anything complicated.

2	**tablespoons bright red paprika**
1	**teaspoon cumin**
1	**teaspoon coriander**
½	**teaspoon curry powder**
½	**teaspoon black pepper**
¼	**teaspoon allspice**
1	**teaspoon chili powder**
¼	**teaspoon cayenne pepper**
½	**teaspoon dry mustard**
1	**teaspoon salt**
1	**teaspoon sugar**
½	**teaspoon garlic powder or 1 large clove garlic, minced (see note below)**

Note: If desired, omit the garlic powder and use fresh garlic instead; simply rub the chicken or fish with the fresh garlic, then sprinkle with the spice mixture. I always AL-WAYS **ALWAYS** use fresh garlic, but many people like the convenience of powdered garlic.

Combine all of the ingredients in a bowl. Use this mixture as a marinade for chicken or fish. For example, sprinkle 1 to 2 tablespoons over a chicken breast, less for delicately flavored foods such as fish and shrimp.

Believe it or not, even spices have calories and fat contents. See, at right, the listing for this marinade.

Per recipe:

Calories: 97.6
Carbohydrates: 18.5 g
Protein: 3.9 g
Fat Total: 3.8 g
Fat Saturated: .37 g

Basmati Rice and Variations

SERVES 4

Basmati rice is a lovely, aromatic, long-grained rice that originated in the mountains of India. It is distinct and deliciously fragrant; regular long-grain, grocery-store variety rice is not a substitute.

WHITE BASMATI RICE

1⅓	**cups white basmati rice**
1¾	**cups water**
½ to 1	**teaspoon salt**
1	**tablespoon butter (optional)**

Pick over the rice to be sure there is no extraneous matter floating around, then place the rice in a bowl and wash in several changes of cool water, swishing it around with your hand, until the milkiness disappears. After it has been cleaned, let the rice sit in some cool water for 10 minutes or so, then drain the rice in a strainer.

Place the water in a heavy saucepan with a tight-fitting lid and bring the water to a boil; add the salt, optional butter, and drained rice. When water returns to the boil, cover the pot and turn heat to low. Simmer over low heat for 15 minutes, then turn heat off. Let rice stand in the covered pot for another 15 minutes to cool slightly and absorb any excess water.

BROWN BASMATI RICE

1	**cup brown basmati rice**
2	**cups water**
½ to 1	**teaspoon salt**
1	**tablespoon butter (optional)**

Pick over the rice to be sure there is no extraneous matter floating around, then place the rice in a bowl and wash in several changes of cool water, swishing it around with your hand, until the milkiness disappears. After it has been cleaned, let the rice sit in some cool water for 10 minutes or so, then drain the rice in a strainer.

Place the water in a heavy saucepan with a tight-fitting lid and bring the water to a boil; add the salt, optional butter, and drained rice. When water comes to the boil again, cover the pot and turn the heat to low. Simmer the rice for 30 minutes. Lift the lid to see if all the water has been absorbed; if not, continue cooking for another 5 to 10 minutes. If all of the water has been absorbed, replace the cover and turn off the heat. Let the cooked rice stand in the covered pot for another 20 to 30 minutes to cool slightly and allow the grains to separate.

Per serving (without butter):

Calories: 121
Carbohydrates: 26.5 g
Protein: 2.4 g
Fat Total: .11 g
Fat Saturated: 0 g

Per serving (with butter):

Calories: 141
Carbohydrates: 26.5 g
Protein: 2.4 g
Fat Total: 2.4 g
Fat Saturated: 1.4 g

Per serving (without butter):

Calories: 116
Carbohydrates: 24.9 g
Protein: 2.4 g
Fat Total: .58 g
Fat Saturated: 0 g

Per serving (with butter):

Calories: 136
Carbohydrates: 24.9 g
Protein: 2.5 g
Fat Total: 2.9 g
Fat Saturated: 1.4 g

SPICED BASMATI RICE

1⅓	cups white basmati rice
1¾	cups water
1	tablespoon butter
1	small onion, sliced very thinly
1	teaspoon cumin seeds
1	large clove garlic, minced
½ to 1	teaspoon salt
¼	teaspoon cayenne pepper (optional)

Pick over the rice to be sure there is no extraneous matter floating around, then place the rice in a bowl and wash in several changes of cool water, swishing it around with your hand, until the milkiness disappears. After it has been cleaned, let the rice sit in some cool water for 10 minutes or so, then drain the rice in a strainer.

In a heavy saucepan with a tight-fitting lid, heat the butter over a medium flame until it has melted. Add the onion and sauté until the onion has browned slightly, stirring often, around 5 to 8 minutes. Add the cumin seeds and garlic and stir for 30 seconds or so, until the garlic has cooked slightly. Add the salt, water, drained rice, and optional cayenne pepper. When the water comes to a boil, cover the pot and turn the heat to low. Simmer for 15 minutes, then turn heat off. Let rice stand in covered pot for another 15 minutes to cool slightly and absorb any excess water.

SAVORY BASMATI RICE WITH SPICES

1⅓	cups white basmati rice
1¾	cups water
½ to 1	teaspoon salt
1	tablespoon butter
6	cardamom pods
1	2-inch stick of cinnamon
6	whole cloves
1	bay leaf

Pick over the rice to be sure there is no extraneous matter floating around, then place the rice in a bowl and wash in several changes of cool water, swishing it around with your hand, until the milkiness disappears. After it has been cleaned, let the rice sit in some cool water for 10 minutes or so, then drain the rice in a strainer.

In a heavy saucepan with a tight-fitting lid, heat 1 tablespoon butter over a moderate flame until the butter has melted and is hot; add the cardamom pods, cinnamon, cloves, and bay leaf and sauté for 30 seconds or so, until you can smell the spices and see them gently frying. Add the drained rice and sauté with the spices for 30 to 60 seconds. Add the salt and water. When the water comes to a boil, cover the pot and turn the heat to low. Simmer for 15 minutes, then turn the heat off. Let the rice stand in the covered pot for another 15 minutes to cool slightly and absorb any excess water. Remove all whole spices.

Per serving:

*Calories: 155
Carbohydrates: 29.2 g
Protein: 2.9 g
Fat Total: 2.6 g
Fat Saturated: 1.5 g*

Per serving:

*Calories: 145
Carbohydrates: 27.4 g
Protein: 2.5 g
Fat Total: 2.5 g
Fat Saturated: 1.5 g*

213

Perky Corn Bread

SERVES 4

Hot, fresh corn bread is a natural with homemade soups and stews. It also satisfies that craving for bread while giving you a high-fiber and low-fat alternative.

My college roommate, a razor-thin man from Tennessee, used to make excellent corn bread every week and would say, "The only reason to have corn bread is to see how much butter you can get on each slice." Although I agree with him in sentiment, perhaps a modicum of moderation might be helpful!

Per serving (of four, using egg whites and 1 whole egg):

Calories: 265
Carbohydrates: 41.6 g
Protein: 13.1 g
Fat Total: 5.3 g
Fat Saturated: 1.3 g

¾	**cup yellow cornmeal**
⅔	**cup bread flour or unbleached white flour**
½	**cup raw wheat germ**
1½	**teaspoons salt**
¾	**teaspoon baking soda**
1½	**teaspoons baking powder**
2	**egg whites and 1 whole egg or 4 ounces egg substitute**
1	**cup low-fat buttermilk**
¼ to 1½	**teaspoons cayenne pepper**
	a small (9-inch) skillet
	Pam®

Preheat the oven to 400°.

Place the first 6 ingredients in a large bowl, mixing briefly.

Place the eggs or egg substitute in a separate bowl; add the buttermilk and cayenne pepper, mixing well. Make sure there are no lumps of cayenne floating about.

When the oven is hot, place the skillet on a medium-high flame on the stovetop and allow the skillet to become *very* hot (around 2 to 3 minutes—it may even begin to smoke). When the skillet has heated, turn off the flame.

Immediately pour the buttermilk-egg mixture into the cornmeal mixture; fold quickly but do not overfold. When the batter is completely wet (that is, without dry streaks of flour running through), spray the skillet with Pam® and then immediately pour the batter into the hot skillet, smoothing out the top with the spatula. Place the skillet in the top portion of the preheated oven and bake for 20 to 25 minutes.

Slice the hot corn bread into quarters and serve with sharp cheddar cheese (and/or butter!), if desired.

Variation

- If desired, pour the batter into molds for corn sticks or muffins.

Pico de Gallo

This must be made with fresh summer produce. A great condiment to have around for lunches, chips, or even with breakfast (huevos rancheros).
And even if it's not MADE IN TEXAS it's still darn good.

2 to 4	tomatillos
2	cups fresh tomatoes, peeled and seeded (see note below)
2	green onions, minced
1	clove garlic, minced
1	teaspoon red pepper flakes
1 to 3	tablespoons sugar or honey
3	tablespoons diced green chilies
¼	cup chopped cilantro
	salt to taste
	lemon or lime juice to taste

Note: To peel tomatoes, bring a large pot of water to a boil, then add the tomatoes and turn off the heat. Allow the tomatoes to sit in the hot water for 30 to 45 seconds. Remove the tomatoes and rinse them under cold water. Using a small paring knife, core the tomato and peel off the skin, which should come off quite easily.

Remove the papery husks from the tomatillos and wash them well. Slice the tomatillos into quarters and place them in a food processor; blend them briefly, until they have been chopped into ¼-inch pieces. Add the remaining ingredients and blend until you have a chunky sauce (do not puree!) Refrigerate until ready for use.

Per serving (approximately ½ cup):

Calories: 68.5
Carbohydrates: 15.8 g
Protein: 2.6 g
Fat Total: .5 g
Fat Saturated: .073 g

215

Salsa Rojo
(Picante Sauce)

I first made picante sauce one evening when it was raining, cold, and miserable; I was in the middle of preparing a Mexican meal and discovered I had no salsa. Since I was loathe to venture outside and go to the store for a single bottle of sauce, I ferreted out the ingredients and made some myself in no time. I was more than shocked at how easy and tasty my homemade version was! Since this is a cooked sauce, it is not imperative that you have fresh tomatoes; canned will work, although a combination of canned and fresh would taste best in the dead of winter. The quantity of red pepper flakes is a matter of taste; if desired, fresh jalapeños could be used instead, but only by those who know what they're doing!

1	**18-ounce can or 2 cups tomato, peeled, seeded, and chopped**
½	**cup green bell pepper, finely diced**
2	**cloves garlic, minced or put through a garlic press**
½	**cup onion (white, yellow, or green), diced**
1	**teaspoon red pepper flakes**
½	**teaspoon oregano**
1 to 3	**tablespoons sugar or honey**
¼	**cup red wine vinegar**
¼	**cup chopped cilantro**

Per ½ cup serving:

Calories: 50.6
Carbohydrates: 11.8 g
Protein: 1.6 g
Fat Total: .47 g
Fat Saturated: .073 g

Combine the first eight ingredients in a saucepan and bring the mixture to a boil over a moderate flame. When the sauce is simmering, reduce the heat to low and let it cook until the onion and pepper have softened, approximately 5 to 8 minutes. Remove the pan from the heat and let it cool a bit. Add the cilantro when the salsa is just warm. Refrigerate the salsa and serve with chips or as a condiment to Mexican meals.

Salsa Verde

SERVES 4

Green salsa is a refreshing variation over the omnipresent red salsa. It is light and piquant, not overpowering. Try a green salsa instead of picante sauce next time you have tacos.

6	**tomatillos**
	juice of 1 lime
1	**small tin green chilies, drained**
1	**green onion**
1	**clove garlic**
½	**cup cilantro (loosely packed, whole leaf)**
½	**teaspoon salt**
¼	**teaspoon cayenne pepper (or more to taste)**
1	**teaspoon cumin**

Wash and remove the papery covering from the tomatillos. Place all of the ingredients into a food processor and blend until you have a fairly smooth sauce, but maintaining some texture. Place the salsa verde in a bowl and refrigerate.

Per serving:

Calories: 40
Carbohydrates: 8.7 g
Protein: 1.9 g
Fat Total: .41 g
Fat Saturated: .04 g

Cucumber Dip

1	**cup nonfat yogurt**
½	**cup nonfat sour cream**
½ to 1	**teaspoon salt**
2	**teaspoons Dijon mustard**
⅔	**cup cucumber, finely diced or shredded**
2 to 3	**tablespoons fresh tarragon, chopped**
1	**tablespoon lemon juice**
½	**teaspoon white pepper**
1	**teaspoon sugar**
1	**tablespoon finely chopped chives or green onion**
⅓	**cup tomato, peeled, seeded, and finely chopped (optional)**
1	**tablespoon drained and chopped capers (optional)**

Place the yogurt and sour cream in a bowl and stir with a fork until it is smooth and creamy. Add the remaining ingredients. Taste for seasoning and refrigerate.

Per serving (⅓ to ½ cup):

Calories: 76.7
Carbohydrates: 12.5 g
Protein: 5.8 g
Fat Total: .36 g
Fat Saturated: .1 g

Variations

- Use dill, basil, lemon balm, cilantro, or chives instead of tarragon.

Spinach Dip

SERVES 4

Per serving:

Calories: 106
Carbohydrates: 16.3 g
Protein: 7.6 g
Fat Total: 1.3 g
Fat Saturated: .1 g

4	**cups fresh spinach, stemmed and washed**
1	**cup nonfat sour cream**
½	**cup nonfat yogurt**
1	**tablespoon reduced-fat mayonnaise**
1	**tablespoon Dijon mustard**
1	**teaspoon sugar (optional)**
⅛	**teaspoon minced garlic**
1 to 2	**green onions, diced (optional)**
3	**tablespoons fresh basil, thyme, or tarragon**
	salt and pepper to taste
	lemon juice to taste

Bring a large pot of water to a boil and turn off the heat. Add the cleaned spinach and stir gently to make sure all of the spinach is heated through. Immediately drain the spinach in a large colander and rinse under cold water. When it is cool, take the spinach between your hands and squeeze out any excess water. Set the blanched, squeezed spinach aside.

Puree the sour cream in a food processor with the yogurt, mayonnaise, mustard, garlic, onion, sugar, and herbs until thoroughly mixed, around 5 to 15 seconds. Add the drained spinach, blending briefly to chop the spinach. You can blend until you have reached the desired consistency (either a smooth puree or a dip with more recognizable pieces of spinach).

Place the mixture into a bowl and adjust the seasoning. Refrigerate and serve with crudités or chips.

Basic Tomato Sauce

This is a great basic tomato sauce for pasta, lasagna, or anything you need a to-mato sauce for. It is rich without being heavily flavored, so the taste of tomato is king.

1	teaspoon finest-quality olive oil
½ to 1	teaspoon fennel seeds
2 to 3	large cloves garlic, minced or put through a garlic press
3½ to 4	cups Italian plum tomatoes (either fresh, canned, or a mixture of both; see note below), peeled, seeded, drained, and chopped
¼	cup dry white vermouth or dry Marsala
	fresh black pepper
	salt to taste

Note: The easiest way to make this recipe is to use 1 28-ounce can of Italian crushed tomatoes as the base, and add fresh chopped tomatoes to make up the rest.

In a heavy saucepan, heat 1 teaspoon of olive oil over moderate heat; when the oil is hot, put in fennel seeds. Cook the fennel for 10 seconds or so, then add the garlic, stirring and cooking for about 20 seconds. Next add the tomatoes and vermouth, bringing the mixture to a slow boil. Reduce the heat to low and cook for 15 minutes. (If you are using exclusively fresh tomatoes, the cooking time will be approximately 25 to 35 minutes.) The sauce should not be watery, but simultaneously it should not be dry; continue to cook until some of the liquid has cooked away. Add a grinding of fresh pepper and salt if desired. Set aside to cool—the sauce will thicken slightly as it cools.

If you're using exclusively fresh tomatoes, you may wish to add 1 teaspoon or so of sugar to take the "edge" off the acidity from the tomatoes.

Per recipe:

Calories: 290
Carbohydrates: 46 g
Protein: 9.9 g
Fat Total: 6.7 g
Fat Saturated: .91 g

Information and
Sample Menus

Ingredients and Techniques

ancho chili—Ancho chilies (dried poblano peppers) are shriveled flat pods nearly black in color; they are triangular in shape (sort of), not elongated, narrow chilies like Anaheim peppers. They can be roasted before using by holding one with tongs above an open flame, turning it frequently until the skin changes from black to a dark red-brown and begins to smoke. Quickly remove the core and seeds, then chop the chili into small pieces using a very sharp knife, being careful not to burn your fingers since the chili will be hot. Place the chopped pepper in a small bowl and add just enough water to cover; allow the chili to rehydrate for 20 minutes before using in a recipe. Alternatively, you could just seed, chop, and rehydrate the chili without roasting, but this has a more acidic, green taste rather than a roasted, smoky, earthy taste. Ancho chilies are found in the Mexican section of a grocery store or in the bulk herbs section of your natural food store.

basmati rice (white and brown)—Basmati rice was virtually unknown fifteen years ago in the U.S.; now it is found almost everywhere from regular supermarkets to natural food stores. Basmati is a variety of rice usually grown in the northern India and Pakistan regions; it is highly aromatic, fine-grained, and much superior to regular long-grained rice in taste and smell. Brown basmati is also much more flavorful than regular brown rice, emitting a popcornlike aroma when being cooked. Both California and Texas have marketed their own American-grown basmati rice not very creatively named "Calimati" and "Texmati." The best white basmati (in my opinion) is purchased in large burlap bags weighing a minimum of 5 kilos (11 pounds), available in Indian markets.

blanch—A term used when a raw vegetable is put into boiling water and cooked for 30 seconds or so. The vegetable is then immediately removed from the boiling water and rinsed in cold water to halt the cooking process.

brewer's yeast—*See* **nutritional yeast**.

canola oil—One of the oldest food oils known to man, rapeseed (canola) has been cultivated for millenia. Plant scientists located a toxic gene in the rapeseed plant and removed it; the result was what we now call canola. Canola oil is very high in monounsaturated fats which have been linked to lowering LDL cholesterol levels. It is a light, almost flavorless oil which is excellent for salads and sautéing.

Chilean mushrooms—*See* **mushroom powder**.

chili paste with garlic—This is a typical Southeast Asian ingredient: a blend of garlic, vinegar, toasted sesame oil, and LOTS of hot chilies. It is very hot, so the only way to really judge your tolerance is to start slowly at first, adding perhaps ¼ teaspoon at a time until you've reached your limit. Some chili pastes from Thailand also have dried, ground shrimp paste as well (called *trassi*), which is equally tasty.

cilantro—A fresh herb, also called Chinese parsley, green coriander, or Mexican parsley. It is the green top of the coriander plant available in nearly all grocery stores. Dried coriander is *not* a substitute for cilantro. A substitute for cilantro could be parsley, Italian parsley, or fresh mint leaves.

five-spice powder—A licorice-like blend of ground spices containing star anise, ginger, cinnamon, fennel, and pepper. It should be used with restraint, because too much of it will overpower the taste of the dish. I think it's an odd blend to have come out of China, but there you are. Quite tasty if you like star anise, which luckily I do!

garam masala—Garam masala could best be described as the "house blend" spice for Indian cooking. Every family has a slightly different recipe as do the various regions and states of India. Curry powder is not a substitute for garam masala. Here's a quick version:

1	*tablespoon black peppercorns*
1	*tablespoon whole cloves*
2	*sticks cinnamon*
3	*tablespoons cardamom seeds (not whole pods)*
¼	*cup whole cumin seeds*
¼	*cup whole coriander seeds*
1	*whole nutmeg, cracked into pieces*
1 to 2	*dried red chilies (optional)*
1	*bay or cassia leaf (optional)*

Place the spices in a heavy skillet and roast them over a medium flame until the spices have emitted a lovely, toasted aroma. Remove the pan from the heat and place the spices in a coffee grinder; grind the spices until you have a fine powder. Place the ground spices in an airtight jar labeled "Garam Masala."

(For more information about garam masala and Indian spice blends, consult Yamuna Devi's *Lord Krishna's Cuisine: The Art of Indian Vegetarian Cooking*, Dutton Publishers.)

gingerroot—The tuber of the ginger plant. This is easily available in the Chinese or gourmet sections of most grocery stores. Dried ginger powder is not a substitute for fresh gingerroot.

herbes de Provence—A mixture of herbs commonly found in the Mediterranean Provence region of France. This combination usually has thyme, marjoram, savory, rosemary, basil, and sometimes lavender flowers and fennel seeds. It is easily available in any gourmet market and some supermarkets. Here's a quick way to make your own:

> **2 tablespoons thyme**
> **1 teaspoon each marjoram, savory, rosemary, basil, fennel seeds,**
> **and lavender flowers**

Mix and place in an airtight jar.

hoisin sauce—A smooth Chinese seasoning made from pumpkin, it is sweet, dark, and has the consistency of thick ketchup. It will keep indefinitely if kept in a glass jar and refrigerated. A substitute could be oyster sauce, plum sauce, or some ketchup mixed with a bit of tamari.

Marmite (and **Vegemite**)—A concentrated yeast paste. This salty, dark-brown spread adds a "meaty" taste to vegetarian dishes and sauces. It can be found in an English or Australian specialty market, large specialty grocery stores, in some health food stores, or even Indian markets. Marmite and Vegemite are good sources of vegetarian vitamin B-12.

mince—A technique for chopping something very finely. If the recipe calls for mincing, it means to chop as finely as possible this side of pureeing, not to dance around the kitchen in an affected manner.

mushroom powder—I don't know if anyone has actively marketed mushroom powder as an ingredient, but it is excellent for adding a "meaty" taste to vegetarian dishes. Dried Chilean mushrooms (found in health food stores in bulk) are too tough to be really edible if they are simply rehydrated. But if you place the whole, dried mushroom in a coffee grinder and make a powder, you can place the powder in a sealed glass container and add a tablespoon or so to soups and sauces to give them a fuller, heartier taste. Of course, any dried mushroom will work for this, but many gourmet dried mushrooms are too expensive just to grind up and use as a soup base.

nutritional yeast—Sometimes confused with **brewer's yeast**. Brewer's yeast is literally a by-product of the brewing process, whereas nutritional yeast is specifically grown for use as a food and nutritional supplement. Some nutritional yeasts contain vitamin B-12 (an important and sometimes elusive component for strict vegetarians), and some do not; check the nutritional profile carefully. Nutritional yeast, like Marmite and Vegemite, is yeast; it adds a heartier, fuller, "meatier" taste to vegetarian dishes. Some people do not like the taste of yeast though, and others have health problems that require them to strictly monitor their intake of anything containing yeast. At any rate, when one is first experimenting with nutritional yeast, the best rule of thumb is to go slowly; only add a teaspoon at first, then, when you've adjusted to the taste, add more as desired. People often prefer to lightly roast the yeast in a pan before using it to give a smoother taste. To roast, place the yeast in a skillet and roast over a medium flame, stirring constantly until it changes color from yellow to tan and has a toasted aroma.

olive oil (extra virgin)—Olive oil is probably the oldest oil known to human-kind. The first cold pressing is called extra virgin; this is considered the premium oil by cooks. Extra virgin olive oil maintains the integrity of the olive; it is frequently yellow to deep green in appearance and has the taste of olives, either fruity, robust, or flowery, depending on where and under what conditions the olives were grown. Olive oil is high in monounsaturates (as is canola oil). Besides the Italian, Spanish, and French olive oils available in many gourmet markets, be sure not to overlook the premium oils grown in California—as the American palate has become more discriminating, the olive growers have taken note and are producing excellent oils.

oyster sauce—A Chinese condiment not unlike hoisin sauce. Some oyster sauces contain only oyster flavoring, whereas others contain real oyster extract. Check the label carefully. Oyster sauce is slightly sweet and slightly salty and not in the least fishy. It is wonderful in vegetable stir-frys.

tamari—Sometimes erroneously called soy sauce (shoyu), tamari is the first, real, "natural" soy sauce. Tamari contains only soy beans, salt, and water; it is brewed slowly and has a deeper, more complex taste than plain soy sauce. Soy sauce (shoyu) has wheat added to it which speeds up the brewing process, enabling sauce makers to produce more sauce in less time. Soy sauce contains volatile substances that "burn off" during cooking, usually requiring the cook to add more soy sauce and concurrently add more salt; tamari is a more stable product, meaning that the taste remains in the food and the cook thereby adds less salt. Tamari is slightly less salty than soy sauce and can be found in any natural food store.

tamarind—Tamarinds are sour brown seed pods common to the Middle East, India, and Southeast Asia; the pods are soaked in hot water and squeezed through a sieve to produce a smooth, brown paste. Tamarind pods can be found in the southern United States grouped with the Mexican produce in many grocery stores. You can also find tamarind bricks and tamarind concentrate at Indian grocers. Personally, I buy the tamarind concentrate since it is just as good as preparing the dried pods yourself, is infinitely easier, and quite inexpensive. Tamarind has a sour-sweet taste, not unlike sour plum jam; a substitute for tamarind would be slightly sweetened lemon or lime juice.

toasted sesame oil—Not to be confused with regular pale sesame oil. Toasted sesame oil is dark tan in color and has a nutty, strong taste and smell, meaning that a very small amount will flavor an entire dish. Since such a small quantity is used at any given time, purchase as small a container as possible to ensure against rancidity. Keep all oils in a dark and cool location.

Vegemite—*See* **Marmite**.

Equipment

What with the abundance of kitchen equipment stores around selling thousands of specialty items, I'm often asked what I think are the best utensils of the lot. The following list contains some handy items to have around, some for which I've specified the brand names. The comments below are my opinion only. I've also taken this space to answer an oft-asked question . . . how not to cry when cutting onions.

convection ovens—Convection ovens cook merely by circulating hot air quickly in a small space. There's nothing artificial about this method of cooking and in fact it has a great many advantages: namely its ability to brown food, to seal in juices of foods like fish and meats, and to cut the time of ordinary cooking by half.

coffee grinder—Even if you don't drink coffee, a coffee grinder is great for grinding spices. Freshly ground spices are as different from preground spices as dried herbs are from fresh herbs. So far my Krups® coffee grinder has been used every day for the past eight years and has worked without fail. That's a pretty good testament in itself.

cutting board—I prefer wooden cutting boards since they don't seem to dull the knife as quickly as plastic boards.

food processors—I've had the same Cuisinart® for the past twelve years—it was the first Cuisinart® model sold. I just bought a new stainless-steel S blade and a new work bowl; the motor works perfectly and has worked perfectly for twelve years. I think nowadays all processors do pretty much the same thing, with the only real difference being the size of the work bowl. When purchasing a new machine, seriously consider how large a bowl you will need; for most purposes, a standard processor is more than sufficiently large.

garlic press—OK, OK. There is only *one* garlic press I think is worth the money. It's made by Good Grips® and has three distinctive features: 1) it is made of heavy aluminum and is easy to hold onto, 2) it has holes big enough for the garlic to get through (which many garlic presses do not), and 3) THE MOST IMPORTANT! It has a red plastic self-cleaning attachment! Anyone who has spent any amount of time sticking a toothpick through the teeny-tiny holes of a regular garlic press will immediately understand the relevance of this feature.

gas versus electric ovens—I've baked in both gas and electric standard ovens and find them pretty much the same, since the purpose of baking is to surround the food with heat, and whether this heat comes from an electric source or a gas source doesn't seem to make too much difference. There is a slight difference with the physical action of heat rising in a gas oven, but this is very slight. Most electric ovens nowadays are self-cleaning, which unquestionably is a plus.

gas versus electric ranges—Gas ranges are best. Period. Next question?

ginger grater—To begin with, what *is* a ginger grater? A ginger grater is a small gadget (about a 5- × 3-inch rectangle), with a slightly curved interior, and containing hundreds of ⅛-inch "spines" or "tines" speckling the inside surface. When the peeled gingerroot is rubbed against these spines, the fibrous particles of the root break down into an ultrafine paste in seconds, with the added benefit that it is a hand tool and requires no electricity.

There are two types of ginger graters, porcelain and metal. I've used both, and have no distinct preference; the porcelain tines can occasionally become broken, necessitating the purchase of another grater. But the metal graters can retain the fibers of the gingerroot while grating, causing an accumulation of cellulose to clog the tines. Either way, it beats mincing the root with a knife. Ginger graters are inexpensive and can be used to grate daikon, carrot, or any other root vegetable with the same ease.

knives—The selection of knives is a *very* personal one; some people swear by Brand A and others by Brand B. My personal preference is for Wüsthof® knives, the German-made, stainless-steel blade flanked on either side by an ebony handle. Wüsthov® knives have three steel rivets running through the handle and are beautifully balanced; some people, however, prefer a lighter weight knife. You'll hear other people and chefs praising the finesse of Henckels® knives. As I said, choosing a knife is very personal. What is really important is that: a) you feel comfortable with the knife, b) you can afford the knife, and c) it sharpens easily and maintains an edge. Go to a large kitchen supply store and look around at the different brands of knives—feel them, ask questions about them, see which brand appeals the most to you. After all, *you* are the one who will be using it—if you're not comfortable with it, you'll never use it, regardless of the high praises of someone else.

Insofar as the quantity of knives is concerned, on the whole I only use about four knives—I see no real need for a different knife for every function in the kitchen. You could easily spend a thousand dollars on knives alone, but to what end? A good French chef's knife (8-inch or 10-inch) fits most people's uses; a small paring knife is imperative for small, detailed work, and a boning knife is quite useful. Other than a serrated bread knife, what is there?

mandoline—A mandoline is one of those French "cutting gadgets"; it slices, juliennes, makes waffle-cuts, etc. In other words, it's one of those hand slicers that have interchangeable blades for different functions. It's about 12 inches long and 4 inches wide. The real French-made metal mandolines are expensive and are a status symbol in some kitchens. I was given a simple German-made gadget (made by Börner®) similar to a mandoline, except that it has fewer blades and cannot make a waffle-cut. The purpose of this thing is to slice equally thin or thick slices with the simple up and down movement of the hand—and it works beautifully. Any food processor with slicing blades does the same thing, but if you're only slicing a couple of potatoes you may not wish to dirty up the entire processor work bowl, and this is where your handy-dandy mandoline steps in. Mandolines are also great for finely chopping onions in no time; this helps somewhat with the Onion-Crying Syndrome (see **onions** below).

Mandolines and mandoline wanna-bes are dangerous items; they have exposed blades which should never be left lying around, especially if you have children. These gadgets are great time-savers in the kitchen, but they are to be used carefully by adults. Used correctly and in the right hands, they are a boon to chefs; in the wrong hands, they can cause severe damage. They are inherently no more or no less dangerous than a knife, but they look harmless—and therein lies the danger. Mandolines should be treated with the same respect you treat a straight razor blade.

microwaves—I know this is silly, but I have a problem with a machine that alters food on a molecular level. Call me foolish, call me silly, but call me *safe*. I don't own a microwave and try to stay away from them whenever possible.

onions—How can you cut onions and not cry? There are several ways, the first and best being: have someone else chop the onion. Forgoing that, the most effective method I've found is to cut/mince/slice a cold, refrigerated onion. This goes against the storage practice for onions, however, since most onions will begin to mold and go soft if stored long-term in a refrigerator. But if you buy onions frequently (say, once a week), and only store two onions at a time in the refrigerator, you'll probably never have them mold. I can honestly say that when chopping onions, whether by hand, with a mandoline, or in a processor, nothing beats the simple action of merely chopping a cold onion for reducing (if not eliminating) the Onion-Crying Syndrome.

pots and pans—Yet another very personal choice. My favorite pans are without doubt Cop*R*Chef®. These pans have a stainless-steel interior, covered with an aluminum layer, then finally a complete, pure copper exterior. The interior doesn't stain and stays bright with a gentle scrub; the aluminum layer helps distribute heat quickly, and the copper exterior distributes heat evenly. They are expensive and will last for your entire life. The copper exterior, however, does require some polishing if it is important for you to have "bright copper kettles." For myself, I clean them three times a year or so. A dull copper pot cooks exactly the same as a bright copper one, so why bother spending all that time polishing? I also like the heavy French-made Le Creuset® series; these are also wonderful pans that are practically indestructible.

wok—Nothing can beat a wok for Asian cooking, whether it be Chinese, Thai, or Vietnamese. A standard skillet just doesn't do the same thing, though it is an adequate substitute. I've owned electric woks and standard woks that sit atop the range, and I think I get better results from the stovetop version because I can achieve a higher temperature than with the electric. I currently use a cast-iron wok made by Nordic Ware®; its only drawback is that it weighs a ton. Nothing like lifting weights while you cook, *n'est-ce pas?*

Recommended Books

Everyone should own a copy of *Laurel's Kitchen* by Laurel Robertson, Carol Flinders, and Brian Ruppenthal (published by Ten Speed Press). This book is invaluable as a resource guide for nutrition and whole-food recipes.

There are a whole host of wonderful books written before the facts were in about a high-fat diet, or were written as a textbook for a particular style of cooking (such as Yamuna Devi's mammoth dissertation on Indian cuisine); the following are a few of my favorites not in any order and not necessarily those with the lowest fat.

Tajassara Recipe Book, by Edward Espe Brown. A Shambhala publication.
Madhur Jaffrey's World of the East Vegetarian Cooking, by Madhur Jaffrey. A Knopf publication.
Lord Krishna's Cuisine: The Art of Indian Vegetarian Cooking, by Yamuna Devi. A Dutton publication.
Good Food from a Japanese Temple (now retitled *The Heart of Zen Cuisine*), by Soei Yoneda. A Kodansha publication.
The Complete Book of Spices, by Jill Norman. A Viking Studio Book publication.
The Complete Book of Herbs, by Lesley Bremness. A Viking Studio Book publication.

And of course, the entire canon of Julia Child is a treasure trove of information about cooking techniques, culinary history, and extraordinary recipes as only the imitable Mrs. J. C. can make. They may, however, be rather high in fat.

Sample Menus

Here are a few ideas for menu combinations and theme parties—pick what looks best and will fit your guests' needs! Add your own touch—a green salad, a fresh vegetable, French bread, corn on the cob . . . the possibilities are endless!

A Winter's Repast

Black Bean Soup
Hearty Navy Bean Soup
Savory Stuffed Potatoes
Seafood Gumbo
Pleasant Peasant Stew
Wild Rice Soup

A Summer Cookout for Family and Friends

Grilled Chicken with Mango Relish
Shrimp Kabobs with Bay
Butterflied Pork Chops with Green Peppercorn Marinade
Lamb with Rosemary
Dijon Potato Salad
Baked Onions
Roasted Peppers
Five-Bean Salad
Sword-Fish Swordfish
Greek Turkey Kabobs
Berry Cobbler

Kid's Night Out

Shannon's Banana-Nut Muffins
Fish Fingers
Barbecued Chicken
Parmesan Chicken Breasts
Vegetarian "Hamburgers"
Tuna Casserole with Fusilli
Apple Crisp

Mexican Fiesta

Gazpacho
Mexican Quiche
Green Chili Chicken
Fresh Pico de Gallo, Salsa Verde, and Red Salsa
Chicken Enchiladas
Mexican Rice Casserole
Black Bean Enchiladas
Chicken Tostadas
Ginger-Honey Custard

A Trip to the Orient

Vietnamese Chicken Soup
Szechuan Shrimp
Chinese "Hot" Noodles
"Fried" Rice
Chinese Peanut Chicken
Chi Mei's Green Beans (Almost)
Hunan Eggplant
Beef Stir-fry
Cantonese Five-Spice Fish
Seafood Stir-fry
Shrimp Stir-fry
Siamese Salmon
Ridiculously Simple Japanese Tuna
Szechuan Eggplant

Cocktail Snacks

Spinach Dip
Cucumber Dip
Beef Kabobs
Pasta Salad
Chicken Kabobs
Shrimp Kabobs with Bay
Baba Ganoush

Vegetarian Visitors

Savory Stuffed Potatoes
Lentil Lasagna
Vegetarian Chili
Mexican Quiche
Imperial Navies

Chinese "Hot" Noodles
Stuffed Peppers
Stir-fry Greens
Spiced Basmati Rice
Quiche Athenée
Ratatouille
Broccoli with Garlic
Black Bean Enchiladas

A Trip to Madras

Savory Basmati Rice
Indian Chickpeas in a Savory Sauce
Zucchini-Tomato Curry
Indian Shrimp with Tomato Sauce
Rice Pilaf
Tandoori Chicken
Muglhai Lamb
Cucumber-Cilantro Raita
Indian Spiced Fish

Middle Eastern Extras

Tabbouleh
Lebanese Lentil Soup
Middle Eastern Chicken Kabobs
Spiced Basmati Rice
Cucumber-Cilantro Raita
Chickpea Salad

Americana

Broccoli Soup
Turkey with Cranberry-Orange Sauce
Wild Rice Pilaf
Baked Onions
Wild Rice Soup
Seafood Gumbo
Savory Stuffed Potatoes
"Oven-Fried" Catfish
Chicken with Fresh Herbs
Pork Tender Sauté
Spaghetti Squash with Rosemary

Viva Italia!

Spinach Lasagna
Chicken Cacciatore
Pasta Salad
Quick Pasta with Red Clam Sauce
Parmesan Chicken Breasts
Fresh Pasta Sauce with Zucchini
Sole Florentine
Eggplant Parmesan

Parlez-vous Français?

Chicken Dijon
Sautéed Fish with Peppers
Lamb with Rosemary
Dijon Potato Salad
Navy Bean Salad with Vinaigrette
Ratatouille
Risotto
Salmon with Herb Dressing
Broccoli Soup
Red Pepper Soup
Chicken with Lemon-Caper Sauce
Fresh Turkey or Chicken Sausage

The Dog Chapter

or

The Lowest Point in My Culinary History

A *True* Shaggy Dog Story with a Recipe

containing:

Dog Cookies for Christmas
(Part I)

I DIDN'T WANT to do it.

Every fiber of my being resisted, but Bonnie was adamant. "We've *got* to do it," she stated, "anything else just won't make sense. And it won't take that long—just an evening." She reached over, grabbed my arm, and gave it a gentle shake. "Oh come on—it'll be *fun.*"

Fun. Anytime someone says "It'll be fun" a neon warning sign complete with sirens goes off in my head flashing "Like hell it will." I had carefully orchestrated against such an event, but here I was on the precipice of relenting and agreeing to perform the repugnant.

"And I've got a recipe from my sister-in-law who raises prize silkies, and she says her dogs just go ape over them."

A vision flew through my mind of a *National Enquirer* headline complete with a color photo depicting a monkey with a dog's head grafted on top:

Prize Dogs Turn into Chimpanzees—
Owner Cries, "It Must Have Been That Banana They Ate as Pups"

Time was running out—it was already mid-November, and Christmas wasn't far off. The words "You're right, Bonnie. We should do it," escaped my mouth against my better judgment, finalizing the newest twist to this dreaded holiday project. I was committed. It was too late in the game to argue. I had a headache and my nerves were raw at the thought of baking . . . *dog cookies.*

Bonnie Tetley was hired as the marketing consultant for my company. On a bright October afternoon we sat in her living room battling the problem of what to give my clients as a small "thank-you" gift, a mere token of gratitude, something that would be more thought than gift for the Christmas season. I only had two criteria for the gift: 1) that it be inexpensive, and 2) that it didn't require me to do any work.

"I don't care really," I said, "a nicely printed holiday card would be fine with me. It's simple, quick, and even though it's hackneyed, it does the job."

Bonnie scowled. Bonnie was aghast. Bonnie looked at me with horror and amazement. Quite a feat for the cheeriest person in Texas. "A *card*!? A **CARD**?!? You must be out of your mind! Your business is a *service-oriented* business—chefs coming into people's homes and cooking wonderful homemade meals for them. How can you think of something so impersonal as a card? No, no, no . . . that will never do." She shook her head with impatience.

I shrugged as Bonnie turned away, physically dismissing my idea. Nicely printed cards were by far my favorite because they were *easy*.

We were at a standstill. We had gone over at least a dozen alternatives each of which hinged on me hand-making something and distributing it, and I balked every time because I knew I had a thousand things to take care of in early December without the added burden of baking miniloaves of nut bread or churning out two hundred chocolate truffles. I had shot down every idea Bonnie had come up with because they all required my participation, a fact not lost upon Bonnie. I wasn't adverse to *some* participation, mind you, participation on the level of addressing cards or tying holiday bows, but the specter of spending added time in the kitchen baking hundreds of *anything* sent a shiver down my spine. I had no brilliant ideas to offer. A silence ensued.

Bonnie, sighing at my stubbornness and shifting in her chair, looked down at the morning newspaper lying on her coffee table. I thought she was about to ask me to leave. Her eye spotted a column she'd read that morning. Her face was the definition of "a mind at work."

"How many of your clients are . . . dog owners?" she asked.

Strange question, I thought. "Quite a few," I stated softly, mentally going down the list of clients we served, "probably more than half. Maybe even three-quarters."

"Hmmmm . . . " Bonnie muttered, "dog owners *love* to get things for their little darlings."

"That's true." I thought of the myriad of dogs I'd had to contend with during my rounds at client's homes. Dogs that barked at the sound of a blender, dogs that thought being under my feet was the greatest fun imaginable, dogs that yapped at the mere fact I existed. And, of course, all of the dogs in my neighborhood who, to my immense frustration, use my yard as a bathroom. My stomach knotted and my brow furrowed.

"Did you see this article about gourmet dog biscuits in this morning's paper?"

"No," I said. "Articles about dog biscuits give me indigestion when I'm having my morning tea."

"There's this place," Bonnie began, her energy swelling, "that sells gourmet dog goodies. They've got . . . well, all kinds of stuff."

Gourmet dog biscuits for the client's gift? Great! I thought. Problem solved! We buy fancy dog biscuits, wrap them up, and stick a quick note on them. Inexpensive, unusual, and requiring very little work from me. With my personal criteria having been met I said, "That's perfect! Great!" And in a trice the matter was settled—gourmet dog biscuits for the pampered poodles and simpering Shih Tzus. The dog owner would be surprised by such personal attention to the smaller components of their households and the doggy would get a present for the holidays as well. The Perfect Idea.

So why was my stomach in a knot? Even with this Perfect Idea, I had some reservations; not about the gift, but about the *dogs*. I would rise above it . . .

Dog Cookies for Christmas (Part II)

Bonnie Tetley and I sat in her living room discussing what progress had been made with the gourmet dog biscuit idea. Although the gorgeous mid-November day belied the fact that Christmas was lurking just over the horizon, time was nonetheless running out. She still hadn't bought the gourmet doggy treats and was a bit evasive when I asked, "What have you found out about those dog biscuits?"

Bonnie hesitated. Then she cleared her throat. Bonnie smiled wanly. Obviously she was preparing me for a change of venue. "Well . . ." she began, "I've been thinking about this. I've been everywhere and looked at all of these different treats, and they just didn't feel right. None of them looked personal enough. They just . . . well, you know, you're in a service business where you make things. It just doesn't feel right for you to give a store-bought gift to someone. It would mean so much more if we could make something ourselves."

Firmly I declared, "I don't want to make anything for the clients. I don't have time."

"Hang on, hang on. Listen to this. Your business is chef service. Chefs come into people's homes and cook wonderful, homemade meals. Your entire business is established on making everything from scratch."

"Yeah. So?" I wondered. Even though I didn't know where she was going with this, I didn't like where she was leading. "I thought we'd decided that we were going to buy some dog biscuits . . ."

"Well, the more I thought about this, the more it seemed wrong. We've got to *make* something for the clients—and everyone makes Christmas cookies this time of year—"

My spine stiffened visibly. Bonnie increased in speed.

"So, since we can't really buy something because your business is built on handmade fresh things, how about we make something? We can't *buy* anything—surely you can see that?"

My lightning-quick reasoning immediately parried her thrust. "The clients get tons of edible gifts at the holidays. It's like bringing coals to Newcastle. I cook for them all year long."

"I'm not talking about making something for the clients. I'm talking about making something for their dogs."

My heart stopped and my eyes bulged as it dawned on me what she was suggesting. "Dog biscuits?!?" I screamed. "You want me to make *dog biscuits*?!?"

"Now just wait a minute. Think about this." Bonnie's speech increased in speed, as if by saying it faster it would hurt less. "We'll make something for the dogs . . . you know, nothing much, just a token. It won't take that long—just an evening. And think of the marketing mileage we can get from it! Not only will your clients be thrilled, but what if they start talking to their friends about it. Word could get around . . . you may get an article in the newspaper about it!"

"Dog biscuits?!?" I screamed again. My carotid artery throbbed. "You want me to make *dog biscuits*?!?"

"Now just wait a minute. Think about this. We make something. It's not difficult and it won't take very long. We could say something like, 'We know you never have any leftovers with **our** food, so here's a doggie bag for the littlest member of your family.' Your clients will be so impressed that you thought enough of their little darlings and that you went to the trouble to actually bake dog treats for them. You can't buy that kind of public relations. This is what being a business owner is all about, going the extra mile. Doing that little extra. And your clients will never forget it. They'll start talking about you and you'll probably get new clients from it. And besides which, it'll make a good story to tell to someone. 'Remember the time we baked *dog biscuits*?' you'll say. What a great opening for your next interview—the next time someone does a story on the company. This could be a *great* marketing scheme for you."

Although my resolve was weakening, a small voice in the back of my head was screaming, *"Dog biscuits?!? You want me to make dog biscuits?!?"*

"People get Christmas cookies, so these will be dog cookies." Bonnie was adamant. "We've *got* to do it," she stated, "anything else just won't make sense. And it won't take that long—just an evening. Oh, come on—it'll be *fun*. And I've got a recipe from my sister-in-law who raises prize silkies, and she says her dogs just go ape over them."

Her face was aglow with excitement. She had thought this detour in marketing through from beginning to end and, unfortunately for me, she had a valid point. I crumbled. "You're right, Bonnie. We should do it." So why did I feel I'd just been run off the road into a ditch?

Prepping for Puppies

"Here are the ingredients . . ." Bonnie began.

"Just a sec . . . let me get a pencil and paper." I put the telephone down. My mind raced. Nothing could be so loathsome to me as the idea of making dog cookies. The fact that I would be reduced to baking dog biscuits, after the years of countless, sumptuous meals of gourmet precision my hands had prepared, was an indignity not to be borne lightly. Even the prestige of adding the line "Experienced Dog Cookie Baker" to my résumé paled beside the ignominy of my situation. My cynical side (known for its superb logic) whispered, "Some things are better left unknown. You could live your whole life without making dog cookies. Just like you could live your whole life without seeing an abominable snowman. Same thing."

"Go ahead," I said.

Liver. Oatmeal. Eggs. Wheat germ. Oil. Puree everything. Form into biscuits and bake. Simple enough. A recipe that spoke my language. Maybe this doggy treat business wasn't going to be such a trial after all.

* * *

"Eight pounds of liver, please."

The butcher looked at me strangely. "Eight *pounds?*"

I nodded. He placed piece after dripping piece of the sliced organ meat into a plastic bag. Three and a quarter pounds. Five and a half pounds. He picked up a particularly large chunk—the scale topped at eight and a quarter pounds. "That's fine," I said.

He wrapped the plastic bag in paper and handed it to me. "Anything else?" he asked with a raised eyebrow, expecting me to provide an explanation for the unusual quantity of liver I had just procured.

"No, thank you," I said as I thought, "This is more than enough. Eight and a quarter pounds more than enough, to be exact."

As I stood in the checkout line my mind was a ferment of discontent. We were scheduled to bake the infernal biscuits that evening. "Twelve hours from now this will all be behind me," I thought as I handed the bulging, squishy package of liver to the unsuspecting cashier.

I returned home and prepared the "dog batter." Since I was making a double recipe (doubling my fun!), I placed half the ingredients into the food processor and stood watching the liver gradually disintegrate. I had a repulsed feeling in my gut as I stood staring into the swirling pink mixture, not really focusing on the contents, gazing at the mahogany brown organ metamorphose into a salmon-colored puree. My stomach practiced its Olympic gold medal trampoline act. I suddenly acquired an objective outlook on my emotions and wondered, "This is an abnormal reaction. It's just liver. I'm seen liver a hundred times before. What happened in my childhood that makes me so disgusted with internal organs? Why does my stomach turn every time I think of liver . . . or sweetbreads . . . or gizzards . . . ?"

The Haggis Trauma

I was a painfully quiet fifteen-year-old, particularly with strangers. Growing up in a small town in Illinois I was nothing if not isolated. When forced to speak in unfamiliar situations, I could at best muster three- and four-word sentences, frequently spoken just above a whisper.

During this period my piano teacher had arranged for me to accompany a voice student from Bradley University; this student was a soprano who needed a pianist to accompany her with a song at (for what I thought was) a Scottish Rite Cathedral. The intinerary for the evening was she would pick me up at my home, we would go to the ceremony, we would have dinner, she would sing, then we would return home. I was mystified as to what secret Scottish rite I would be witnessing . . . some ancient Celtic initiation? Something akin to a Freemason ceremony? What occult mysteries would I be privy to? My heart rose with anticipation! In preparation for the evening of Mystery, I'd not eaten so that I'd be ready to partake fully of every facet of the Sacred Rite.

It was the dead of Winter. The sun had set at 4:25 P.M. that afternoon, and every minute awaiting my adventure hung thick and electric in the air. When the singer ultimately picked me up to escort me to the ceremony, I was resplendent in my polyester patterned sport coat, polyester brown slacks, and two-toned platform shoes. It was, after all, the mid-1970s.

Visions of Scottish Rite Cathedrals I had never before entered sprang before my eyes: large, cavernous, columned edifices where solemn rites of ancient esoteric religions were practiced. Would I find ornate gargoyles lurking in the recesses with bulging eyes, mouthing silent screams? Would this be akin to one of the great cathedrals in Europe? Would I be taken to an Illinoisan Notre Dame? Or the Chartres of Peoria? Could it be possible we'd be dining at the St. Peter's of Pekin? As the prima donna drove us down the dark road, I looked out of the frosted automobile window—gray, bitterly cold, and ice everywhere. I held my breath in anticipation as the car careened down the inky, winding, unknown paths during the heart of winter.

We circled down a gravel drive barely illuminated by the car's headlights. Skeletal trees raised their arms skyward, shaking their icicle fingertips in warning, "Go back! Stay away! Woe to ye who enter here!" We stopped at a single-story, ranch-style building without windows. We were in the Middle of Nowhere. (Nowhere was a popular place in central Illinois.) She turned the car's engine off.

"Is this it?" I croaked. My mind raced, "What about the Cathedral? What about Scottish Rites?" Where was I?

My companion for the night said, "Get out."

Clutching the sheet music in my hand, we exited her car and quickly walked the frozen distance to the black building, the only light being the winter-blue sky, suggesting a ghostly path to follow. My feet were nearly frozen and the "crunch-crunch" of our footsteps on the ice-encrusted snow echoed appropriately the bitterness of the evening. We came upon a heavy door; her gloved hand grasped the handle. She eyed me suspiciously as if to warn me of something, but hesitated and opened the door slowly. A flood of fluorescent light spilled onto us.

I looked into the interior with my eyes wincing from the brightness, hearing raucous laughter, foreign sounds, loud recorded music, and spying men in skirts. Crepe paper streamers swirled from the low ceiling and in the distance through the haze of cigarette smoke I could see the largest bottle of Cutty Sark I'd ever seen positioned on a dais. People were signing chits of paper and putting them in a box; I surmised the gigantic bottle of Scotch was going to be raffled off later on during the evening's festivities. This wasn't the Scottish Rite I had had in mind.

We entered the hall amid short, plump women with cat's eye glasses (most of them wearing pants, ironically) and the men in kilts. I noticed through the fog of smoke long, industrial tables laid with industrial plates and industrial silverware. Industrial paper tablecloths. Industrial coffee cups turned upside down. Everyone was drinking punch or some unknown brownish liquid out of industrial juice glasses. The room was void of any semblance of comfort and was built without sparing any effort to make it industrially miserable.

A jolly man with heavy black sideburns and thick glasses came toward us carrying a small amber drink in his hand. My new friend obviously recognized him for they embraced. He winked in my direction and said, "Och aye, lassie, whoos this laddie yuv gut in yer wake? Nut yer bruther?"

My "date" for the evening immediately lost her normal American speech and responded, "Och, hees noo kin'v mine. He's th' accomp'nst."

"Th'kumpnist? He's luks too wee a bairn to play th'thing."

"Och aye, but Ah rrr-r-r-rreckon he'll doo."*

[*Translation: "Hello, my dear. And who, may I ask, is this charming young man you have with you? A relative, p'haps?"

"Oh no, he's not related, though I'd be proud to have him as a brother. He's my accompanist for the evening. And a damn good one at that, too."

"But he looks so young! So handsome! So like a Grecian sculpture! The bone structure! Such grace! Are you sure he's from earth and not heaven? Such a royal bearing! Such majesty! Are you sure he's not a descendant of European nobility?"

"I know it's difficult to believe, but he's my accompanist!"]

They laughed.

I was shown to our industrial table and resigned myself to an industrial folding chair. My eyes watered from the sea of cigarette smoke and my feet smarted from the thawing process. "How long will this last?" I wondered. "And when will we eat?" My stomach growled. I glanced down the long line of industrial tables, speckled on either side with a few old industrial women and men too tired and old to make the cocktail rounds. I sat meekly in my industrial chair in my patterned polyester sport coat, sitting on my hands for warmth, wondering if I'd be able to play the piano when the time came.

After the collegiate singer made her hellos through the crowd she finally positioned herself across from me. I was getting thirsty and noticed there were no industrial water glasses to be found. Through the din of laughing and piped Scottish music, I yelled, "Is there any water?" She looked at me briefly and shook her head, holding up her hands as if to say, "Haven't got any." Or, translated for that evening, "Och, nut gut eny yu silly boy. Doo Aye luk lahk a waitriss?"

Thirstily awaiting the progression of dinner and the ensuing "performance," I saw a mimeographed menu by my napkin. What culinary wonders were we to partake of that eve?

"Haggis, mashed neeps, champit tatties, green beans."

At least I knew what green beans were.

Through the noise I yelled at my companion, "What *is* this?" and pointed to the menu. She didn't hear me so I sat silently, big-eyed and parched.

Eventually it was time for the presentation of the haggis. A drum roll sounded. Everyone stood up and sang "Auld Lang Syne" with teary eyes and quavering voices, then all stood erect as the bagpipes announced the real beginning of the Feast of the Scots. Men in kilts below and 1950s tuxedos above came through the hall, displacing the cigarette smoke that filled the air like heavy moorish fog, brandishing their swords like true Celtic warriors. Leading this procession was a man in full Scottish regalia carrying a brownish gray lump on a silver platter decorated all round with sprigs of parsley and holly. When they reached the center of the room everything stopped; the din ceased and people held their breaths. The collective anticipation of the moment was infectious and even I, who had no idea what on earth was going on, waited eagerly to see what they would do next.

An old man said a prayer in Scots Gaelic and a bearded man with red hair plunged his sword into the heart of the gray-brown mass while people cheered. The tenor of the evening returned its normal pitch with more lighting of cigarettes and yelling in dialects.

"Are we going to eat now?" I begged. "Soon," my singer companion replied. Or, translated, "Soooon."

Soooon wasn't soon enough. Thirty minutes later women in print dresses and calico aprons came pouring out of the kitchen balancing plates full of food. My hunger had practically subsided by then but my thirst was unendurable. "Will they bring water?" I cried. My friend for the evening looked across the table at me blankly and mouthed, "Can't hear you!" Or, translated, "Och, laddie—speek up! D'ye 'spect me to hear yur whispers?"

I returned to the menu. Mashed neeps. Champit taties. Haggis. What could this all mean?

Eventually one of the print-dress women swooped down and presented me with my meal. I stared at it. Even in the school cafeteria I had never seen anything quite like it. At the bottom was a nebulous gray-brown lump which looked as if it had been spooned out with an ice cream scoop. Next to that was a whitish lump (same ice cream scoop), and next to that some gray-green beans, a sprig of wilted parsley, and finally another ice cream lump that looked suspiciously like mashed potatoes. "What's this?" I yelled to my companion.

"That's mashed potatoes," ("Duh," I thought) "and those are green beans, and that's haggis, and that's rutabaga."

Rutabaga! *Rutabaga!*

"What's this?" I queried again, pointing to the brownish mass. "Haggis," she responded. It looked too suspicious to eat unknowingly. "What's *in* it?" I asked, feeling myself very clever for asking. "Just eat it," she smiled and began conversing with her neighbor at the table.

Tentatively I took my fork and scooped up a bit of the haggis; it was soft and had no distinct color. Beige? Tan? Antique ivory? Buff? None of these terms seemed to be quite accurate. I sniffed it. No particular smell besides that of smoke.

I lifted a spoonful toward my mouth. I opened my mouth. I put the haggis in my mouth.

What happened next I shall never forget to my dying day. Inside my mouth was a tepid paste thicker than the thickest peanut butter. As soon as it touched my mouth it stuck. To everything. It had no distinct taste save that of fried onions masked in brown-gray felt. But whatever this haggis was, it had a life of its own. Through no natural force would it condescend to being swallowed, and since I was practically dehydrated from lack of water by that point I couldn't form enough saliva to wash it down. The haggis was a terrorist and my tongue had just been taken hostage. I desperately searched the table for a glass of water but couldn't find one. Beads of sweat formed on my forehead. The haggis, having taken my tongue prisoner, was now forcing a coup d'état on my teeth. My heartbeat quickened. With my mouth glued shut I couldn't ask for water, so with Herculean effort I dispersed the haggis from one large glob sitting on my tongue to a mass encompassing my entire palate and gasped, "WATER. When are they bringing WATER?"

My companion smiled. "I don't think they have water," she said, her voice quite musical. "They'll bring around some coffee at the end of the meal."

My eyes watered from the plethora of smoke and the thought of sitting for thirty minutes with the indescribable lump in my mouth awaiting industrial black coffee to wash it down. I looked across to the prima donna to see how she was progressing with her blob of brown paste; I observed that her haggis remained untouched as she jovially conversed with her neighboring dinner companions. I heard my parent's maxim to "clean my

245

plate" echo in my ears; my eyes bulged and my stomach sank at the thought of attempting to put yet another spoonful of haggis in my digestive system. To each side of me and down the industrial tables I watched in horror as person after person placed spoonful after spoonful of the hateful haggis into their mouths, laughing and carrying on as they did so, appearing for all the world as if they were enjoying it. "Where are they putting it?" I wondered. "And how are they swallowing it?!"

Suddenly that enormous bottle of Cutty Sark began to have deeper significance in my adolescent mind.

The rest of the evening was a blur. I vaguely recall playing the piano as she sang, occasionally moving my tongue just so the cement wouldn't harden, and then the cold ride back home.

Ultimately I was safely ensconced in the icy dark, a passenger in a car exiting the Middle of Nowhere. I peered out the crystalized windows watching the edifice of Scottish Rites sink into the dark, needing only a surrounding mist and a ghostly chorus to convince me I had just visited the dark side of Brigadoon. As there was still three-quarters of the haggis stuck to my palate, I summoned my courage to ask yet again the question that was burning to be answered: "What was *in* that haggis?"

My companion merely giggled and drove on.

We arrived back at my home. I entered the house and stood ten feet away from my mother with a desperate look on my face. "Good Lord!" she said, "you smell like smoke! How was it?"

I was beyond caring about the smoke by that time, and she'd never believe "how it was." After gulping down a half gallon of water and brushing my teeth and tongue five times, I swooped upon the dictionary and looked up the word "haggis."

> **hag•gis** (hag' is),n. *Chiefly Scot.* a traditional pudding made of the heart, liver, etc., of a sheep or calf, minced with suet and oatmeal, seasoned, and boiled in the stomach of the animal. [1375–1425; late ME *hageys* < AF*haegeis, equiv. to *hag-* (root of *haguer* to chop, hash < MD *hacken* to hack[1]) = -*eis* n. suffix used in cookery terms]

I would like to add another definition.

> **hag•gis** n., a gray-brown mass invented in medieval Scotland, later marketed and packaged as tile grout.

Performing the Dirty Deed

"A fifth of Bombay gin," I responded.

"No, *really*—is there anything I can bring?"

"A fifth of Bombay gin."

"I'll see you tonight at seven-thirty, right? 'Bye now." Bonnie rang off.

The moment had come. It was the Eve of Dog Biscuiting, and I was left high and dry. Literally dry, since I wasn't joking about the gin.

The afternoon progressed as usual, with increasing rawness being exhibited from my temper and nerves. I mentally went down my To Do list: 1) the nauseating liver puree was in the refrigerator, awaiting its transformation from a disgusting mess to divine dog cookies. At least the organ meat part was done. All that was left was: a) bake the damned cookies, b) sort, c) bag, d) tie a bow on, e) attach a card to, and f) deliver the damned cookies.

I rolled my eyes and thought, "Good for business. This is supposed to be good for business."

The clock eventually read seven-forty-five: the moment of truth had come. I turned on the radio only to be assaulted by canned Christmas music.

Bonnie entered all smiles and enthusiasm. I had preheated the oven so that I'd lose no time getting the chore finished. She took off her coat and put down her purse. I was keenly aware she wasn't escorted by Mr. Bombay Gin.

"What size should we make them?" Bonnie asked as she tied on her apron. She was having a ball watching me spoon out pureed liver drops onto the baking sheet.

"I'm not going to make small, medium, and large, if that's what you're driving at," I snapped. I was bound and determined that Bonnie could lead me to the oven but she couldn't make me enjoy it, particularly without any reassurance from my old friend Mr. B. Gin.

"Well, it doesn't matter," she said. "It's just a token gift after all, we don't need to give them more than five or six treats per dog. They're pretty small anyway," she added, referring to the size of biscuits I was making.

Bonnie didn't notice my annoyed glare aimed in her direction. Any criticism directed toward the size of my dog cookies was not appreciated. I calculated the number of liver drops I could get per baking sheet—roughly fifty. Ten across and five up. I had two baking sheets, which made one hundred per batch. With six drops per client and one hundred clients, I would need at least six hundred liver drops!

"Six biscuits per client? Isn't that a bit excessive?" I responded. Premonitions of baking dog biscuits for the next four hours sent a tremor down my leg.

"Look at them," Bonnie stated. "If we give any fewer than six we'll look as cheap as all get-out."

Cheap or not, I was rebelling against the probability of baking dog cookies ad infinitum. My initial criteria of keeping it simple and not requiring my participation was dissolving with each passing second.

"But what about that client who's got thirty dogs?" I quickly rejoined.

"Thirty dogs?!" Bonnie gasped. "Whad'ya mean, thirty dogs?!?"

"I'm certainly not going to make a . . ." I paused, quickly doing the multiplication in my head, "a hundred and eighty of these things for them alone!! We'll be here all night!"

"What've they got thirty dogs for?"

"What do you mean what've they got thirty dogs for? They raise them. Purebreds."

"Purebred whats?" Bonnie pursued.

"How should I know? Purebred somethings. What are we going to do about them is what I want to know."

Bonnie paused. "Where do they keep them?"

"I don't know!" I barked. "Behind their house, I expect." There was only one aspect about owning thirty dogs that immediately pooped, er, *popped* into my mind.

"Well," she chirped, "we'll just have to figure out something to do with them. Give them an extra big bag of cookies or something. Maybe one treat per dog. We'll figure it out later."

Later. Later. When was later? My anticipated date with Mr. B. Gin at the end of my Dog Biscuiting seemed further and further away.

The first batch went in. "Well," Bonnie said as she clapped her hands, "this isn't so bad!"

I glowered. Bonnie was busy tearing the colored plastic and getting ribbons assembled, and there I was, making, forming, and baking the Infernal Dog Cookies, the most humiliating moment of my culinary history. "Not so bad?" I muttered. "Look who's making the damn things."

Bonnie tore equal portions of green and hot pink cellophane squares and piled them neatly on the countertop. She hummed along with the radio, which was serenading us with a reggae version of Handel's "Hallelu-jah Chorus."

"When are you going to deliver them?" Bonnie asked.

"It's what . . . Thursday night," I began. "I've got a full day tomorrow and meetings on Saturday, and I'm not going to work on Sunday, so they'll have to go out on Monday."

"Monday," Bonnie repeated. "That'll be fine."

"That'll have to be fine since that's when I'm getting around to it," I said under my breath.

Five minutes had passed. My temper began to subside. *("Hal-le-lu-jah . . .")*

"If I take all of the doggy treats and go in planned routes, it shouldn't take me . . ."

I stopped and sniffed the air. A certain odor emanated from the kitchen.

"Good Lord," Bonnie muttered. Her nose wrinkled. "What's that smell? Do you smell something?"

I most assuredly did. The smell of liver. Cooked liver. Overcooked liver. A very penetrating and nauseating smell, the smell of a dog-food factory.

"Good Lord is right!" I said. "What a stink! That's disgusting!"

Bonnie suggested that we not think about it and suggested we continue cutting ribbons and cellophane. How we were supposed to ignore the creeping odor wasn't explained.

Soon the timer went off and we inspected our first batch; little two-inch hard, brown droplets. They had no distinct shape, just kind of a plopped mess. The baking process hadn't smoothed them out like real cookies; they had merely changed from a dull pink to a dull brown. The odor was either less noticeable or our senses had adapted to the stench. I placed them on a wire rack to cool.

"You've got to admit, it's pretty funny, I mean, us making these things," Bonnie giggled. "Three months from now you'll look back on this and laugh. Just wait—you'll see!"

Bonnie began assembling the dog treats, placing them in individual piles to be wrapped and ribboned. "One two three four five six, one two three four five six," counted Bonnie under her breath. She quickly placed the dog cookies in separate piles, whispering as she went. "One two three four five six . . ."

"Three months from now the kitchen'll still stink of liver." ("Forever . . . and Ever . . . [biddy-bop mon] Hal-le-lu-jah . . . Hal-le-lu-jah, Mon!")

Epilogue—Hallmark®
Says It Best

Several days had passed. It was the Monday following the Festival of Dog Biscuiting, to be exact. I wasn't sure where to begin—how should I tell Bonnie about what had happened to the dog biscuits?

Rrrrrring. "Hello, Bonnie?"

"Oh, hi Jay. What've you been up to? Did you have a nice weekend?"

"Um, well . . . " I began, welcoming this opportunity for stalling, not knowing how to break the news to her, "I've been turning the sprinkler on Asterisk and Octothorpe."

"You've been what and what?"

"Turning the sprinkler on Asterisk and Octothorpe."

Bonnie paused. "I'm sorry, I've not got any idea of what you just said or what you're talking about. You've been turning the sprinkler on *who?*"

"Oh, I was just trying to keep one of my neighbors from walking her dogs on my lawn—"

"Oh! Speaking of dogs—"

"—and the two of them are named Asterisk and Octothorpe," I continued, not giving Bonnie a chance to interrupt my flow. "I guess the owner thought it was cute to call them that. Anyway, I thought if I turned the sprinkler on her when she was walking the dogs, she would get the message and cross to the other side of the street."

"Did you say 'asterisk'?"

"Uh-huh."

"And the other was—archo-what?"

"Octothorpe," I corrected. "It's the pound sign on a telephone—you know, one of those crosshatch thingamajigs."

"*That's* what it's called? I just thought it was called the 'pound sign.' What's it called again?"

"Octothorpe. Octo, meaning eight, and thorpe, meaning thorns. The pound sign has eight 'thorns,' hence the name octothorpe. She named these dogs Asterisk and Octothorpe after the star and pound key on the telephone. Some sense of humor, huh?"

"I suppose . . . eight . . . hmmmm . . . I wonder, why Asterisk and Arto-whatever?"

"Beats me. Probably because both are symbols with things perpetually coming out of them."

"You turned the sprinkler on them—" Bonnie paused. "Oh!" she cried, "you got me sidetracked! What about—"

"Those dog cookies?" I interjected.

"Yes!" Bonnie exclaimed. "I can't believe you're talking about some Archothorn. Did you get them all delivered? Did the clients go wild over them? Have you made new clients because of them? Did the dog owners say how their dogs like them? Did they ask you for the recipe?"

"Well, not so far. Actually, uh . . ."

"Did you get them all delivered?"

"Well, no . . ."

"No?!?! But you got *most* of them delivered, right?"

"Well . . . actually none of them have been delivered yet."

"None of them delivered?" Bonnie was aghast, again. "I thought you said you were going to get them all out today!"

"Oh I was, but . . . we've got a little problem."

"Problem? What problem? They're all wrapped aren't they? They've got the right names on them, haven't they? Did your car break down? What?"

"The wrapping is fine. It's just that . . . um . . ."

"What? What? What?"

I could barely contain myself. "Did your sister-in-law mention anything about keeping the biscuits refrigerated or anything?"

"No." I could hear her frantic breathing over the telephone. "Why?"

"I've checked all of the dog treats and . . . um . . . they're covered with mold."

A pause. "You're joking."

I couldn't help but laugh. "I wish I were. They've all molded. We can't use any of them."

"Molded," Bonnie repeated in dumbfounded amazement.

"Yup, molded." It was with great restraint that I kept from chanting, "I told you so." Even if I hadn't told her that the biscuits would mold, I *had* told her making dog cookies would be a pain in the posterior.

It was way past the eleventh hour for this project and my patience had worn thin.

"What are we going to do?" Bonnie asked.

"I don't know. We've not got any time. Whatever we do, it'll have to be done within a day or two. It's already the holiday season."

After some additional discussion confirming the profundity of moldiness in the dog treat department, we agreed to have some nice cards printed wishing the client a happy holiday.

"I wish I'd thought of something like that months ago," I remarked.

A silence ensued. Although I couldn't see Bonnie over the telephone, I could nonetheless tell she was glowering into the receiver.

And Now for . . . The Recipe

Dog Cookies

Dogs go ape over 'em!

1	**pound liver (more or less)**
2	**cups oatmeal (or a mixture of oatmeal and cornmeal)**
1	**tablespoon oil**
¼	**cup wheat germ**
2	**eggs, with or without the shells**
2	**baking sheets, greased or sprayed with Pam®**

Preheat oven to 350°.

Place all ingredients in a food processor. If your blade is very sharp, you can include the eggshells. Process until smooth.

Drop the mixture onto a greased baking sheet by heaping teaspoonfuls, tablespoonfuls, or pour the entire mixture in a gigantic blob on the sheet. Put on a gas mask while baking.

The baking times are:

Small cookies: 12 to 14 minutes.
Big cookies: 14 to 16 minutes.
Full sheet: 25 to 30 minutes.

Remove when done. **Cool and refrigerate or freeze in an airtight tin or plastic bag. Do not leave at room temperature. They *will* mold.**

Index